The

Secret Legacy of Biblical Women:

Revealing the Divine Feminine

Melinda Ribner

MW00326017

Copyright © 2012 Melinda Ribner
All rights reserved.

ISBN: 0985468300
ISBN 13: 9780985468309

Library of Congress Control Number: 2012906395

Praise for
The Secret Legacy of Biblical Women:
Revealing the Divine Feminine

"Melinda Ribner has written a book that is imaginative, bold, and filled with practical wisdom for our lives. She brings alive the feminine archetypes that lie dormant within us. She wrestles with, engages, and energizes those archetypal forces until they become available as our allies in the healing of our hearts and of this world. *The Secret Legacy of Biblical Women* is a treasure of Wisdom, written with great heart, prophetic vision, and passionate beauty."

Rabbi Shefa Gold,
Author of *Torah Journeys: The Inner Path to the Promised Land.*

"What a glorious book! Melinda Ribner reveals the "missing link" to humanity through her provocative interviews with the matriarchs of the Bible, initiating us to the vital, transformative messages directly spoken by them. A consummate teacher of Kabbalah, Ms. Ribner has referenced her magnificently crafted edition with years of Torah study. Her book is destined to become the premiere classic for ushering in the wholeness of masculine and feminine forces that so many have searched for in our spiritual journey."

Ellena Lynn Lieberman,
Author of *The Principles of Dynamic Manifestation*
As Received Through the Akashic Records

"I have waited my whole life for a book that would elevate woman like this holy book does. We may all know the stories of our biblical mothers, and yet we do not feel that we know them as people. When Ribner gives a voice to our biblical mothers, they become real and approachable and we are uplifted and inspired. This book offers us answers to questions that we have had as well as those we did not even know how to ask. Most importantly this book is a practical guide to help us live more meaningful and beautiful lives. This is must reading for every girl and woman of all faiths, but it is equally important for men to read this book as well so as to increase their appreciation of the women in their lives."

Yitta Halberstam Mandelbaum,
co-author *of Small Miracles series*

"Melinda Ribner's new book, *The Secret Legacy of Biblical Women*, is revolutionary! With authority, clarity, and compassion, Ribner, a teacher, healer, and spiritual guide, courageously gives us a multilayered gift. Her insights into our biblical foremothers are practical and mystical, her meditations sacred and therapeutic. By exploring these women, Ribner connects us to them and helps us become the strong, intuitive, and spiritual women we essentially are."

Zelda Shluker,
Managing Editor, *Hadassah magazine*

"Mindy Ribner is prophetically honest. She speaks Truth not only to Power but more importantly to herself. As the rabbis say, 'Words that come from the heart enter the heart,' she speaks from the innermost heart of Jewish women, biblical women and of the Shechinah. 'The Shechinah speaks from her throat,' as God told Abraham about Sarah, 'Listen to Her voice.'"

Yitzhak Buxbaum,
author of *Jewish Spiritual Practices,
The Life and Fire of the Baal Shem Tov*

"*The Secret Legacy of Biblical Women* by Melinda Ribner is a ruach hakodesh inspired book that has the power to activate and awaken the awe, wisdom and ecstatic living force of sacred feminine energy in both women and men."

Rabbi Gabriel Cousens, M.D.,
Author of *Torah as a Guide to Enlightenment.*

"All the glory of the king's daughter is in her inner dimension (Psalm 45:14). Melinda Ribner in her path-breaking new book, *The Secret Legacy of Biblical Women* brilliantly weaves narrative, Midrash, mystic truth, and dialogue in a fashion that has never before seen print form. Readers are treated to hearing thoughtful observations spoken in the first-person from our famous principal female characters of the Bible. These musings are not drawn solely from academic book research. Rather, Melinda Ribner has thoroughly employed her own intuitive gifts to derive insights that help fill gaps in a way that traditional homilies have not. Each chapter flows with teachings from a most high source. All over our Jewish world, women now are finding their voice in a way that paves the way for the Messianic Era. Melinda Ribner has furthered our progress by revealing for us in dialogue fashion deep inspirations that cannot help but foster both greater self-awareness as well as better group dynamics for Jews in these difficult times. One would be well-advised to use this remarkable contribution both for personal learning as well as collective understanding among several readers. The inner dimension of women is all the more glorified thanks to Melinda Ribner's wonderful input to Jewish knowledge."

Reb Rahmiel Havyim Drizin,
author, teacher, and frequent contributor
to www. Kabbalahonline.com

"It is said that some stories which never happened are true, while others may actually have happened yet are not really true, since they teach us little or nothing of any value No-one needs to vouch for the literal veracity of every idea or statement in the book, because its purpose is not to provide dry academic history. Rather, it comes to inspire us in our Torah practice through opening up a new dimension of the Chassidic pathway of connection with the true Tzaddikim. While numerous works are available about the great male Torah role-models in all the generations, Melinda Ribner, one of the leading Torah teachers and spiritual guides of our time, has created a new genre in which, through her deep sensitivity to the subtle nuances of the biblical texts and midrashim, we can take a fresh look at the great women of Israel not as statuesque figures from the past but as real people who responded heroically to actual life challenges.

This work will surely empower many women who seek to nurture and actualize their Israelite neshamah (soul), and it will also greatly enrich many Jewish men, who will find a wealth of insights that will help them better understand the strength and greatness of their own mothers, wives, sisters and daughters and the vital role of Jewish women in drawing the Shechinah to dwell in our midst."

Rabbi Avraham Greenbaum,
author of *On Wings of the Sun*

"The Talmud states that in merit of the righteous women, our forefathers were redeemed from Egypt. In this generation too says the Lubavitcher Rebbe it will be in the merit of the righteous women. This is why it is so important to read this book by Melinda Ribner so that women the world over can bring about true redemption. NOW!"

Rabbi Aaron Raskin,
author of *Letters of Light by Divine Design,*
Rabbi Congregation B'nai Abraham,
Brooklyn Heights, New York

"Mindy Ribner's book is a timely gift to a world that is re-examining the relationships between masculine and feminine forces that shape so much of our reality. Her writing is infused with vitality and passion, and saturated with rich wisdom from the Jewish tradition, filtered through her own, most feminine being. Her words are urgently needed, not only by women, but by men who are striving to understand and honor the enduring interplay between the masculine and the feminine."

Daniel Raphael Silverstein,
Trainee Rabbi, Spoken Word Artist & MC

Dedication

I dedicate this book to my sweet and beloved mother Corinne Ribner of blessed memory, who left this world on July 30, 2009. That day was *Tisha B'Av*, a traditional day of mourning, the Jewish holiday commemorating the destruction of the Holy Temples in Jerusalem. I know that there is a hidden message in the timing of her death that will reveal itself to me in deeper ways each year. What first occurred to me was that my mother was like the Holy Temple. Just as the Holy Temple was and is the foundation of Jewish life, my mother was my foundation.

I thought I knew my mother but I did not. I spoke to my mother almost every day of my life. She insisted on the daily phone call. After each conversation, she would often end with "I love you." When she would call me "my sweetheart," which she often did, and when she would smile toward me, I would feel bathed in love.

Yet it was only in her death and its aftermath that I had a glimpse of who she really was. The courage, the generosity of spirit, and the pure faith she displayed during her illness and dying was beyond anything I knew about my mother. She was clear, calm, loving, and accepting. Where did she have this strength? She always told me that she had a private relationship with God that sustained her since childhood.

My mother was most interested in this book. She cared about this book as if this book could be redemptive to all women, even to her, and especially to me. She encouraged me to find my own voice as a woman. "If I would be courageous, brutally honest, and authentic, I could do something that would be important." She would admonish me with those words when she thought I was becoming too scholarly and selling out my voice as a woman to gain legitimacy in the male-dominated Torah world.

Like many women of my generation who embraced feminism, I devalued the feminine and imitated men so I would gain power and influence that men seemed to have. I feared the economic dependence of most women in my mother's generation, so becoming self-sufficient was a priority. Admittedly, even in my pursuit of spiritual knowledge and growth, I ran to learn from one male rabbi to another, to study one book by a man or another, not valuing my mother's wisdom as much as I should have.

It was only in the wake of my mother's death that I realized and acknowledged that it was my mother who was my greatest spiritual teacher and my best friend, as she often reminded me, especially when she offered me instructive criticism that I may not have requested. It was my mother who transmitted to me the deep sublime women's Torah that is not found in books all the while so lovingly and patiently guiding me to reclaim the feminine. I wished I had acknowledged her more when she was alive in a body.

Like the biblical women before her who are the contents of this book, my mother was also sadly not acknowledged and appreciated enough for the wonderful loving person she was. I pray that this book and its dedication be a testimony to my mother and to biblical women who have modeled to me how to stand courageously in this challenging world. May this book serve as a merit to the soul of my beloved mother and make her smile from her heavenly station. I also pray that this book will inspire others to share their appreciation and gratitude to their mothers, and to all women who gently embody the love and depth that is unique to women and too often is unappreciated.

*   *   *

This book is also dedicated to the other members in my family:

To my beloved, precious, and loving father Isaac Ribner of blessed memory, to my beloved awesome uncle Dr. Richard Ribner of blessed memory, to my beloved aunt, my father's oldest living sister, Bernice Rogow, an inspiring and living model of the feminine, to my dear beloved brother Stephen Ribner, one of the most positive representatives of men on the planet today, and to his "girls," my lovely nieces, Jessica, Joni, and Robbi Ribner: May you each be inspired by this book to embody all the beautiful and positive attributes of the feminine.

*   *   *

Acknowledgements

Acknowledgements to my teachers, Rabbi Shlomo Carlebach of blessed memory, Rabbi Yitzchak Kirzner of blessed memory, Leah Cohen of the Jewish Renaissance Center, and all my *hevruta*, all the men I have studied Torah with privately over the years. Acknowledgements to Monica Tan for the cover design and to my dear mother Corinne Ribner of blessed memory for the painting used for the cover.

Acknowledgements and appreciation to the following organizations and individuals who supported the publishing of this holy book:

Organizations: Am Kolel, Sanctuary and Renewal Center (www.sanctuaryretreatcenter.com), Radio Free Nachlaot, Kol Hevra Magazine (Emunawitt14@yahoo.com)

Supporters of women's Torah: Diana (Hana) Tuminago, Sue Garland, Irene Baydarian, MJ Ackerman. Beth Baker, Andrea Hyatt, Loreleii Kude

In honor of mothers, aunts, and teachers: Linda Nathanson Lippitt in honor of Sarah Yehudit Schneider, Geela Rayzel Raphael in honor of her mother Natalie Lois Robinson and in memory of mother-in-law Rose Geiger Paul, Alexandra Sipocs-Kocsis in honor of Kocsis, Sipos, Woznica, and Goldstein women, Shelly Goldberg in honor of her mother and aunts, Joan Marie Ellis in honor of the Ellis- Rollins family.

In memory of mothers, fathers and friends: Marcia Dane in memory of her mother Eunice Epstein Sykes, Ellisheva Amaris Chana bat Sarah in memory of mother, Joan Helen Heid, Marianne Liebman in memory of mother Flori, Marsha Shapiro in memory of Francis Rogow Becker, Rinah Karson in memory of her mother Edith Seline Steintz, in memory of Eugene and Sonia Amster, and Hannah, Yetta, Bessie, Shirley, Harry, and Lynnette Kline, and grandparents Minnie and Morris Amster and Max and Theresa (Tova) Kline by family, Bernice Rogow in memory of her mother Sarah Axelrod Ribner and her husband of blessed memory, Harry Rogow, Stephen Ribner in memory of mother Corinne and grandmother Sarah Burger Ribner, Carolyn Jarashow in memory of mother Gertrude Baker, David Kinberg in memory of mother Ethel Kinberg, Melinda Ribner in memory of friends Yaffa Golden and Melinda Elliot. Sarah Blum in memory of her mother Zelda Miller Bean.

Table of Contents

Author's Note

There are holy precious moments in one's life when one receives guidance from deep within to reclaim oneself in a new way and alter the course of one's life. These wake-up calls from our very souls leave their imprint upon our lives forever. We are different than we were before. Others may notice the changes that have occurred within us, but then again, it is sometimes simply our secret.

I remember exactly where I was sitting when I was called upon to write this book. It was during a typical Shabbat afternoon class on the Torah portion of the week that happened to be named " Chaya Sarah'" (the Life of Sarah). This biblical text actually begins with an account of her death. In his talk, the rabbi revealed a little known secret about how Sarah died from the Zohar, the major Kabbalistic commentary on the Bible. When Sarah saw in a vision that her husband was planning to kill her only precious beloved son on Mount Moriah, it was more than she could bear. The Zohar reports that Sarah died of grief and anguish. She gave a few piercing cries and died.

How many times had I learned about this most prominent biblical story, the sacrifice of Isaac by the hand of his father Abraham, without ever considering the impact of this act on Sarah, the mother, and on women to this very day. The Bible says, "Take your son, your only son Isaac, whom you love, and go to the Moriah area. Bring him as a burnt offering on one of the mountains that I will designate to you" (Genesis 22: 2). Almost everyone who studies and writes about this event talks proudly about the faith of Abraham and Isaac to meet this greatest spiritual test of their lives in this act of sacrifice. It is even recorded in the Jewish daily prayer book and read by hundreds of thousands of people each day. But little is said of Sarah, the wife of Abraham and the mother of Isaac.

As I listened to the rabbi's talk that day, the story of Sarah's death unexpectedly became very alive, extremely relevant and important to me. I found myself in the text in a way that I had never experienced before. I was shocked. I was horrified. I was deeply saddened. Sarah, the spiritual mother of the Jewish people, the mother of all converts, a prophetess of the highest order, a righteous holy woman died alone of grief and anguish! How could that be! How could the act of sacrificing his son be considered Abraham's greatest demonstration of faith when it resulted in Sarah's death? Where was the sensitivity to the heart of the feminine? Weren't Sarah's feelings important? Much of what I had previously accepted and even treasured about Judaism seemed to crumble before me.

Sarah's pain suddenly became my pain. The account of Sarah's grief and anguish triggered my own. What happened to Sarah was not something that occurred in the very distant past, but somehow the same lack of acknowledgement for the heart of the feminine was still happening today to women and men all over the world. I certainly have had more than my fair share of trials in this lifetime. There have been so many times when I felt dishonored, when my feelings were not respected, when my voice was muted because I was a woman. Admittedly, there have been times when I even felt being a woman was a bit of a liability. Overwhelmed by deep emotion, I would sometimes chide myself to think more like a man, be strong like a man, rather than feel and be sensitive like a woman.

As I sat listening to the rabbi that day, I was speechless. I was afraid if I spoke, I would actually cry. So much was churning within me. My most vulnerable feminine heart had been opened. I was emotionally distressed, yet I was also inwardly exhilarated. I knew right then that I had to claim my voice as a woman in a way that I had not yet done. In those precious awesome holy moments, I received a wake-up call for a new understanding and direction for my life work. At that very moment in time, it became profoundly clear that the women of the Bible like Sarah had something to teach me about being a woman, a Jew, a human being that I did not yet know and needed to know. Furthermore, I sincerely doubted that I could fully receive this transmission from a man, no matter how sensitive and compassionate he might be. Biblical interpretation has been primarily in the domain of men. I intuitively knew that there were depths of interpretations about biblical women that had never been adequately expressed before. This was the legacy of transmission that I was now called upon to claim. With tears in my eyes, I prayed deeply to be worthy of writing this book.

At the time, I had been a serious student of the Bible for more than twenty five years yet I was actually surprised by my empathy with Sarah. For the most part, I must confess, I had previously even sided with the Biblical patriarchs over the matriarchs. I had identified with the universal vision of Abraham. I had blamed Sarah for the Middle East conflict between the Arabs and the Jews attributing it to her decision to send Ishmael and Hagar away. I had blamed Eve for the eating of the forbidden fruit, tempting Adam and bringing evil into the world. I blamed Rebecca for deceiving Jacob. Had Isaac blessed his son Esau, the one he intended to bless, not only would Esau have become a better person, the Jewish people would not have suffered so much, and on and on. It seemed to me that it was the women who were responsible for all the chaos of the world. Like many modern women and men, I rejected the feminine and identified with the masculine.

Though having written four books on meditation and Kabbalah, I had not been particularly interested in the stories of biblical women nor in gender issues previously. My interests were in the field of Jewish meditation, mysticism, spiritual development, and healing, rather than feminism and egalitarianism. More than anything, throughout my life, I was looking for the direct experience of God. Unable to find the intensity of spirituality that I yearned for in synagogues of my youth, my search of God led me to many exotic places that included even living in an ashram for several years. In 1977 during the funeral of my beloved grandfather, I received a powerful call to return to Judaism and become Torah observant. The rabbi's eulogy included the following words to the family: " He leaves behind him a lineage of devout Jews." Those very simple words penetrated my heart and altered my life dramatically. Deep inside, in that very moment, I wanted to be one of those Jews. I did not want to break the chain of the Jewish people.

I did not want my grandfather to have to answer in heaven for a Hindu granddaughter. Pledging myself to be whole-hearted about Judaism I was immediately ready to jump in and take on an intensive Jewish spiritual practice as required by the tradition. My previous experience of living in an ashram taught me the importance and value of spiritual discipline and commitment. It was this promise that I made to myself, to my grandfather Avraham Dovid ben Yakov Shimeon and to God at my grandfather's funeral that kept me connected to Judaism through all the years and challenges I would face later in life.

When I returned from the funeral, I discovered that a room in a friend's beautiful large West Side apartment was available for me to move into immediately. I moved out of the ashram that very day. I began my Torah observance of Shabbat on the next Saturday. A few days later, I found myself guided to a Jewish bookstore where I stumbled upon a few books with alluring titles such as *Duties of the Heart* and the *Way of God*. I highlight the names of these books here because they may also be an important resource for many of you. These books changed my life! Judaism to me now became an authentic inner spiritual mystical transmission that offered me the promise of a life permeated with truth, holiness and love.

I soon found my spiritual home in a small orthodox synagogue on the West Side of New York City led by the charismatic Rabbi Shlomo Carlebach of blessed memory who happened to be a leading composer of Jewish music, a master storyteller, a brilliant Torah scholar and powerful spiritual transmitter. The prayer services with him were ecstatic and even thrilling with lots of singing and dancing. The weekday Torah learnings with Reb Shlomo were also very wonderful. In a very romantic setting, a darkened room illuminated with the light of candles, Reb Shlomo transmitted his Torah to us. " Please open your hearts, I do not know what I am going to say" was the way he usually began his teaching, as he gently strummed on his guitar, and sang a niggun, a wordless melody. He would then speak softly seemingly channeling the very words people listening to him needed to hear. As the Talmud states, " Words of the heart enter the heart". The Torah that Reb

Shlomo taught was always so beautiful and sweet. I would meditate, become deeply relaxed and be filled with love and light as I listened and received the learning.

This orthodox synagogue was also unique because it was primarily female. During the High Holidays when tickets needed to be purchased, the number of women would be more than twice that of the men. I still recall how remarkable and unusual it was to pray in an assembly that was predominately female. The women in those early days with Reb Shlomo were also an unusual group of creative, accomplished, deeply spiritual and beautiful women. Many of us had had spiritual experiences outside of Judaism as well so we enjoyed the intensity of prayer that Reb Shlomo offered us. The spiritual sisterhood among the women, nurtured by Reb Shlomo in the shul, was very vibrant, important to the women as well as to the survival and vitality of the synagogue. Though the women were each there primarily because of the spiritual joy we experienced in the *davening* and learning of Reb Shlomo, we had fun with each other. Life long friendships between the women formed during that special time. I am still good friends with a few of the women from this sisterhood between the mid 1980's until Reb Shlomo's death in 1994.

Because this was an orthodox synagogue, the women sat separately from the men, and did not participate actively in the prayer service itself. That did not bother me, because the separation allowed me to be more fully immersed in prayer and bond with the other women. The women were not spectators as they frequently are in most orthodox synagogues. If anything it was the opposite. The men would too often be found to be gazing at the women singing and dancing fervently.

The women may have been feminists in the workplace. In the synagogue, it would appear that we let go of feminism. It was not so important to us that we were not counted in the minyan (prayer quorum). As women, we were happy that we did not have the responsibility to be present for prayer services by a certain time. " Let the men do the external service", I would tell myself. The women can be occupied with the more inner and important work of prayer. Besides, we women were mystics and more concerned with the higher worlds than this world. We knew that we counted in the higher places where it really mattered. Reb Shlomo was often speaking about the unique holiness of women so we always felt elevated. I mention this former time in my life because it impacted on some of the perspectives on the feminine that are reflected in this book.

If I had attended another kind of synagogue, more egalitarian, I might have acquired certain skills for participating, along with the men, in communal worship. Instead, in the beginning of my time in the shul, I learned to shop and cook for hundreds of people at a time for *Shabbat* and holiday celebrations. I did not know much about cooking before, yet I accepted this responsibility, knowing that the meals with our teacher were very important. The kitchen became a holy place where I learned how to be a Jew. Rather than feeling demeaned for doing "women's kitchen work", I felt honored and blessed to be serving and contributing to the community in such a direct and intimate way. Previously, in the ashram, preparing food was valued as a profound honor granted only to those highly esteemed within the community who had years of rigorous meditative practice behind them.

It may also be important to highlight that it was in this synagogue that I began to teach Jewish meditation and Jewish spiritual healing. After teaching there for a year, I was invited to teach at synagogues of all denominations in NYC and Brooklyn. I taught in many places until I gained a following and formed my own group that I called " Beit Miriam". The other books that I have written record some of the pioneering work I did in resurrecting ancient Jewish meditative practices for people today. In 1989, I received semicha (ordination) directly from Reb Shlomo to do this work. This was a powerful transmission, albeit a controversial one. Many people stormed out of the synagogue during the ceremony. To honor and empower a woman as a spiritual teacher was not something that was done in the orthodox Jewish world at that time. Spreading the practices and the joy of Jewish meditation was my spiritual calling and even the primary source of my livelihood until that Sabbath afternoon in around 2005 when I heard this teaching about Sarah's death.

Overwhelmed, terribly sad, and grief stricken, I came home that evening to process all the feelings that were triggered within me through writing what would become *The Secret Legacy of Biblical Women*. As Sarah was my inspiration for this book, I would like to share the initial process with you. On that very evening, unbeknownst to me, I began my writing on what would be the chapter on Sarah in this book. I asked myself the question of why the story about Sarah's death made me so unbearably sad. How does a person actually die from grief and anguish upon hearing of a terrible event? I had experienced tremendous grief in my life, but somehow I survived. What takes place within such a woman that she would actually die from grief? What was Sarah experiencing in the last moments before she died? How and why did she really die? Did Sarah have a message for generations to come when she died, and when she lived, for that matter? I sat with these questions, and listened deep inside for answers.

As I reflected and meditated upon the death of Sarah, it was almost as if time and space collapsed and I could commune with the soul of Sarah. I do not claim to be a channel of Sarah. I did not hear any voice. What took place was most likely my own projection, and my imagination, yet nevertheless, the experience of communing with Sarah seemed to provide me with direct insight into the life and death of Sarah in the most astonishing way that I never imagined possible.

The answers I received to these questions and so many other questions about the life of Sarah that night are featured in the interview section of the chapter on Sarah. I meditated and communed so deeply with Sarah many times and then I repeated this process with each of the biblical women in this book so much that I began to imagine them actually talking to me.

When I first began to commune with Sarah about the experience around the circumstances of her death, I was actually frightened, as if I had been given a ticket to the abyss. I wanted very much to empathize with Sarah at that time in her life, but I did not want to fully enter into her experience. I was even afraid that I might also die. Was I a strong enough vessel to contain such depths?

Through the power of my empathy and intuition, I leaped across the void to have a glimpse of the kind of pain that Sarah might have felt in the moments close to her death. There are no words to describe this kind of pain when life no longer makes any sense. The death of her most precious and only son, who she birthed in her old age, by her husband, was more than she could bear.

This pain is beyond words. Only cries, screams, and whimpers can hint to its depths. That is why the oral tradition in Torah says that Sarah died with cries and whimpers. At the heart of Sarah's pain was betrayal. It was not just that it was the loss of her most precious son Isaac, whom she had waited so long to bear in the most miraculous way. Sarah and her husband Abraham had dedicated their lives to instill in those around them life-enhancing principles of love that arose from the belief in one God who loves life and all of creation. Sarah had dedicated her life to end the idolatrous practices of child sacrifice so prevalent in her time. This bond between her husband and son to commit this horrific act by her husband was a total betrayal of everything Sarah embodied and advocated. How could she have continued to live in this world after this event!

Like Sarah, have we not all experienced betrayal of some sort in our life? Living in this world the beautiful soul who is our true essence is betrayed countless times in a myriad of ways in a lifetime, but unlike Sarah, most of us survive, shattered, or strengthened by the pain of our betrayal. Sarah died. What I understood from my night of communing with the soul of Sarah was that Sarah, the mother of the Jewish people, was not a victim whom we should pity, but rather she was our spiritual mother and a brave heroine whom it is incumbent upon us to honor in her life and in her death. She did not die in vain. Her life and death have an important message for women and men today.

When I connected my soul with that of Sarah that night, I also realized for the first time that our holy mother Sarah, the first mother of the Jewish people, died alone, abandoned by her husband, her son, and even by her community. Her husband Abraham had sent her to Hebron prior to this event. He most likely did not want to deal with her reaction, her tears, and her protest that might interfere with his resolve to do what he had been commanded to do. What made Sarah's death worse for me was that her pain was not acknowledged at the time she died and not sufficiently throughout history. The rabbis praise her, talk about her greatness, her strength, her righteousness, and that is wonderful, but very few if any talk about the meaning of her death. To me, her death was a powerful message, speaking louder than any words could ever do. I made a pledge to Mother Sarah that night that I would be a mouthpiece as best as I could be to express what had not yet been heard.

I did not fully realize until much later that my tears and pain arose from a source much deeper than the actual death of Sarah herself. My tears touched upon the tears of all women and men who have been oppressed, who have lived in a world where the voice of the feminine has been silenced, whose wisdom has been unacknowledged, whose freedom has been compromised, and whose loving heart betrayed.

In time, I came to understand that I cried that night for the Divine Feminine, known as the *Shechinah.* According to Kabbalah, all the tears of our heart and soul are ultimately for the feminine expression of divinity, or *Shechinah,* the Divine Feminine that has remained hidden. Because She is hidden, and She is in exile, our world is imbalanced. Our priorities are confused. We are each disconnected from each other and from our true selves. Our mother earth is ravaged.

Sarah, the mother of the Jewish people, is particularly significant because in her time she was honored as a priestess and as an embodiment of the Divine Feminine. Her level of prophecy was deemed higher than that of her husband. The death of Sarah and the manner in which she died marked the diminishing of the matriarchal societies of which Sarah was one such matriarch. After Sarah, with a few exceptions, women who had been the spiritual leaders of the world were gradually relegated to supporting roles. Even Rebecca, the daughter-in-law of Sarah, no longer spoke directly to her husband, and resorted to deception to realize her prophetic goals. Patriarchal societies soon replaced matriarchal ones.

For thousands of years, patriarchy has reigned. The voice of the feminine has been muted. The wisdom of the feminine has been hidden. Mother earth is erupting in tornados, floods and hurricanes. World economies are collapsing. Wars, terrorism, and random acts of violence are multiplying. The world is quickly now realizing the limitations of masculine power to solve our problems. A call for the awakening to the heart of the feminine has been uttered in our time throughout the world in a way never heard before. What has been hidden will soon be revealed. We live in auspicious times.

Preface

Since the days of Abraham and Sarah, Judaism has taught the world about the unity and oneness of God. God is one, and as such God is neither male nor female, but with attributes of both. Judaism identifies the masculine aspects of the Divine as *"The Holy One Blessed be He," "Ha-Kodesh Boruch Hu," Kodesh,* or "holy," meaning transcendent and separate from the world, and it identifies the feminine aspect of the Divine as *Shechinah,* as the immanent, indwelling, and manifest Presence of God in the world. Despite the dual-gender concept of God, the Creator of the World, the Majestic Awesome Being, the Ground of All Existence, who birthed creation and loves all of creation, is almost exclusively depicted, publicly at least, as male in most Western prayer communities. God as female was primarily associated with pagan idolatrous nations that preceded Abraham and Sarah's mission to unify the world to the worship of one God.

For thousands of years, our institutions, our religions, even our concepts of God have remained primarily patriarchal. Everyone, whether Jew, Christian, or Moslem, is always talking about "Our Father in Heaven." For many, God is only masculine and seems to reside somewhere in the heavens. This masculine God offers protection and blessing to those who pray to Him. Yet if God is our father, what happened to the Divine Mother? Where is She? How can there be a father without a mother? Is God only in the sky and not here on the earth? Is God not also in our midst, and within us? What does God's oneness really mean?

Outside of Kabbalistic and Jewish renewal circles, it has been almost taboo to mention the Divine Feminine, let alone pray to Her. There is only one beautiful biblical reference to God as a mother found in the writings of the prophet Isaiah (49:15). "Can a mother forget her nursing child and have no compassion on the child she has borne? Though she may forget, I will not forget".

According to Kabbalah, the body of ancient esoteric Jewish wisdom, there is a primal drive in the universe to restore the Divine Feminine of High and the woman on this earthly plane back to her proper place as well, so the feminine, both divine and human, is in proper balance with the masculine in both the spiritual and physical universes. Because the external world is already quite adapted to the dominance of the masculine, the values and wisdom of the feminine will have to rise to create the balance needed for peace and harmony. This book is primarily a guidebook for facilitating the rise of the feminine spirit and the revelation of the Divine Feminine. As long as the feminine presence within each person and within the world is not honored, there cannot be peace between men and women, between various groups of people, and with our mother earth, our common home.

Isaiah's prophecy's "The light of the moon will become like the sun," (Isaiah 30:26) predicts that women and the feminine spirit within all will rise to transform the world for the better. For the past half a century, many people throughout the world believe that this transformation has begun to take place. Was feminism the millennial movement that Isaiah predicted?

As a social political movement, feminism aspired to give women equal opportunities and rights as well as fundamentally transform the world and liberate it from sexism, racism, and class distinction. It is interesting and important to note that Jewish women such as Bella Abzug, Gloria Steinem and Betty Friedan spearheaded and largely shaped the feminist phenomenon in the 1970's. Feminism successfully opened many doors for women at the time and made radical changes in our society. As liberating and empowering feminism might be to many, it would appear however that it was not the prophesied movement. Our problems as individuals and communities, either materially or spiritually have not been solved.

One of the reasons that feminism failed to achieve its most lofty goals of world harmony and peace, in my humble opinion, was because it was non-theistic at its core. Because its spiritual roots were in communist theology and humanistic philosophy rather than Torah, feminism could not and did not resurrect the path of feminine spirituality nor could it reveal the Divine Feminine as needed and predicted in ancient prophecies. It was not within the scope or mission of feminism to do that. According to Kabbalah, it is the revelation of the Divine Feminine that will heal the world.

Quite simply, it is not enough that women can be engineers, doctors, lawyers, rabbis and even presidents of nations. Entry into these professions by women does not necessarily assure that these women embody the feminine heart and wisdom in their positions of influence and power. It does not necessarily indicate a rise in the feminine when more women enter into the work place to occupy jobs formerly filled by men or engage in other activities that had been formerly dominated by men. In addition to opening doors into the marketplace, feminism encouraged women to be sexually open in a way that had never been advocated publicly before, thereby, reducing the need for marriage. Patriarchal, oppressive, and boring might be adjectives frequently used by many feminists to describe the institution of marriage. In my mother's pre-feminist generation, a higher percentage of women chose marriage over career. It is true that they did not have the career options as women today, but also equally true that there was greater value placed on marriage and bearing children than today. In my baby-boomer generation, most women, whether they are married and single, enter the marketplace of work.

In our increasingly secular world, it has even become politically incorrect to be only a stay-at-home mother or housewife. When I am on the Upper West Side of Manhattan, I can't help but observe the large number of baby carriages being wheeled by women clearly other than the mothers of the children. I do not think that it is primarily for economic reasons that many of these women entrust their little ones to other women. If money were the primary issue, couples would have relocated to Brooklyn or even Queens. Rather, having a career holds greater value than raising children. In a similar vein, I have met women, wives and mothers, who are even embarrassed to reveal to others that they have no career outside of the home. The traditional work that women have done in the home is not held in high esteem.

Ironically, because of its emphasis on egalitarianism, feminism may have indadvertedly actually contributed to the devaluing of the feminine by not recognizing or appreciating the truly important distinctions that exist between masculine and feminine. In fact, it has now become confusing for many to know what is meant by the terms 'masculine' and 'feminine', much less embody them within ourselves and celebrate these unique gifts within each other. Are there significant differences, other than anatomical, between men and women? Are we the same or are we different and how so? This confusion has increased stress in relationships between the sexes as well.

One of the challenges that I have seen in my therapy practice for women today is that the "problem solving and negotiating" skills they have acquired in their work that have made them successful there will not serve them in their personal relationships with their husbands or lovers. Usually, it backfires, creates friction, and actually dampens the love and passion between them. Informed by my knowledge of Kabbalah, my clinical work as a therapist in my private practice with men and women is devoted in large part towards helping men and women understand, relearn, reclaim and honor the unique differences between men and women. When they learn to do this, they restore harmony and passion in their relationship. For example, many women need to learn how to embody the beautiful and receptive qualities of the feminine without becoming a doormat or defensive. Men, on the other hand, need to embody the beautiful bestowal and directional qualities of the masculine without becoming domineering or insecure.

It has taken me many years to appreciate the difference between secular and kabbalistic ideas about the empowerment of women. Succinctly stated, as I understand, feminism promotes egalitarianism, seeking to eliminate the differences between men and women, between all people, so everyone will be equal and there will be fairness in the world. Kabbalah highlights the differences between men and women, between the Jewish people and other people and seeks to restore the proper balance between each of them so there will be harmony and peace.

Many women like myself have been looking today for the new paradigm beyond feminism to help them actualize themselves authentically and more fully as women. Kabbalistic wisdom is an ancient yet timely road map for this kind of spiritual transformation for both women and men. With the exception of Chassidic groups like Chabad, the study of Kabbalah has been until fairly recently largely restricted to married men over forty years of age. Within the body of knowledge known as Kabbalah there are predictions that its study will become widespread in pre-messianic future times. It would appear that we do live in auspicious times for it is only in the last fifteen or twenty years that we have seen books on Kabbalah written in English widely available.

The wisdom of Kabbalah revealed in this book through the examples of biblical women offers positive and clear definitions for what is meant by masculine and feminine that are quite different than those generally considered in modern times, and are particularly relevant for women and men today. For example, the quality of loving and giving is more commonly associated with women in modern culture, but this quality, according to Kabbalistic teachings is masculine, and more associated with men who embody the essence of masculinity.

The quality of strength or that of setting boundaries might be associated with masculine as men have greater physical strength, but this quality is actually feminine. Each chapter in this book highlights a unique feminine quality demonstrated by a biblical woman as well as how this quality shaped her contribution in making the world a better place for all. The feminine path for the revelation of the Divine Feminine is clearly outlined through detailed spiritual practices attributed to each woman as well.

It is important to highlight that in ancient times, even up to medieval times, Jewish women had their own prayer gatherings independent of men.

Their prayers addressed the God of biblical women. As modern woman tried to fit into a male-dominated world, attend the same places of worship, and use the same prayer book, women lost contact with the oral tradition of feminine spirituality that women had transmitted to each other for thousands of years. This book also revives this ancient and relatively unknown tradition of connecting with the mothers that has been almost lost in our day.

As if responding to the call of the Divine Feminine Herself, hundreds and thousands of women today of all faiths all over the world meet at the time of the new or full moon in sacred circles to share their visions, dreams, and prayers in possibly the same way that thousands of women must have done in ancient times. Not quite finding themselves spiritually or emotionally fulfilled in either egalitarian or patriarchal religious settings, women today are gathering to explore alternative ways to create greater love, healing and abundance for themselves and the planet. These female-only or female-guided gatherings are significant because they help to foster an awakening to the ancient wisdom of the feminine that has been hidden within us for thousands of years. Because this is largely uncharted territory, many women may seek to return to pagan times when the Goddess was supreme. Perhaps this is because they do not know how or have not yet been able to uncover the Divine Feminine within their own Western prayer tradition. Yet She is there if you know how to look for Her. This book, *The Secret Legacy of Biblical Women: Revealing the Divine Feminine* shares the spiritual keys needed to reveal the Divine Feminine in our midst today. Let us now go forward to birth together a new order, building on everything that preceded us, rather than regressing backward to a fantasy of the good old days that in truth were not so good in so many ways. Now is the time to find a new harmonic balance between the masculine and feminine, both divine and human, and not to simply retreat to the embrace of the feminine alone.

After teaching Jewish meditation for more than twenty-five years, it was only when I began to offer alternative meditative gatherings for the Sabbath and holidays that I realized that I had inadvertently stumbled upon a powerful and awesome path of feminine spirituality that was different than what I was experiencing in synagogue. Because *Halacha* (Jewish law) was honored, these Beit Miriam gatherings I led attracted men and women from all affiliations within Judaism. Most of these participants might not have observed *Shabbat* or the holidays otherwise though several were observant and connected to synagogues but were looking for something exciting and different. No prayer book was used, but meditation, Kabbalistic teachings, and dyad interactive exercises enabled participants to receive the particular spiritual transmission of the holiday. While I was quite experienced in facilitating feminine approaches to spirituality for many years, it was only a preparation for what was to become for me a "game-changer" in Jerusalem, a mystical peek experience of such magnitude that my understanding of the feminine and Judaism was radically transformed and deepened. This was indeed another major transformational wake up call that also impacted on the writing of this book.

Long after I began writing this book, I moved to the Old City of Jerusalem so as to be blessed with the privilege of praying daily near the *Kodesh Koddeshim*, the Holy of Holies, that place closest to the holiest place in the ancient Holy Temple in Jerusalem. I spent several months praying each day before sunrise in the tunnels that have been excavated by the Wailing (Western) Wall in Jerusalem, where the holy women of Jerusalem gather to pray and weep in what Judaism considers the most holy place on earth.

It was there I had a most profound revelation of the *Shechinah,* the Divine Feminine. It may sound crazy, but I felt that She indeed spoke to me and informed me of the following: God's covenant with the Jewish people is real. There is no replacement for it. In the right time, all the prophecies will be fulfilled. She, the *Shechinah,* the Divine Feminine, the indwelling Presence of the Divine, is faithful. She has been waiting patiently, since the beginning of time, behind the veil of physicality that covers Her, to be redeemed from Her hiding to fill the world with love and blessings. When

She is fully revealed in the world, our hearts will be opened, and there will be love and peace on all levels. Evil will have no jurisdiction.

She is eternally unified with *Ha-Kodesh Boruch Hu,* the Divine Masculine, yet from time to time, when our hearts are truly open, it is She who gives us a glimpse of Her beauty and Her love. This is more than enough to sustain and strengthen us until the great messianic day of Her revelation. This book is devoted to Her revelation and to that great day when the *Shechinah* is revealed and Her residence in the hearts of every human being and on the Temple Mount in Jerusalem is reestablished magically and peacefully.

The Book and its Design

Whether one is secular or religious, whether one believes that the author of the Bible was God, or the work of men, most will acknowledge that the men and women of the Bible are not simply people, but that each is a distinct archetype. As archetypes, biblical women help us discover ourselves anew as well as tap into the forces buried within us that are needed to come forth to heal this world. Biblical women are not just familiar archetypes. Each woman in her own way is a reflection of a key archetype that has been hidden and suppressed, even violently, by patriarchal religions for thousands of years: the archetype of the Divine Feminine.

Though biblical women were allotted very few words, if any words at all, about their lives in the Bible, biblical women changed the world and Western religions as we know them today due to the independent and courageous choices they made. Through the imaginary interview format that is the heart of this book, each biblical woman becomes alive to the reader as she tells her story in her words and speaks directly to the needs and concerns of people today. In our time when there are very few models of spiritual leadership, the opportunity to be in the presence of these holy women, to receive their wisdom and their love, even if it is only in one's imagination, is quite profound. By reading their stories and hearing their words, we are guided to live our lives more fully and complete the redemptive work that these women began thousands of years ago.

Scholarly and faithful to the esoteric teachings within Judaism, this book is also a very practical offering of profound Jewish wisdom on issues that are important and relevant to people today such as love and sexuality, faith, healing, family relationships, marriage, and growing through challenge while also revealing little known biblical and Kabbalistic prophecies about future times. Through its group discussion guidelines, meditations, and spiritual practices within each chapter, this book becomes an invaluable practical guidebook for personal growth for women and men of all backgrounds.

In this book, Eve, Sarah, Rebecca, Rachel, Leah, Bilha, Zilpa, Dina, Miriam, Batya, Chana, and Esther have a voice to tell their stories, and transmit the wisdom and love that is the heart of the feminine. Each of these women have their own story, as we each do, but their lives were not independent of each other, nor are ours. According to Kabbalah, the feminine soul reincarnates and undergoes a journey that culminates in the redemption of the world. They began a journey of the feminine and they ask that we complete it for them, for ourselves, and for the world.

Each chapter in this book devoted to a biblical woman is based on extensive research. In the writing of this book, it has been important to me that I be faithful to the *Midrashim* (legends codified in the Oral Torah) as well as additional rabbinic commentaries about each woman. In cases where there were contradictory *Midrashim,* I took the liberty to select the one that resonated deepest within me and my understanding of the biblical woman I researched. Because my research was extensive, I have placed additional Kabbalistic and *Midrashic* commentaries on each woman in a separate section in the book for those who want to deepen their understanding of each woman from a Kabbalistic perspective. It is through the Kabbalistic resources that one will gain a further appreciation of the development of the feminine and how important and essential her revelation is to Judaism and the world.

The imaginary interview with each woman required me to be in an elevated clear state when I could meditate deeply upon the gathered material. The content of the interview was not planned in advance. I simply wrote what I heard, what I received in guidance to questions that I felt drawn to ask. Many times, I personally was surprised by what came through me.

You may agree or you may not agree with what has been written. I fully expect that some of what is written will be controversial and even provocative to many people in different ways. That is good. It is my hope that the material will be a springboard for your own thinking, exploration, and discussion with others. This is a book to be studied and savored like a good wine. I encourage people to learn this book with others and to even take turns reading the interviews out loud with each other so readers can experience each biblical woman within themselves. Discussing the supplemental material on each chapter such as the qualities of the feminine that each woman embodied, the spiritual and meditative practices associated with her, and the follow-up questions will make this book even more meaningful to men and women. This book would be a wonderful addition to support the content at *Rosh Chodesh* (new moon) gatherings or other community group meetings. Each month can feature a biblical woman who expresses the energies of the month. Using this book as a companion guide with my other book *Kabbalah Month by Month,* which reveals the Kabbalistic energies for each month of the Jewish calendar, would be optimal.

Chapter One

Eve's Gift of Love

Secrets of Holy Intimacy

Eve

"A woman lives for love. This is good and a sign of her strength and not a weakness. In her heart of hearts, a woman cannot tolerate superficiality. So honor your depths. Yearn to surrender and be penetrated with Godliness. This is a greatest joy."

—*Mother Eve*

Eve (Chava)

The First Woman, Mother of all Living

Upon the simple reading of the Bible, many blame Eve (woman) for bringing evil and death into the world. As the story goes, Eve ate the forbidden fruit and then gave it to Adam to eat. The punishments for this "sin" were metered out to all accordingly. Adam and Eve were cast out of the Garden of Eden. The serpent that tempted the woman to eat the forbidden fruit was cursed to crawl on its belly, eat dust, and have enmity between him and womankind for all time. Because of Eve's action, a woman would now experience pain in childbirth. She will need her husband more than her husband will need her and her husband would rule over her. Finally, because man listened to the voice of his wife, he now has to work by the "sweat of his brow" to survive.

Others reject this biblical story as misogynistic, a story that was written by men to justify the oppression of women in all cultures throughout time. Yes, it is true that women have indeed been oppressed and man has had to work for his "bread," and the serpent crawls on the ground. But is there a much deeper reading to this story?

According to Kabbalah, the secrets about creation and future prophecies are encoded in this story of Adam and Eve. Whether we take this story of Adam and Eve literally or metaphorically is not so important. What is important is to understand the wisdom contained within this story. First, we need to know this story and all the commentaries about it, so as to enter into it, and allow it to become our story as well. That will be easy, for the

1

story of Eve, the first woman, known in Hebrew as Chava, the "Mother of All Living," is the archetype for women of all times.

Adam and Eve Were Initially a Single Nonphysical Being!

The first basic thing the Bible tells us we need to be mindful of in our understanding of this story is that Eve and Adam were originally one being that was called "Adam." "Let us make man in our image, after our likeness.... So God created man in his image, in the image of God He created him, male and female He created them" (Genesis 1: 26).

Creation began with one being, Adam, so all people would know that they have the same creator. According to Kabbalah, Adam, the original being, contained the souls of all people, men and women of all nations, for all generations to come. Remember that we too today are each a part of this original being known as Adam.

The first instructions to this bi-gendered being known as Adam were to be fruitful, multiply, and rule over the fish, the birds, and every living thing (Genesis 1: 28). When Adam received these instructions, Adam was a singular being, male and female, so it would appear that Adam could reproduce asexually. Adam was originally placed outside of the Garden of Eden and then was taken and placed within the Garden to work and guard it (Genesis 2: 15). Adam was then instructed to freely eat of all the trees except the fruit of the Tree of Knowledge of Good and Evil, for if he were to eat of this fruit, he would die (Genesis 2:17).

"It is not good to be alone," God says. "I will make him a helper (*ezrah genedo*), opposite him" (Genesis 2:18). Adam requires a mate like all the other creatures. To help Adam overcome his feelings of isolation, Lilith was first given to him, prior to the creation of Eve, according to Jewish legends. Lilith is not mentioned in the Bible, but is prominent in Kabbalah and *Midrashic* (orally transmitted) sources. Lilith was created separately from Adam and never assumed bodily form like Adam did after "the fall." The legend is that Lilith insisted on full equality and consequently abandoned

Adam because Adam was unwilling to yield to her demands. With the use of the ineffable name, Lilith flew to the Red Sea, away from Adam. Lilith, said to be spurned by Adam, is still overcome with jealousy of humankind, and capable of injuring babies. Even to this day, people secure amulets to protect infants from her. Also, according to legends, Lilith arouses men to commit the sin of wasting seed, a terrible sin that is said to cut off a man from the experience of the *Shechinah*.

According to the Bible, the best helpmate that Adam needed would not be separate from Adam but would come directly from him. This woman was always there, they were one being, they were adjoined back to back, and she was not even noticed. Now she was to be separated from the body of Adam. It was part of the divine plan from the beginning that they would be separated, but it was important that they first share the memory of being part of one being. This deep connection did not work with Lilith because she did not share a common root with Adam.

Hashem (God) cast a deep sleep upon Adam and took one of his sides (Genesis 11:21). And man said, *"This time* it is bone of my bones and flesh of my flesh. This shall be called woman, for from man was she taken" (Genesis 11: 24). Now man and woman stood separate from each other, face to face, so as to now be able to help and challenge each other to grow. The main act attributed to this woman was that she ate from the Tree of Knowledge of Good and Evil. God had commanded Adam to not eat of this Tree. Adam told Eve to not eat or even touch the Tree, but Eve ate and then gave the fruit to Adam to eat. The reasons for Eve's eating from the forbidden tree will be explored in depth in the interview that follows. You will have an opportunity to decide whether her defense for this action resonates with you.

The interview with Eve contains much kabbalistic and *midrashic* wisdom within it and is presented in a way that is easily accessible. The kabbalistic commentary of this chapter has been placed toward the end of the book for those who are interested in deciphering this most important primal story on even deeper levels (see pages 205–218).

For information about Eve in the Bible, read excerpts in Genesis 2:22-23, 3:2-3, 3:7, 3:20, 3:22, 4:1

Invocation

For those who truly seek to love and who are ready and willing to enter into the depths of life itself to transmute what is dark into light, connect with Eve, the Mother of All Life. The mother energy of Eve (Chava in Hebrew) is loving, intense, and powerful. She will not settle for trivialities and superficialities and neither do you.

Mother Eve will guide and empower you to lift up the fallen divine sparks (called *nitzotzot* in Hebrew) that call out for healing in all of life experiences. Eve asks you to complete this work and participate in the birthing of a new order of consciousness that is both loving and responsible.

Interview with Eve

Question: It is so awesome to be in your presence. What is your message for the women of today?

Eve: I love you and I bless you. You are a part of me as I am within you. You may feel that you have your own personal identity but you are much more than you know yourself to be. You may also feel that you are no different than a male, because in your present world you can do everything that a man can do and more, but know firsthand, always remember, and be mindful that you are a woman. As a woman, you have a special and unique mission in the world. You are beautiful. You are powerful. There is much that you as a woman must do to bring this world into the proper balance and harmony. Please know that women share a bond that cannot yet be totally revealed. My heart is full of blessing for everyone that this revelation of the feminine occurs as soon as possible.

Question: Thank you for that wonderful introduction and blessing. Would you please begin by telling us about yourself?

Eve: In the first story of creation recorded in the Bible Adam and I were created as one being. We were joined together, yet we did not face each other, we were back to back in a state of unconsciousness. We were not really connected, or close to each other. The Holy One caused a slumber to fall upon Adam and I was then created as a separate conscious entity.

After I was separated from Adam, my size was reduced. I did not quite face him. I was smaller than Adam yet I was conscious of life in a different way than Adam. I needed him and he needed me. I stood opposite him, so as to stimulate and challenge him. It was and remains my responsibility as Primordial Woman to help Adam to do what he was meant to do, which is reveal his own inner light. And his job was and is to enable me to reveal my outward light.

If I did my job well, I knew that I would be restored to my full stature as at first, and I could then face Adam in a loving relationship of mutuality and respect. This is what I wanted the most. It had been my hope and prayer from the beginning of time to the present time that my original size will be restored and I stand face to face in a full loving relationship with my husband.

Question: But why did you do it Eve? Why did you eat from the Tree of Good and Evil?

Eve: Like women throughout the ages, I have always been guided throughout my life by the desire for love and relationship. Men like to love, but love is life to a woman. There is a deep yearning in the heart of the feminine for love. Please know this about me when you seek to understand why I did what I did.

I know that I have been blamed for bringing sin into the world. I have been blamed for bringing chaos and death into the world. My action has regrettably been used to oppress women. The suffering endured by women of all cultures throughout time is an unfortunate legacy, a profound burden, and even sacrifice that women, including myself, have bore since the beginning of time.

In the future, my legacy will be redeemed. What I did and what women have done for all of humanity has not yet been understood or fully appreciated. I know that the truth will become clear in the right time. When it is understood, all of humanity will have profound appreciation and respect for me and all women. All will know that what I did was necessary to move life forward. May my legacy be redeemed in your times.

Question: Does not the Bible say "Of every tree of the garden you may eat, but of the Tree of the Knowledge of Good and Evil, you must not eat, for if you eat of it, you will die" (Genesis 2: 16–17). Adam even told you to not eat of the Tree or even touch it.

Eve: Firstly, Adam had been given the prohibition against eating of the Tree when he was alone, before I was created. Because we were back to back at that time, I did not hear this command directly. After I came on to the scene as a separate entity, life had radically changed for us, offering us new possibilities. It was now a new order and together we could do more than before. When I touched the Tree inadvertently because the serpent pushed me against it, and nothing happened, I did not know whether I could believe Adam. When I ate the outside of the fruit and also nothing happened, I then ate the whole fruit. My consciousness was then radically altered. There was a painful separation between me and Adam then, so I gave him the fruit and we were united again.

Question: You did not yet answer the question. Why did you do it Eve? Why did you eat from the Tree of Good and Evil? I would like to understand your motivation.

Eve: My goal was for knowledge of God, for union with the Divine. Without this God knowledge, my life was empty and meaningless. The fruit looked good and I knew that it would make one wise. The serpent told me that my eyes would be open and I would be like God knowing good and evil. As the helpmate to Adam, it was clear to me that my job was to stimulate Adam to grow in his knowledge and service of God. I wanted him to more fully realize his awesome potential and do what he was created to do. It is the nature of woman to stimulate man to grow. Without this stimulation, man would not develop.

Adam was a great, even a magnificent being of light, but I knew that was only because he was created that way. He didn't do anything to earn or deserve what he had. He simply received all the wondrous light that was so generously bestowed upon him. He could be so much more than he was, but only if he was able to grow through challenge and struggle. More importantly, while he was joyfully basking in the light, there were sparks of divine light trapped in darkness. It was his job to restore these sparks to their source, but he was blinded by his own light and could not perceive darkness. Because I was diminished myself, I felt the pain acutely of those who were not unified with the Holy One. It was my job to inspire Adam to do what he was supposed to do and to be all that he could be.

Question: Please explain.

Eve: Adam had been given the responsibility of tending all that was in the Garden. By doing this holy work, Adam and I would merit the light that was so lovingly and completely shining upon us. As a woman, I knew more than Adam how important it was that we participate and earn what is given to us. To just receive is shameful. We can't just take and take and not give back. I understood that by eating of the Tree, our consciousness would change, but we would be able to give and to love in a deeper way. Life would not be easy, I knew that, but life without change, life without love is not meaningful to me. In my heart I believed that what I did was what God originally wanted. God did not want Adam and me to be simply puppets with no free will. That is why God placed the Tree in our midst.

Question: Eve, you make it sound like the eating was a good thing. How can that be? You brought sin into the world and with it suffering and death. It was a sin wasn't it?

Eve: I understand that this act has been considered a sin by most people. Some people even call it the original sin and believe that all evil in the world is derived from this one act. Perhaps we should have waited until *Shabbat,* but my love for all of creation was too large. The cosmic residue of light, the fallen sparks that were left out of the garden, were calling out for love and healing. They were experiencing a profound immeasurable pain from their disconnection from God. There is no greater pain than this. I was willing to personally enter into the darkness, into what you call evil, for the sake of love. Such is the nature of a woman who loves. Women do this all the time.

Question: You make it sound like this act was one of total altruism. Was there another motivation underlying your decision to eat of the forbidden tree?

Eve: Ultimately, quite honestly, I wanted to bring Adam closer to me. I knew that as Adam developed, we would be better able to be together in a more direct and complete way. The kind of relationship that he could have with me would be much different and better than he could have with Lilith, which was based entirely on the desire for physical pleasure and nothing else. Yet Adam was still, however, spending time with Lilith, playing with her and wasting his seed with her. I was alone too much of the time. This is why the serpent could approach me and try to seduce me.

Question: What was your relationship with the serpent?

Eve: Adam had befriended the serpent and let him spend much time with me. The serpent awakened lust within me. He injected his impurity into me. At the time, I did not know or understand what was happening to me when I was with him. The serpent was the male version of Lilith. Since Adam desired Lilith so much, I hoped that my contact with the dark energy of the serpent would make me more attractive to Adam. More than anything, I wanted to attract Adam to me, so we could do what the Holy One wanted us to do, to co-create, to procreate and fill the world with light and children. Regrettably I absorbed some of the filth of the serpent and then transferred it to my children, especially to Cain. I never loved the serpent. I only loved Adam. Adam is my eternal soul mate. My relationship with the serpent was only a means to fulfill a holy purpose.

Question: Eve, was it not a sin? Did you not do something wrong? Were not you, Adam, and even the serpent punished?

Eve: On the surface reading of the Bible, it looks like we were each punished in very specific ways. In actuality the punishments ascribed to us were exactly what we needed to heal and fulfill us on the deepest level. The Holy One does not ever punish but rather the Holy One fulfills the desires of all. Everything that the Holy One does is for good. What happens to a person is always what is needed for growth. I accept and rejoice in that truth, and so should you.

Let's look at the punishments: that man should suffer through his labor and that woman should suffer during her labor. What is labor but manifest co-creativity? What God ordained was good for us. It was what we really wanted. It was not only good for Adam to work, it was essential for him to work in order to earn life in this world and "the World to Come." Adam needed to work rather than spend his time chasing Lilith, which was empty pleasure that would amount to nothing positive. There is no merit without toil. As it is said in the holy writings, "In proportion to the toil is the reward." After the "sin" he now was finally clear about the importance of his mission to make this world a dwelling place for the Divine.

Question: What about the curse of pain in childbirth? Women still suffer from the pain of childbirth.

Eve: After the eating of the Tree of Good and Evil, I was given the name Chava, which means "Mother of All Living." What an honor and privilege! Previously I was simply called woman. I did not have a real name. Now I was elevated to the holy status of mother. If it was really such a sin, why would I be rewarded with this glorious name?

Regarding the punishment of pain in childbirth, people assume that pain is bad, but pain is not bad if it is serving a positive and holy purpose. Life is all good. The pain of childbirth is particularly exquisite for it cracks open the heart, soul, and body of a woman so she receives a higher and more profound revelation of God. Through giving birth, a woman becomes like God. She is the creator of life. After the pain of childbirth, she is better able to mother her child as this child has come through her.

Birthing like much of life is not something that a woman can control, but something that she must allow to take place within her and through her. When a woman learns to relax, trust, and ride the wave of bodily sensations during birthing, she is filled with awe. She bears witness directly to the Divine Mother's holy work taking place within her. Always remember relax, let go, and open to the love that flows through you by virtue of being a woman. If a woman becomes very frightened when giving birth, there will be more pain than necessary. A woman's pain in childbirth and life in general diminishes when she learns to surrender to that which is greater than herself. Please keep your beautiful heart open, even when you are sad and frightened. It is much better to feel the depth of your feelings, breathe through them and release them rather than build a hard shell around your sensitive and beautiful heart that will only block off the flow of love to you. Your safety paradoxically lies in your openness, your vulnerability and willingness to surrender to the depths of who you are.

At her very core, every woman must learn not to resist life but rather to courageously and open-heartedly embody the beauty of life and awesomeness of the *Shechinah* for all to see. The Divine Mother is revealed through every woman, whether she is birthing a child, nurturing relationships, or involved in creative projects that foster greater connectivity and love in her world. When a woman opens herself to embody Her, she will feel ecstatically joyful and grateful for the awesome gifts and even the challenges that have been given to her as a woman.

Question: What about your husband "ruling" over you? That does not sound good to me.

Eve: This was also not a punishment. I actually wanted Adam to "rule" over me. When a woman allows a man to demonstrate leadership, they are both uplifted. When a woman is honoring of her man, he becomes more honorable. If a man does not offer a woman direction, she has no need for him. I know that may not sound politically correct to many women and men in your modern time. Please understand that I did not want to be independent like Lilith, neither do most women. It is quite simple. A woman was created to receive from a man. She has been blessed with a womb that is a portal to the Divine. Her very womb is an internal compass to guide her forward as a woman. She will draw the right man toward her if she only listens and allows the arousal to occur within her.

Within the womb of most women is a deep hunger for a man, a soul mate, and ultimately a husband. To this man, a woman will joyfully open, surrender and allow him to enter her, penetrate her and permeate her with light and love. The feminine heart yearns for this depth of love. That is the main reason why I ate of the Tree. Adam was a great light. Even angels worshipped him. Adam was my husband and soulmate, so naturally I yearned to open my heart, my body, and my soul in surrender to him. When my husband was giving to me, it was good for both of us, and we were both happy and joyful.

Question: How is your story relevant to people today?

Eve: Because each man has a bit of Adam's light and each woman has a bit of my love, when they come together, they can experience the same joy that we did. The experience of oneness makes men and women very happy and the world is uplifted as well. Marital relations are a kind of re-union, through which men and women not only remember, they return and reclaim the original state of oneness that Adam and I had. Remember, the key to joy and fulfillment for a woman lies in her surrender, in her openness, her willingness to be vulnerable, to receive, and share.

Question: It sounds like you are recommending that women be sub-ordinate to men.

Eve: You clearly do not understand what I am saying at all. Ruling does not mean dominating or controlling. Ruling is about giving, bestowing, leadership. A man who is connected to the Divine and living to his potential is a true giver. It is his joy and it is his nature to provide direction for the woman and to give or, so to speak, rule with generosity. As I said earlier, within the heart and body of most women is the desire to receive from a man she can trust to give to her the highest light of God. Such a woman yearns to become impregnated with light and love, to nurture and grow it within her, so as to give the world something infinitely greater than what she had received. Our very anatomy reveals these deeper secrets. For example, a man gives a drop of semen, and woman receives it, transforms it, and then gives the world an infant human being, created in the image and likeness of the Divine. Need I say more?

When a woman opens and truly allows herself to surrender and receive the divine light her husband gives her by his very being and all that he does, she is then also better able to nurture herself and others. Everything around her comes alive and blossoms through her nurturing. Such a woman has a special radiance. When a woman is happy, her husband is happy, her children are happy.

Question: What about men who are not so generous? There are men who are cruel to women. Should woman allow themselves to be subordinate to them?

Eve: If a man does not demonstrate the capacity to be a bestower of light and love, there is no reason for a woman to remain with him. Of course, she must never allow herself to remain in a relationship where she is abused or feels even less than her husband. There is no holy purpose in that.

A man who seeks to dominate and control a woman, rather than give the light of his God consciousness to her, is disconnected from the Holy One. He pretends to be strong, but he is actually insecure and weak. He secretly fears and may be even jealous of the inherent spiritual beauty, awesome power, and Godliness of a woman. This kind of a man is actually more concerned with receiving than giving. No matter how masculine he may externally appear to be, he is more like a female than a man. But unlike a beautiful woman, his receiving is not for the sake of giving, so he is further weakened by his own selfishness, rather than strengthened. Only when a man becomes a giver is he strengthened.

Question: What about religions that are oppressive to women? Should women simply accept their second class status?

Eve: Unfortunately, it is true that there are manmade religions or aspects of true religions that are oppressive to women. Rather than honoring and elevating women, they treat them as second-class citizens. These religions even blame me for their evil actions. This is their projection and I am not responsible for that. They must know that when they do not honor, love and cherish women, they do not act in ways that are pleasing to the Holy One and the *Shechinah*, the Divine Feminine. The Holy One loves women and chose the woman to be the channel to bring life into the world. Is this not an honor and privilege?

Question: Is there additional advice on this topic that you would like to give to women at this time? Many women are angry and suffer from low self-esteem because of this mistreatment.

Eve: As a general rule, a woman must never allow herself to be defined by those who negate her intrinsic beauty and seek to subjugate her. Look at me, people throughout time have said such evil things about me. Follow in my footsteps and be unafraid. Please do not allow yourself to be at the effect of those who seek to denigrate you simply because you are a woman. It is a big mistake for a woman to judge herself by the criteria of a predominantly masculine culture that honors the qualities of the masculine at the cost and diminishment of the feminine. In societies that value power over love, a woman might easily feel embarrassed, even ashamed, because she feels more deeply than a man. This is wrong. The beautiful loving heart of a woman is a divine gift, a blessing to all and must be cherished rather than ridiculed.

Women, please remember your true beauty and your power lies in your willingness to embody the light and the loving heart of the Shechinah. No one can take that away from you, though they may try. Delight in being a loving beautiful woman. If you suffer from low self-esteem, it is only because you have not internalized this truth sufficiently. Being a woman must be celebrated continually. Being a woman is a privilege.

Question: How did you feel when Adam blamed you for eating of the Tree? Did you not feel betrayed?

Eve: I was so happy when Adam ate of the fruit I gave him to eat. After I ate of the fruit of the forbidden tree, our consciousness was radically different from each other. He expressed his love for me by eating of the fruit so we would once again be united with each other. But when the Holy One questioned him, he blamed me for the change in his consciousness. I was so very disappointed in Adam. I could no longer trust him. Yes, I did feel betrayed, but even more I felt sorry for him. He showed himself to be so weak by blaming me, his wife, rather than simply explain the reason for eating of the fruit and take responsibility for his actions.

Question: Does what happened between you and Adam affect men and women today?

Eve: Yes, it does, unfortunately. It is important for both men and women to understand the effect. Because Adam blamed me as he did, there is still a residue of concern within all women throughout time wondering whether they can trust men. Will a man be strong enough to stand up for love, for truth? All women ponder this question and even at times test their men.

Similarly, because I gave to Adam to eat from the forbidden tree, I have come to understand that many men are still so afraid of the awesome depths of women that they have difficulty loving them. Because of their own feelings of inadequacy and insecurity, they may even be jealous of women and threatened by their innate spiritual power. So much healing needs to happen between men and women. When the healing between men and women is complete, there will be peace in the world.

Question: You had three children with Adam. One of them Cain slew his twin brother Abel.

Eve: Regrettably, Cain was jealous and angry when his offerings were rejected and his brother's were accepted. He did not and could not appreciate the difference between the two offerings. Whereas he had offered a small amount of the inferior portions of his crop, actually the leftovers after he had eaten, Abel had offered the finest of his flock before enjoying any personal benefit. Is there not a difference? Furthermore, in making the offerings, Cain was arrogant and selfish and Abel was humble and generous. As a result, Abel's flock prospered and Cain's produce dwindled, which only added to Cain's feelings of jealousy.

Because he was the firstborn, Cain felt a sense of entitlement that he would rule over Abel. The Lord then warned Cain directly about the power of jealousy to lead to sin and gave him the opportunity to change and do better. But Cain was so consumed with anger he could not hear this divine call for repentance.

As his mother, I want you to know that Cain did not mean to kill Abel. It was not his fault. If it was anyone's fault, it was mine. Cain did not know that there would be death as a result of his actions. We had never witnessed death before. My son Cain unfortunately contained within him much of the sperm remaining in my body from my encounter with the serpent. He was not really the son of Adam. He did not resemble him at all. Abel was also not really Adam's son either, though he contained less of the sperm of the serpent.

Abel's death was a great loss to me. At this time of tragedy, Adam deserted me, rather than comfort me. He left me for 130 years. During this time period, he consorted with Lilith, creating demons and the souls of people who would incarnate later but would not be blessed with pure living divine soul. These souls have incarnated into human bodies throughout time and they cause great evil in the world. These people may look human but they are not fully human. These evil souls continue to live, causing chaos even in your time as well. These souls whether they inhabit Jewish bodies or not can be known by their antipathy to the Jewish people.

Question: Adam left you for 130 years!

Eve: Yes. Even though Adam deserted me for 130 years, I waited patiently for him to return to me. I did not return to the serpent. I knew that Adam would eventually come back to me because it was divine will that we would be together. We are soul mates. Adam did eventually return to me and I birthed Seth, who was the perfect expression of our union. Seth was born with the likeness of Adam, not like my other previous children. The children of Seth would carry on our mission of perfecting the world. Adam and I gave everything we knew to Seth.

Question: Many women today are still waiting to be united with their soul mate. Do you have some words for them?

Eve: My heart is with women who are not married or in a bad marriage in which they are not loved. I know this pain intimately. It is truly heartbreaking that so many women and men are not wedded to their true soul mate. This is an expression of the exile of the *Shechinah,* the Divine Feminine. When a man and woman are married to their proper soul mate, they bring oneness into the world and reveal the *Shechinah* in their midst. Because each woman contains a part of me and each man contains a part of Adam, every marriage restores the union between Adam and me. Every marriage has the possibility of bringing good and healing to the world.

When there is a breakdown in marriages, improper sexual relationships, or there are many lonely single people, disharmony is brought to the world. It is not good. Men are given the commandment to marry, because they need it. It is more within the nature of a woman to marry. They do not need the commandment to marry.

Question: Do you have any guidance for a woman?

Eve: Generally speaking, a woman is naturally more evolved and sensitive than a man. She loves more deeply and knows how integral love and relationship are in life. Women must be patient and do whatever they can to help men evolve. That is what I did and continue to do through women today.

The heart of the woman, whether she is single or married, is still patiently waiting and even yearning for the time when she can gracefully receive the light of the highest consciousness. A woman finds her fulfillment in the act of surrender to life, to the beloved one, found in her soul mate, human and divine. An open loving heart is the most joyful way to live.

Question: Not all women are so spiritual or patient nor do they want to surrender and be submissive as you recommend.

Eve: Yes that is true. For some women, Lilith is more of their ideal than I am. They admire the rebelliousness of Lilith and her ability to challenge Adam. Many of these women celebrate their independence and pride themselves on all their accomplishments, but this is not the truth of a woman's heart. I suspect that inwardly many of these women are angry, bitter, critical, and resentful because they simply do not know how to receive from the universe. Rather than live openly and gracefully as I advocate, they try to control reality. Their own needs and desires are too often foremost in their minds. They are all about taking, controlling, and manipulating others for their own selfish purposes, rather than sharing the beauty and goodness of life with others. Is there not a difference between receiving in order to share and simply taking solely for one's own benefit?

Woman who embody Lilith qualities may know how to use their sexuality in order to successfully seduce men like Lilith does, but they cannot love them nor do they even want to love them. Love requires vulnerability and surrender and that is too frightening to these women. There is a protective shell around their hearts that does not allow them to experience the surrender and joy of love. There is an unfortunate legacy of the wounded and defensive feminine that has been transmitted from mother to daughter throughout the generations.

Question: What can women do to heal their defensiveness?

Eve: All women need to be sweetened by love, human and divine. A woman must know this about herself. Without this sweetening, she will be embroiled in negativity, and be unable to free herself. Yet, by strengthening her connection to the Divine through prayer, meditation, and doing good deeds, she will be opened to receive the love of the *Shechinah,* the Divine Feminine. A woman must learn to surrender to love and not to her fears. Love has the power to shatter the invisible energetic walls around her heart. Fear will only imprison her even more. By opening her heart and allowing herself to be vulnerable, a woman learns to trust and love herself, life itself, and God. The beauty of a woman lies in her receptivity, openness, and vulnerability, and not in her neediness or fearfulness.

When she is sufficiently healed, her open loving heart and light will draw to her a trustworthy man who can give her the love and pleasure she was created to receive. Until she has been sweetened by divine love, she must, however, be discriminating in her relationships with men. Not all men are worthy of her trust. A man may be equally self-serving and disconnected from the Divine as she is. Yet, when she discovers the power of love within her, she can be vulnerable because she knows that her safety truly comes from God. Her vulnerability becomes a gift she can offer to others. She no longer fears love, but knows, deep in her heart, that she has been bestowed with a beautiful loving heart to heal a particular man, those around her, as well as herself.

Question: Please speak about your relationship with Lilith.

Eve: Quite honestly, there was jealousy between Lilith and me in the beginning. When Adam was with her, he was not with me. He often compared me to her, and wanted me to be as sexual and independent as she was. Yet, as much as he desired her, he could never possess her as he could me. I was his alone, though he did not always appreciate me.

Lilith and I have reincarnated through many lifetimes to heal the rift between us. Now with the expanded perspective of time, I can appreciate that there was much that we needed to learn from each other. Over time we have gained a greater understanding, love, and respect for each other. In your modern time, the relationship between Lilith and me is being rectified most completely. Women have embraced Lilith energy in their desire to be independent, sexual, and powerful. But as I said earlier and reiterate once again, this alone will not fulfill them. Women need to embrace my more gentle loving energy as well. It may even be necessary for women to embody both the energies of Lilith and me within themselves.

For example, a woman needs to acknowledge and reclaim the Lilith within her, that is, her shadow dark self, and redeem her with the light and love of her higher consciousness, particularly, if she has no man to share his higher light and love with her. Whether she is single or married, she herself, on her own, must allow the necessary sweetening of the hard shells that have formed around her heart to take place. As a woman travels the path of feminine spirituality, she learns how to do just this. A woman can be strong and loving at the same time. This is very holy work, for in so doing, she redeems herself and the world.

Question: What should we learn from your story?

Eve: Do not lose faith. Remember that deep within you, life is intrinsically good. Beyond the labels of good and evil, beyond pain and betrayal, there is only good. Everything is good. Before we ate from the Tree of Good and Evil, there was only good. The way to return to the consciousness of the Garden of Eden is to see all of life as good and make choices that reflect the goodness of life.

Do not take life for granted. Remember that your time in the physical world is limited. Life in the physical world is precious because it does not last forever. You can re-create life in the Garden of Eden in the special moments of love you share with others. I know that life in the physical world is not easy, but it is nevertheless a great gift and privilege. Always remember that.

Question: Do you have a particular closing message for women today?

Eve: Keep your heart open. As a woman, you have much to teach man about love and surrender and how to truly serve God. Most men do not live and feel as deeply as you do. They are often not even in touch with the lack of depth in their lives. A man is more governed by his routines, his habits, his thoughts, rather than his heart. A woman lives for love. This is good and a sign of her strength and not a weakness. In her heart of hearts, a woman cannot tolerate superficiality. So honor your depths. Yearn to surrender and be penetrated with Godliness. This is a greatest joy.

You are innately beautiful. Honor the divine gifts that you have been given as a woman. When you open to the *Shechinah,* you may embody Her and radiate Her love to all you meet. Know that when you are with your man in holiness in sexual intimacy, you bring peace and harmony to the world. Keep yourself beautiful and attract a man to you. Without the arousal of the feminine, man would do very little in this world. You can not overestimate the influence you have upon your man, your children, friends and the world at large.

Question: Do you have a particular closing message to men today?

Eve: A man is like the sun brilliantly shining light upon all, that is when he is plugged into the Divine. Such a man is focused, assertive, disciplined, and heroic if need be. Like a decisive and fearless warrior, he can stand up courageously to all kinds of challenges and obstacles. His word is his pledge. He can be counted on to carry through with what he has committed to do. He walks his talk. He takes responsibility for his life and never blames anyone for his weaknesses and seemingly failures, particularly his wife.

Such a man is a wondrous being, worthy of a woman's love and adoration. If you inhabit a male body, strive to be this kind of man.

As a man, know that you will be tested in life, even by your own wife. As you pass these tests, you earn respect for yourself and from others. Let your word really mean something. Do not be hesitant to work hard. You came into this world to overcome evil, to do good, and transform this world into a dwelling place for the *Shechinah,* the Divine Feminine. You will do this best when you are married.

If you are married, honor, cherish, appreciate, and love your wife. Like a beautiful flower, your wife needs your love to blossom. Little gestures mean so much to her. If you do actions that reflect these intentions, you will be worshipped by her. If you are not yet married, pray that you be guided to find your true soul mate, the one who will help you to be all that you can be, and then go out to find her in any way you must.

Also, give yourself time to be alone each day, to strengthen your inherent love connection with The Holy One Blessed be He. God is ready to give you all the strength you need to live your life powerfully. Meditate, pray, and learn each day. Do a physical spiritual practice as well. My final blessing and prayer is that women and men come together to rejoice in love and transform this world into a paradise it was intended to be.

Concluding Response to Mother Eve

(It is suggested that this be read out loud by the reader or group)

"Mother Eve, thank you for your wisdom and your love. We have learned so much about the beauty and heart of the feminine from you. Most importantly, we have learned how to honor and cherish the feminine within ourselves and the world. We now identify more with the moon rather than the sun. Like the ever-changing moon, we as women demonstrate to all the art of openness, receiving and willingness to change and grow.

It is our nature and joy to be beautiful holy vessels who draw to us the love and light we need to be creative in this world. We are no longer ashamed of our vulnerability and longing for love and God. We were created for love. We create through love. We are not afraid of the power of our love. We do not fear love. Our hearts are so full of love. We are dedicated to increasing this love by sharing with others. We will safeguard our homes, our relationships and our mother earth. Like you, Mother Eve, we are not afraid to enter into places of darkness within ourselves and others for the sake of love so as to reveal the light and love of the Shechinah inherent in all. May we each do our part in redeeming the Shechinah from Her hiddenness and exile, so the world will be a better place because of our love."

Prayer to the God of Mother Eve (Chava)

Reader: *May the God of Mother Eve grant me the vision, the courage, the strength to enter into places of darkness so as to heal and redeem what is wounded, what is hidden, within me, others, and the world. May I be blessed to help restore all I encounter to a greater light, openness, and love.*

What Quality of the Feminine Does Eve Demonstrate ?

In the interview section of this chapter, Eve states it succinctly: "Love is life to a woman." It is for love that Eve ate of the fruit of the Tree of Good and Evil. Love may be the deepest motivation within a woman who embodies the feminine energy of Eve. Eve also initiated free will for humanity. Freedom and love are intertwined. There can not be love without freedom. One can not be coerced to love.

A woman is a co-creator with the Divine. Because the woman has been endowed with a greater sensitivity, she was given the privilege of birthing new life out of her very own body. Life springs out of a woman, and as such she experiences herself more connected to others and to "mother" earth.

In addition to the privilege of being a vehicle for the physical, emotional, and spiritual birth of a human being, a woman can birth a new consciousness that expresses a greater connectivity for the world. It is for this reason that the woman is considered to be a more refined sensitive being. Humanity looks to the feminine for this kind of revelation of Godliness. The Divine Feminine, known as the *Shechinah,* refers to the revelation of the immanence of God. Generally speaking, the masculine energy is about conquering new terrain, bestowing good, and fighting evil, while the feminine energy is about revealing love and connection in one's midst, experiencing the deepest light and love in one's own body.

The design of our physical bodies also reveals an important difference between the masculine and feminine. For a man, sexual union takes place outside of his body, his sexual organ becomes rigid, tension builds, and he must enter and penetrate a body that is outside of himself to experience sexual intimacy. For a woman, sexual union takes place inside of her, and she must open to receive the man to allow this penetration to take place within her very body. Love opens a woman to receive the gifts of a man. Her ability to trust herself and surrender to God will shape her receptivity. When a woman is most open, she is vulnerable, beautiful, and courageous.

Love and relationship is most important to the feminine. She should bear no shame of her innate yearning to love and be loved for this is what she teaches the world. By her very being and natural radiance, she lifts up the consciousness of all around her to greater love and receptivity. When the feminine feels loved, and loves and nurtures others, she feels most fulfilled and alive.

Spiritual Practices Learned from Eve
Holy Intimacy

Judaism may be the only religion that affirms that marriage and sexuality bring a person to a higher state of holiness than abstinence. Other spiritual traditions teach that a person who aspires to levels of holiness should be celibate and generally separate from the physical world to be more fully immersed in Godliness. Judaism is different. Because God is both spiritual and physical and beyond either, Judaism is all about making unification between the physical and spiritual worlds, as well as the physicality and spirituality within each of us. Because our sexuality is such a powerful biological and physical urge, and because it also connects us to the deepest and innermost core of our souls, it provides us with the opportunity to make the highest forms of unification. According to Rabbi Moses ben Nachman Gerondi, known as the Ramban and Nachmanides, sex brings wholeness not only to us, but it radiates spiritual energy and healing to the world. Though the sexual act is brief, its effects spread to all aspects of our life.

Sexuality is very important to a woman, possibly even more than a man. For that reason, according to Jewish law, a husband has to provide a woman with sexual relations as she desires during the appropriate times. For example, he can't leave for business trips that would minimize her times for sexual fulfillment. Yet many women are not enjoying sexual relations as much they could. Sexual dysfunction is rampant in married couples today and sex is even experienced as burdensome to many women. It is unfortunately too common for women to have sexual relations as a form of obligation, while others may even refuse to have sex, preferring cuddling in place of sexual penetration.

The purpose of sexual relations is ultimately to give pleasure to the woman. The body of a woman is designed by God with the ability to receive greater pleasure and enjoyment from sexual relations than men. Every woman must know this for herself. According to Jewish law, it is more important for man to satisfy and please his wife than himself. This unique pleasure, joy, and knowledge experienced in sexual union is what Eve wanted and why she ate of the Tree of Good and Evil and gave it to Adam. The *tikkun* (healing) of the feminine asks that women give themselves permission to enjoy sexual relations.

A woman is sensitive to the fusion of love and sex. A women's heart and genitals are more deeply connected than a man. In the act of sexual relations, a woman must allow herself to be penetrated, the man's sexual organ enters her innermost chambers, so it is natural and necessary for her to be more refined, discriminating and less promiscuous than a man. As such, a woman must use discernment to control the gates of what she allows to enter her and never allow a man to enter her who she does not love or want his energy to reside within her. Yet she must also be able to surrender and open her gates, for it is through holy sexuality a woman experiences her true spiritual and physical fulfillment. Her very body is a vehicle for the greatest revelation of Godliness.

A woman who engages in promiscuous sexual relations because she is seeking validation of her femininity, male approval, love from others or for any other external benefit will not feel fulfilled. If she views herself as a sexual object, she will treated as such. Her self-esteem will be diminished from participating in acts of sexuality that are not rooted in love and holiness. It is also possible that a woman or even a girl may also be sexually violated or exploited through no fault of her own. Such women will most likely need to do remedial therapeutic work to reclaim their natural birthright of healthy, enjoyable, holy sexuality.

Sex in Judaism is a most holy act, a way to experience and reveal God in the world. Sexual relations done with the proper intention, as a spiritual act, as a demonstration of love and desire for unity with one's partner, creates protective angels for one's self and community and brings peace to the world. Sexual relations done improperly, during a woman's menstrual cycle, or for the wrong reasons, has negative consequences to one's soul and the world. Sex without connection to love, God, or holiness is simply an animalistic act. There is no real intimacy or healing possible in such an act. Furthermore, sexuality that is purely physical undermines whatever spirituality is present and creates *klippot*, opaque shells that disconnect us from the light of the Divine Presence.

There are three partners in the sexual relationship: a man, a woman, and God. Meditation and intention elevates the sexual act to the most holy act between a man and a woman. In Kabbalah, the bedroom is called the "holy of holies." In Kabbalistic sexual practices, the man is *Ha-Kodesh Boruch Hu* (the Holy One) and the woman is the *Shechinah* (the Divine Feminine).

Through sexual relations, the greatest unification takes place. Holy sexuality requires character refinement and consciousness on the part of both the man and woman. Be mindful of your intentions when engaging in sexual relations.

Meditative Practices of Eve
Proper Eating

As the first "sin" took place through eating, a primary spiritual practice from Eve is eating the right foods with proper intention. Eating is not just physical food, we ingest all kinds of food. What we do for recreation, the movies, the television we watch, the books we read, the music we listen to, the friends and acquaintances we associate with, the work we do, everything we take into ourselves is food and has the ability to strengthen or weaken us. It is necessary that we "eat," but how and what we eat is important and affects who we are.

Be mindful and conscious of what you take into your body, your heart, and your soul. We live in a world of choice. We can purify, elevate, and lift ourselves and others up by the choices that we make or we can hurt ourselves and others. It is quite simple and basic. Love yourself enough to make choices that are nurturing to you. Before "eating," consider whether this food or activity will truly support your well-being. Does it connect you to the Divine? Is it loving and healing? Do you feel better afterward? Do you eat for immediate gratification?

Make an inventory of foods, friends, behaviors, and activities that truly nurture you. Seek to include them in your life on a frequent basis. Similarly seek to reduce and eliminate foods and behaviors that weaken you. If a person is depressed, no matter what has happened in life, she or he needs more spiritual nutrition in their diet like prayer, meditation and Torah study. It may be helpful to keep an accounting in a journal or diary so you can see the progress you make in healing yourself and others through proper "eating." Learn to say the blessings before eating and after eating.

Eating with Blessings

Because of our "fall" we need to eat physical foods rather than live just on spiritual light. The first foods were fruits, and then vegetables, and then fish and animals. As we develop spiritually, we are able to eat lighter foods and eliminate foods that do not nurture the body or soul.

When we say a blessing, we acknowledge God as the Creator and source of life, we align our will with divine will, and we draw down divine light from above to below. The spark of divine light that is in the food is then elevated and returned to the source of all life as it was an agent for blessing. We help Eve to complete her work by eating proper foods with blessings.

Firstly, it is important to eat food that is nurturing to us spiritually. Eat "kosher" or vegetarian, particularly if you are born Jewish or choose to follow the Jewish path. Within the Torah there is a clear definition of the foods that are good to eat, that is, foods that are spiritually easy to digest. We may not understand the reasons for the prohibitions of certain foods, and we may even like the foods that are forbidden like pork, lobster, scallops, etc., so it will be a bit of an act of surrender and discipline to eat within the proscribed categories. Know that these prohibitions are not logical, so do not try to understand them in this way. If they are forbidden, we must have the faith to accept that they will not support us spiritually.

Eat food with blessings and consciousness that you are lifting up the sparks of Godliness in the food. Eat slowly, take a few breaths before you eat, and during the course of the meal. Chew the food carefully. Be particularly conscious when eating animal such as meat and chicken. It is important that you have the consciousness of lifting up the holy sparks in the animal when you eat.

Blessings for Fruit: *Boruch Ata Adonai Eloyhenu Melech Ha'olam Boray Pre Ha Etz*

Blessings for Vegetables: *Boruch Ata Adonai, Eloyhenu, Melech, Ha'olam Boray Pre Ha Adama*

Blessings for Bread and Meals with Bread: *Boruch Atah Adonai Eloyhenu Melech Ha'olam Ha Motzei Lechem Min Ha Eretz*

Key Points for Reflection and Follow-up Discussion on Eve

1. Do you feel that Eve was a heroine or not? Was she simply tricked by the serpent, was she naive, or did she have a more noble intention?

2. Has the simple more traditional reading of the Biblical text of the story of Eve affected your understanding of marriage, childbearing, and sexuality? How so? Has the more empowering interpretation of the story and the " punishments" contained in this book changed your understanding of yourself as a woman or man? If so, in what way?

3. The serpent is generally considered a symbol of evil in the West, responsible for beguiling Eve to eat the forbidden fruit. In the East, the serpent is a symbol of wisdom. The serpent is the kundalini energy hidden at the base of the spine that rises to restore enlightenment to a person. Can you reconcile these two different interpretations? How do you understand " the serpent" ? It may be helpful to read the kabbalistic commentary on Eve prior to discussing this point.

4. Women have been oppressed throughout time and continue to be so even today in many places throughout the world. In some religions, this has even been justified due to the "sin" committed by Eve. How do you understand the oppression of women? If you are a woman, what have you personally experienced or witnessed?

5. In what ways do you feel "less than" because you were a woman? How can you reframe the ways you criticized yourself or women so that you celebrate the positive qualities of a woman?

6. In what ways do you feel good about being a woman or being a man? What are the unique gifts that a woman and a man have? How do you celebrate and appreciate being a woman or a man?

7. How do you experience the energies of Lilith and Eve in your life? Can you be both loving and powerful? If you are meeting in a group of women and studying this book, take turns dancing out the energies of both Lilith and Eve. Lilith is the dark, powerful, sexual, seductive energy, and Eve is the powerful, loving, mothering, compassionate energy. Can you embrace both energies as a part of you? Can you be loving and soft when needed and also dark and fierce when necessary?

8. How does a couple transform sexual relations to be more holy, more of a knowing experience, a revelation of the *Shechinah,* rather than simply a means for consensual physical or emotional gratification?

Chapter Two

Sarah's Discernment

The Strength of Integrity

Sarah

"Your insight and wisdom is different than a man's. It is foolish to imitate men and try to fit into their version of reality. The world is in great need of what you have to offer."

—*Sarah*

Sarah

Prophetess and Mother of the Jewish People

Sarah, deemed to be one of the most beautiful women who ever lived, was the first mother of the Jewish people, and also considered a prophetess in her own right. Along with her husband Abraham who taught the men, Sarah taught the women about the unity and oneness of God. In her time, when matriarchal societies were still prominent, Sarah was considered a priestess who taught the women the secrets of embodying the Divine Presence.

Throughout her life, Sarah demonstrated that there was no separation between the mundane and the sublime. This is the wisdom of the Divine Feminine that was attributed to Sarah. When Sarah was alive, it is said that her tent was perpetually open, her candles burned from one week to the next, and the bread she would bake would never go stale. Whether Sarah was doing mundane work such as cleaning the tent or in high spiritual meditation, Sarah was believed to be always connected to the Divine. If you were in the tent of Sarah, you would feel the Divine Presence in an almost palpable way. The clouds of glory hovered over her tent.

Sarah's tent was the prototype for subsequent holy places such as the Mishkon, the tabernacle that was first built while the Jewish people journeyed in the desert, as well as the Holy Temple, built by King Solomon. The same miracles associated with these holiest places were first revealed in Sarah's tent. Sarah is the only woman who has a chapter in the Bible named after her.

Even though Sarah lived in such an elevated consciousness of the *Shechinah,* her life was not without challenges. Because of famine, she traveled into Egypt with her husband, who requested she pretend to be his sister, so he would be safe. Only because of her own spiritual powers, Sarah left Egypt unharmed. When in Egypt Sarah met and acquired Hagar, an Egyptian princess, who would become Sarah's foremost disciple and favored maidservant.

After years of infertility, Sarah offered Hagar to her husband so she could bear a child with Abraham through her. At the age of ninety years, when she had physically lost the capacity to bear children, through a visitation of three angels, Sarah's name was changed and she was blessed with a child, Isaac. When Isaac was around three years of age, Sarah ordered the departure of Hagar and Ishmael from their midst. This act was against Abraham's wishes but he is told to "listen to her voice" and submits to Sarah's demands.

When Isaac was thirty-seven years old, his father is summoned to demonstrate his faith in God by his willingness to sacrifice his son Isaac. Prior to this event, Sarah was sent away to Hebron seemingly uninformed about what was to take place. When Sarah received a vision of the pending death of her beloved son by the hand of her husband on Mount Moriah, her soul expires. If her son had been harmed in a natural way, that would have been devastating, she would have been heartbroken for the rest of her life, she would have sought consolation in God, trusted God's will, but by the hand of her husband, this was too much.

In the Bible, read specifically about Sarah in Genesis 11:29. Genesis 12:15-17, Genesis, 16:5, Genesis, 21: 9, Genesis 23: 1-2 For additional Kabbalistic and *Midrashic* commentary on Sarah in this book, see pages 218–222).

Invocation

For those seeking strength, focus, and the courage to follow your own intuition, meditate and commune with Mother Sarah. She will guide you when you are confused about the best choice to be made. She will inspire you. You will receive the clarity of vision to discern the good from the evil, light from darkness, truth from illusion. Call to the God of Mother Sarah in moments of distress and go forth with integrity and passion to do what you know must be done.

Interview with Mother Sarah

Question: Mother Sarah, there are no words to tell you of our love and gratitude for you. We so much need the blessings of your wisdom and your strength at this time of our lives and that of the world. What is your message to women today?

Sarah: Know your worth as a woman. You are a woman, know that you are a priestess. As a woman, you hold the keys to creation within your body and your soul. Within you are the holy secrets and mysteries of life itself. You have come into the physical world, not for your enjoyment, but to embody the holiness and light of the Divine Presence, called *Shechinah* in Hebrew. Respect yourself and listen to what is in your heart. Your insight and wisdom is different than a man's. It is foolish to imitate men and try to fit into their version of reality. The world is in great need of what you have to offer. Women and men do not know of the awesomeness of the power and the holiness of the feminine. For thousands of years, the path of the feminine, its knowledge and spiritual practices, have been diminished and hidden, but this will soon change.

You are more beautiful and precious than you can imagine. Know that there are many in the higher planes of being who are supporting you. I love you. Call on me and I will help you.

Question: What is the feminine way to connect to God?

Sarah: The feminine path to God is very simple. Programmed within your very cells is the knowledge of how to be a vessel for God. Women know how to do this, opening and receiving, but men may also learn how to do this as well. A woman need not toil as much as a man does for a revelation of the *Shechinah*. She only needs to open herself to who she really is for she is actually an expression and embodiment of the *Shechinah*. Men tend to make life quite complex and abstract but it need not be for women. Give yourself time to meditate, for it is there that you will discover who you really are, what you need to do in this world. Open your heart and the *Shechinah* will reveal Herself to you, from within you.

Question: Is there a spiritual practice besides meditation that I should do?

Sarah: One of the tools given to you as woman or those on the feminine path, Jews or non-Jews, to experience the *Shechinah* is to light candles for *Shabbat,* for holidays, or at anytime at all. There is such wisdom to be received from candle-lighting if you give yourself time to receive. It is really quite simple. All you need to do is simply open yourself to receive. Through lighting candles, you are given the gift of direct access to the holy healing light of God. Meditate on the light of the candle, and let it fill your being. When you are in this consciousness, you reveal the light of the *Shechinah*. Whenever you light candles, take the time to gaze at the light of the candles you have lit. Take time to also reflect on what others need and send healing light to them as well. This is a very magical time for a woman.

Question: There was always light in your tent. How was this possible?

Sarah: The light of the candles I lit was ignited and sustained by my continual awareness of God. My consciousness was drawn inward. I lived for most of my physical life on earth joyfully in a state of consciousness, of deep meditation, and of clinging to the Divine. As I tapped into the eternity of God's light, my candlelight was always lit. In this way, all who saw my tent, or beheld it from afar, would know that God is always present in this world.

Dearest child, my beloved one, the very same spiritual light that sustained my candles is also available to you. It is a gift of the Holy One that the Presence of God may be experienced and manifested in this physical world. The light of the *Shechinah,* the Divine Feminine, is always present if you but see through the veil of physicality.

The external world functions with the light of the sun. Life under the sun is all about doing, accomplishing, and achieving. This is what masculine energy is all about. But the light of the candle is given to the women. The light of the candle illuminates passageways to the hidden and deeper realms of being. It is here that you will find the beauty, and love that you seek. The secrets of God are revealed through candlelight. Remember that the external world with all its fascination, beauty, and excitement will never offer you what you can experience through the subtle but infinite illuminations within yourself. It is for this reason that I remained most constantly in my tent.

Question: In Judaism, women have been given the responsibility of lighting candles to initiate holidays and the Sabbath for the home. If there is no woman present, a man must do this for himself. Why is it important for women to light candles?

Sarah: By the light of a woman's consciousness, she will make her home a place of peace and love or, God forbid, one of strife and misery. The happiness and well-being of her family is a reflection of her consciousness. A woman has the privilege to reveal the spiritual light of the *Shechinah* to illuminate the atmosphere of her home, particularly through the lighting of candles.

Beloved one, know that your thoughts create reality. As a woman, the reality that you create is inhabited by everyone around you. Be particularly conscious what thoughts you want magnified in your life. Everything in life begins with thought. You can choose your thoughts.

If your intention is to bring light and love into your home and into the world, the highest most refined spiritual light will flow through you. The consciousness you open to when you light candles will leave a holy scent in your home as well, that will be felt by all who enter your home. Everyone will know intuitively if God is present in your home. Remember that the more light you share with others the more spiritual light will flow through you.

Question: Do you have some general guidance for people, men and women alike, beginning on a spiritual path or returning to Torah?

Sarah: It is necessary to surround yourself with God-loving, life-affirming people, who will support the highest expression of who you are, and if they are not that, then help them to become the kind of people they are meant to be. At the same time, you may need to separate yourself from those who will not change and seek to undermine you. Muster the courage needed to make important lifestyle changes, to live your life according to the values that promote life and not death. It may not be easy, but know that you always have a choice. The choices you make now will influence the conditions you will have to confront in the future. Choose life. Do not abandon your own inner knowing and your own integrity in order to take care of or please others. If you know anything about my life, you know that I was not a people pleaser and you need not be as well. Your life must be internally validated, not by others, but solely by your conscious connection with the *Shechinah.* Be strong.

Question: Mother Sarah, you traveled with your husband in the desert. What was that like for you?

Sarah: When I occupied a physical body, I lived in the consciousness of God. I was completely attuned to the *Shechinah;* She guided my steps. That was more than enough. I did not have to know where I was going. I experienced the holiness of each moment. I always trusted that where I was, where I went, and whom I met were all a part of the divine plan. My faith sustained me. I was never afraid. My husband had received a divine command to leave our home and I went with him of course.

Question: Many people today are angry to hear that your husband did not protect you when you entered Egypt. He asked you to deny your marriage to him, to say you were his sister, so he would be safe. You were kidnapped by Pharaoh. It seemed like he was concerned about himself and not about you. Were you not afraid or angry?

Sarah: I was not frightened spending a night in the palace of Pharaoh and later in the palace of King Abimelech. I knew that no one can hurt me unless it was divine will. I also had the command of the angelic forces that would protect me and harm those who would try to hurt me. I was not angry at Abraham, for he did not know that about himself nor did he have the same abilities that I had. He knew that I would be safe. No harm would come to me. He did not trust that he would be protected in the same way that I was.

When I was in the palaces, I was treated royally. The Pharaoh and then later King Abimelech wanted to marry me. To make me the queen of their empires, they offered me half of their kingdom, all the wealth, all the luxuries beyond my wildest fantasies. I was not tempted, even though my life would be much easier than with Abraham wandering around the desert. I knew what my spiritual mission and purpose was and that I would accomplish this by being married to Abraham. No amount of riches and honor in the world would make me compromise or sell out what I came into this world to birth. I had total clarity and focus. Abraham and I came into this world to teach people about the oneness of God. Is there anything more lofty and wonderful than that?

My beloved daughters and my precious sons, remember that the physical world is a world of illusions, so be very careful. Remember what you came into this world to do. You did not come here to accumulate material possessions, so why do you give so much energy and time to them. Know your worth. Do not measure your worth by the yardstick of materialism or worldly values. Meditate always on what pleases the *Shechinah* and be guided internally. Maintain your focus and you will be protected and happy.

Question: Be fruitful and multiply is one of the most important and is actually one of the first commandments in the Bible. Mother Sarah, would you speak a little bit about the long period of childlessness that you endured before the miracle of the birth of Isaac? Do you have any words to offer for people going through this challenge or other challenges?

Sarah: When confronting any challenge, a person needs to know that everything comes from God. Therefore, one must seek to find the good waiting to be revealed in whatever experience they are facing. Do not think too much about what you want and what you do not have, but reflect and meditate only upon how you may connect with the *Shechinah* through whatever is happening to you. This connection is the essence of why you are in this world.

Nevertheless, I know firsthand how sad and heartbreaking it is to not be able to bear children. My heart is with you. If this is your plight, you must always remember that there are other ways meant for you to nurture life. You do not need to have biological children to be a mother. Look around you; there are so many people and situations that can benefit from your love and wisdom. If you tune into the Holy One, your prayers will be answered. It may not be in exactly the way you wanted, but if you pray deeply enough, you will be transformed through prayer. You will be happy and rejoice in the blessings that are yours.

Question: Why then did you arrange for Hagar to have relations with your husband?

Sarah: When I became old and it was no longer biologically possible for me to bear children, I finally accepted that it was not my destiny to have a child so I arranged for Hagar to be a surrogate mother for me. I reasoned that if the Holy One did not grant me a child, it must mean that I was to fulfill my destiny in another way. Hagar was my most beloved disciple. I loved and trusted her as I did my husband, so I arranged for her to have relations with my husband. I underestimated the impact of this experience for the two of them. I was naive. I did not expect that I would be betrayed by them.

From this one time of sexual relations, Hagar became pregnant. After all the kindness I had shown her, she taunted me, telling everyone that she would soon take my place as the wife of Abraham and as the matriarch of the Jewish people. She would announce to all the women who would come to visit me that she was more righteous than I was because she became pregnant with my husband at the first attempt while I could not bear a child after so many years. Abraham unfortunately encouraged her as well with these dreadful fantasies. She was my servant, but Abraham treated her as a wife. He might have been taken by her youth and physical beauty, but nevertheless, he did not have my permission to marry her. I of course confronted Abraham. I told him as it is recorded in the Holy Torah, "The outrage is due to you. It was I who gave my maidservant into your lap, and now that she has conceived, I became lowered in her esteem. Let Hashem judge between me and you." He did not fight me. He knew that he did not have the right to liberate and marry Hagar. She was given to me when we left Egypt. Once I had nipped this matter in its root with Abraham, it was then necessary to make it clear to her that I would no longer be abused or humiliated by her. Hagar initially ran away but then returned and bore her son Ishmael. It was not easy for me, I remained childless, but I accepted this challenge as divine will.

After everything I went through, the Holy One had compassion for me. My name was changed to Sarah, which means "princess for the nations," from Sarai, which means "my princess." This was a name that Abraham had given me when we were young. From the moment Hashem changed my name, I was transformed. My youth and my beauty were restored to me. It was a great miracle. I was able to bear a child when I was ninety years old.

Question: Mother Sarah, many people are troubled by your sending away Ishmael and Hagar. Would you please explain what that was all about?

Sarah: There are those who say that my decision to send Ishmael and Hagar away was one of jealousy. You must know that it was not. If it were jealousy, there would be nothing that you could learn from me. The Holy One would not have told Abraham to listen to me if it were a matter of jealousy. What I did was very hard but it was necessary. Abraham and I were charged with a very important mission to spread the teachings of the unity of God and safeguard the holy transmission and revelation of YHVH for all generations. This transmission must be pure and uncontaminated by idolatry. The existence of the world depends on this purity of this transmission. It was very clear that Hagar and Ishmael would not forsake idolatry and that they would have a negative influence on Isaac. Ishmael was already indicating his desire to usurp the birthright of my son. When I witnessed him pretending to direct target practice with his bow and arrow at my beloved son, I knew that he might harm or even kill him. I feared for Isaac's physical safety.

Know that I did what I did to protect the physical safety and the sanctity of my son and all the descendants who would carry the holy transmission of YHVH. I did what was necessary and it was confirmed by God. I am so sorry and pained that so many people have had to suffer until the world wakes up to the truth.

Question: Your decision seems to have created separation between the Jewish people and the Arabs, the descendants of Ishmael. It seems that we are still paying for the decision that you made.

Sarah: My beloved ones, my heart is with you. I know how hard and painful these times are. You must be patient. The situation in the world will have to become more intense until it becomes better. Regarding the difficult situation between the Arabs and the Jews, I cannot and I do not take responsibility for that. I did not cause this hatred. Rather, in sending

Ishmael away, I demonstrated to the Jewish people for all time what they must do to safeguard life and the integrity of the spiritual mission they have. In time the world will acknowledge the unique role that the Jewish people have played. There will be peace.

Remember the prophecy that Hagar received. "He shall be a wild-ass of a man. His hand shall be against everyone." Isaac was too young and not strong enough to protect himself from the influence of Ishmael. Ishmael has been blessed by Abraham, yet his descendants are jealous of the blessings of others. Too often they provoke war with others because of these jealous feelings. You have only to look around your world to see the fulfillment of this prophecy. The jealousy of others will ultimately be the downfall of the people of Ishmael. In the end, they will learn the foolishness of jealousy. It will be the hard way, but they will learn.

Question: Can you offer any other guidance to the Jewish people?

Sarah: There will be war between the Jewish people and the people of Ishmael over the ownership of the Land of Israel because the Jewish people have failed to claim ownership of the land according to the prophecies received by Abraham. The land is a divine gift to my descendants and must be treasured as such. Ishmael cannot be expected to value the holiness of this transmission when the Jewish people do not. When the Jewish people recognize that the Land of Israel is holy, it is unique, it is not like other nations, the people of Ishmael will accept that as well. Then there will be peace.

Question: Everyone talks about how great Abraham was in his willingness to sacrifice Isaac, and Isaac (Yitzchak) in his willingness to surrender his life, but little is said about the impact that this act had on you.

Sarah: I was totally devastated when I saw in a vision that my husband was going to kill my precious and only son. My son was my life. In a single moment's time, my whole life with Abraham seemed like a total sham. This act was against everything I valued in life. The death of my son by the hand of my husband was more than I could bear. So many thoughts and feelings rushed into my head. Why did not Abraham consider what this act would mean to me? How could he be so selfish? Was he unconsciously paying me back for sending Ishmael away? God had told him before to listen to me. Why did he not consult me before planning to do this horrific act?

Question: You died alone, abandoned and betrayed by your husband and your son.

Sarah: Do not worry or be pained on my account. It is true that I was deeply pained for a few moments, but then I knew that I needed to act quickly to save my son. I consciously chose to leave my physical body, in the company of my handmaidens, holy women I lived with for many years, to intercede before the throne of mercy for the life of my son. Let me die. Let me be the sacrifice, and not him. Take me and not my precious son. My prayer was answered. My son lived and I left the physical world. Ask Any mother. She would have done what I did.

It was clear to me that after saving my son's life, my work in the physical world was complete. There was no reason for me to remain embodied. I knew my son and his soon-to-be wife would assume the mantle and continue the holy work that Abraham and I began and I would continue to guide him from the other side. There was nothing more that I needed to do in life, but something very important that I needed to demonstrate through my death. From my death, let it be known that there are things in life worth dying for.

Question: What are we to learn from your death?

Sarah: Please know that I value life. I could not live in a world where life was not valued. My husband and men throughout time seem to need to prove themselves through acts of bloodshed and violence. This is not the path of the feminine that I taught and want to impart to you. The feminine path is all about loving life, revealing Godliness, and even experiencing the holiness of God in one's body. With my death, sadly enough, a new order began for women and men. Women would no longer work in the forefront as I did, but would have to work more behind the scenes, in supportive roles. Not for a long time would the prophecy of the woman be as honored as was mine.

Question: The situation is still similar today. Men are still engaging in war. Do you have any final words for women and men today?

Sarah: You live in awesome and awe-inspiring times. Now is the time to reclaim the path of the feminine that I began. You will be supported from on high by many great ones. Doors to palaces of spiritual delight that have been closed for so long will now easily open for you to enter, but you must stay clear and focused. Know your worth. Keep yourself pure. Love life. Be strong. May you be privileged to lift the veil of the *Shechinah* so Her light may shine throughout the world. May the peace of Her revelation come soon and easily to Israel and the entire world. Thank you for all your good work, my beloved sons and daughters. I support you. I love you.

Calling Out to Mother Sarah

(It is suggested that this be read out loud by reader or group)

"Mother Sarah, we bear witness to your pain. You did not die in vain. Your pain is our pain. We hear a strong message of the value of life in your death. We understand that you could not remain in such a world that your son would be sacrificed. Mother Sarah, we are your children. We honor your voice, your power, and your life. In your lifetime, you were the embodiment of the *Shechinah,* the Divine Feminine. With your death, the voice of the Divine Feminine became more hidden.

We have learned so much about the path of the feminine from your teachings and example. Help us to have the courage and integrity to speak and live our truth like you did. So many of us are looking for our voice, we have been silenced. We do not speak our truth. Too often we avoid conflict and seek to please others rather than assert our truth. Help us to be fearless like you.

In reclaiming the path of the feminine, we promise to value the fullness of life as it is. We will value ourselves and each other above the abstract idealization of life. This is our pledge to you, our Jewish mother. With our love and our discernment, we will redeem the *Shechinah* from Her hiding. With the blessings of the Holy One and you, we will indeed lift the veil that is covering Her and let Her light shine in all Her splendor."

Prayer to the God of Mother Sarah

May the God of Mother Sarah guide me to make the choices that serve my highest good. May the God of Mother Sarah empower me with the strength to remain true to my vision even though it may not be what others would want of me.

What Quality of the Feminine Does Sarah Demonstrate ?

Sarah models a woman who can stand her ground doing what she feels necessary even if it is not popular and even if it is against the wishes of her husband. Contrary to Western concepts of femininity as soft and helpless, Kabbalah sees woman as having a higher level of intuition and inner strength that she must employ in her life for the betterment of the world. It is the feminine energy that is analytical enough to make distinctions and strong enough to set necessary boundaries. It is the power of the feminine to discern what needs to be included and assimilated from that which needs to be separated and released from one's contact.

Not too long after the birth of Isaac, Sarah ordered that Hagar and Ishmael be sent away. This command distressed Abraham terribly. After all, Ishmael was his son and sending him away was against everything that Abraham believed in. The spirit of Abraham was universal, embracing, and inclusive. Blinded by his kindness, he could not see what was happening in his own house. How could he send away his son? Yet he does so only because God tells him to listen and obey everything that Sarah says. Now it is Abraham who will surrender himself, his thoughts, and his feelings to the voice of Sarah. He is told to obey her, even if he disagrees with her. Her insight is deeper than his. She can see more than he can. Sarah was focused, and strong. She did not waiver in this order even though she knew that it was painful to her husband. The Torah says "listen to her voice." It does not say "listen to her words." The voice is more a reflection of the inner essence of a person. The Zohar says the Torah wanted to emphasize that Sarah was on a much higher prophetic level than Abraham. It was not necessary that Abraham understand what she said, but only that he surrender to her wisdom.

Masculine energy is generally not endowed with the same capacity for discernment as the feminine. It would not be logical for a woman to look toward a man regarding a matter with which she has been endowed with greater clarity and perception. Too often a woman defers to the man when she actually knows better. A woman is generally yielding, flexible, and loving, but she must also exercise discernment and listen to her own inner knowing. It may be necessary, however, for her to purify and distill her intuition so that it is heart-based and free of egoism and selfishness.

We learn from Sarah's example that a woman must find the strength within herself to honor her own inner knowing. Many women suffer from low self-esteem when they deny their own truth in order to meet the needs and wishes of others and/or to avoid conflict with them. They may like to pretend to themselves and others that this behavior is selfless, but it is not. When we do not feel good about ourselves, we often seek validation from others, even at the expense of our own truth. This is a common tendency for many women, but is also prevalent with men who have learned that they also need to give themselves up to be loved. When we continue to betray ourselves and what we know as our truth to please others, to be loved and validated by others, our self-esteem is further diminished. We lose connection with our soul. If we find we are overly concerned with what others think of us, we need to remember Sarah. Step back, engage in self-inquiry to reclaim our own knowing and self-worth.

Make an assessment in your life to determine if there are people, activities, and behaviors that you engage in that do not support you in going forward to be the person you want to be. Exercise discernment. You can let go of what does not serve you or the revelation of the *Shechinah* in the world. If it does not seem possible to do this yourself, seek help from friends, clergy, or a therapist. Do not be a people pleaser. Do not give up your inner truth.

What Spiritual Practice Can We Learn from Sarah?

The spiritual practice of candle-lighting—her candles burned the entire week.

Light candles on Friday night, for holidays, and anytime you want to come closer to the *Shechinah*. Meditate prior to lighting candles. Let go of concerns of the day. If you are feeling any anger or resentment, let it go. You must let it go. Before lighting *Sabbath* or holiday candles, try to make amends toward anyone you may be harboring anger toward or who may be angry at you. Forgive everyone. The very act of forgiveness will open you to receive. Know that you only hurt yourself by being angry. Your anger keeps you small, closed, and not able to receive the gifts of the *Shechinah*. As you stand before the candles, pray that you be able to be a channel for the light of the *Shechinah*.

Light a candle for every person in your home, including yourself, and take time to reflect upon the unique light of every member of your family. Meditate and send light to each person you light candles for. Open your heart and be filled with love and compassion for everyone. As you gaze at

the light, pray that your eyes be purified, so you see what is really important for you, your family, and your friends. At this time, you can also see
what others need to shine more brightly in their lives as well. Trust that
what comes into your consciousness is a message. It is a particularly auspicious time for you to send healing blessings to those in need. Visualize each
person as a candle, shining brightly. You have a responsibility to share the
light with others. Teach other women how to light candles.

If you are a married woman, keep this thought in your mind and deep
in your heart, your husband and your children are in need of the light of
Shechinah that only you can reveal and radiate to them. There is much that
you receive from your husband, but when you light candles you can give to
him what he really needs. You can help him to access his soul. If possible,
ask him to stand next to you when you light candles and say "Amen" to
your blessing. It is no accident that you are married to this man. You are
here to uplift him and help him fulfill his life purpose. When he witnesses
you lighting candles, he will honor you as the priestess of the home, and
of his soul.

What Meditative Practice Can We Learn From Sarah?

Sarah was protected by the *Shechinah* (the Feminine Divine Presence) in the
house of Pharaoh and later Abimelech.

When you experience yourself fearful or at any time, repeat the following affirmation and meditation. Repeat several times "I am protected by
the Divine Presence. God is within me and surrounds me. I am protected
by the Divine Presence. " Take a few breaths. As you inhale, the body
opens. As you exhale, you let go of stress and tension. With each breath,
visualize yourself becoming a vessel. Allow yourself to feel empty. Let go of
passing thoughts. Open to the joy of being an empty vessel. Visualize luminous white light entering through the top of your head flowing through
the body. Let this light surround you and then let the light enter into your
body temple. Imagine that you can embody the *Shechinah* as Sarah did.

Key Points for Reflection or Follow-up Discussion on Sarah

1. Do you think that Sarah should have waited to be blessed with a child of her own trusting in the prophecy her husband received without volunteering Hagar to be a surrogate mother? Or was it necessary for her to take the action that she did?

2. Rabbinic commentaries inform us that Abraham was quick to accept Sarah's proposal. How do you imagine Sarah might have felt by his eagerness? Understandably, the request had to come from Sarah, but why was he so eager to have sexual relations with Hagar? Do you think that Abraham caused the rift between the women? Why is there no recorded prayer request for a child as with the other matriarchs and patriarchs? What would you have done in Sarah's situation and why? Would you have waited, or taken an action like she did?

3. Did Sarah have a choice to not send Ishmael and Hagar away, considering the danger that Ishmael posed to Isaac? Was it the right choice to send them away? Whether you agree with Sarah's decision or not, might Sarah be modeling what to do with evil people in our midst who seek to destroy us. Notice that the Bible does not record Sarah bribing, placating, or pacifying the kind of behavior demonstrated by Ishmael. Why not? What do you think? Sarah's approach may not be seen to be "politically correct" in our time, but is it relevant to us today? Can we heal the rift between Sarah and Hagar today by making peace between their descendants? How do we make peace?

4. Several rabbis say that Sarah committed suicide when she asked God to judge between herself and Avraham in the sending of Hagar and Ishmael away. Did she simply die of grief or old age? Or was it suicide to offer her life as a replacement for her son? Do you accept

other interpretations that she died of joy that her son was going to be sacrificed? What do you think? What do you think of Sarah's closing statements in this book about why she died?

5. What challenges do you have in your life for which Sarah is a model? Take time to write about this or share it with another person. What do you want to say to Mother Sarah? If you could talk with her, what would you say to her. What is your pledge to her?

Chapter Three

Rebecca's Higher Truth:

The Art of Spiritual Deception

Rebecca

"A woman is inherently more attuned to what is hidden, inner, and holy, and is guided to reveal or actualize this dimension of reality when necessary by whatever means that are available to her."

— *Mother Rebecca*

Rebecca

Prophetess and Mother of the Jewish people

There is a little known tradition that a righteous person is not taken from this world until a successor has been born. The Bible therefore records the birth of Rebecca prior to mentioning the death of Sarah, even though Rebecca was born after Sarah died. Rebecca, the second matriarch of the Jewish people, the wife of Isaac, was the daughter of Bethuel, the nephew of Abraham, and the granddaughter of Milcah, sister of Sarah.

After the death of his wife Sarah, Abraham sent his most trusted disciple Eliezer to look for a wife for his son Isaac in the land of Aram, his birthplace. The Bible records in great detail Eliezer's scheme and all the events around his search for the woman who would be worthy of being the wife of Isaac and the matriarch for the Jewish people. When Rebecca offered water to Eliezer and to his camels, she fulfilled Eliezer's pre-planned criteria. In acknowledging the miraculous nature of this encounter, Rebecca and her family gave their consent for her to leave her home and marry Isaac, a man who was considerably older than she.

Rebecca is often referred to as a "rose among thorns," a beautiful metaphor in Song of Songs to describe Israel among the nations. As a child, Rebecca was surrounded by negativity, duplicity, and evil, but she herself remained pure. According to hidden Kabbalistic teachings in the Zohar, at the time of her death, Sarah bequeathed part of her soul to Isaac her son and the other part to Rebecca. Rebecca was even considered a reincarnation of Sarah, who was deemed a reincarnation of Eve. When Isaac and

Rebecca first saw each other, they immediately recognized each other as constituting one soul. The Bible tells us that Isaac only found comfort after Sarah's death when he married Rebecca. The miraculous signs that were associated with Sarah were once again restored when Rebecca entered the tent of Sarah.

When Rebecca had been barren for twenty years, Isaac prayed profoundly for a child with Rebecca. His prayers were answered. Rebecca became pregnant with twins. When she was pregnant, Rebecca was unclear about what was occurring within her. The children agitated within her and she said, "If so, why am I thus?" She consulted Shem, the prophet of the time, to understand what is happening within her. "Two nations are in your womb, two regimes from your insides shall be separated, the might shall pass from one regime to the other, and the elder shall serve the younger" (Genesis 25: 23).

When Isaac was old and wanted to bless his sons, Rebecca overheard the plan of her husband and quickly schemed a way to deceive her husband and secure the blessing for her son Jacob. Jacob was initially reluctant to participate in this ruse, but Rebecca assured him that she would protect him. The final biblical comments about Rebecca include her instructions to Jacob to seek shelter with her brother Laban and find a wife for himself there.

For more information in the Bible, read excerpts in Genesis 22: 23 - 27:42-46

For additional Kabbalistic commentary on Rebecca, see pages 222–235).

Invocation

For those who want to overcome their past, to not be limited by their environment, to express what is true in their hearts, connect with Mother Rebecca. Mother Rebecca will guide you to see clearly what is, to discern what is true from what is false, what is good from what is evil, and to trust yourself enough to take the necessary and required actions to express your inner intuition and inner knowing.

Interview with Mother Rebecca (Rivka)

Question: It is a great honor and pleasure to talk with you, Mother Rivka. What is your message for people today?

Rebecca: In "the End of Days," there will be peace. Truth will be clear and all that is not true will be clearly seen for what it is. Be patient. Life has never been easy, but one must have faith and know that it will be good in the end. There will be peace. There will be prosperity.

Question: Thank you for this powerful encouragement. We live in a time of much war and corruption. Our world sometimes seems hopeless and frightening. How did you acquire this faith and perspective?

Rebecca: I was born into a home and place where hypocrisy, duplicity, and lies were everywhere. I knew intuitively at a very early age that I would have to find the truth within myself. In that way, I would be safe and protected. I did not want to be like the people around me. Most people around me would say one thing and then do something else. They would try to appear to be good, but it was easy for me to see that they were not who or what they appeared to be. Most people in my family and my town were selfish, always calculating what they would receive from others, by whatever means necessary. They always had ulterior motives when they did something good. I was less complicated. From a young age, I knew that the greatest joy in life was to serve other people. It was that simple. When I was giving to others, I was happy and I felt safe. I therefore always looked for ways that I could help other people.

Question: Is that why you gave the water to Eliezer and his camels? That is the first story about you in the Bible.

Rebecca: Yes, exactly. Eliezer, Abraham's servant, was a strong man. He could easily gotten water for himself and his camels. But, before he could get the water for himself, I quickly rushed to offer him water as soon as I saw him come near the well. I let him drink to his satiation, and then I fetched water for his camels. I was happy when he allowed me to give to him in this way. He was clearly a stranger in our town. I knew in my heart what a great honor it is to welcome a stranger into your community. And you see how I was rewarded for doing this act. I was selected to marry such a holy person, Isaac, and I could also leave my family and town as well. What a privilege! What a gift. God is so good.

Question: You married Isaac when you were young? How was your life with him?

Rebecca: Being married to Isaac was a great blessing for me. I was able to grow spiritually in ways that I could not even have imagined. We were very close and happy with each other. Even though there was a considerable age difference between us and we came from different backgrounds, we loved and respected each other. As you may note, I was his only wife, unlike the other patriarchs who married more than one woman.

Question: If you were so close with him, as you say, why did you not tell him of the prophecy you received when you were pregnant? Why did you go to Shem and not to him?

Rebecca: I must admit that I was embarrassed by the discomfort that I was having in my pregnancy. I was afraid that it was because I was unworthy of Isaac. Something was wrong with me because of my family background. If I were truly a righteous woman, I would not suffer so exceedingly. I felt that it was best to seek counsel from someone other than my husband. By going to someone objective, I could then receive guidance on how I could improve myself and not have myself diminished in the eyes of my husband.

Question: When you found out the reason and meaning of what was happening to you, why then didn't you tell Isaac? He was your husband and these were his children as well. It would seem that he should know.

Rebecca: The main reason that I did not confide in Isaac later was because I did not want to embarrass or disturb him. My husband Isaac was after all the greatest prophet. His holiness and his level of prophecy were much greater than that of Shem and Eber. I had to assume that if he was supposed to know this prophecy, he would have known. There must be a reason why God did not reveal this matter to him. Please know that it was not easy for me to keep this secret for all the years, but I did so to honor as well as protect my Isaac.

Question: Why did Isaac need your protection?

Rebecca: My husband was so holy, so good, and so pure. He was more spiritual than he was physical. Remember how he was willing to give his physical life to God by the hand of his father without question. Prior to our marriage, he spent fourteen years in the tents of Shem and Eber, totally shielded from contact with evil or the mundane. He rarely spoke about this event, but I know it changed him forever. He was always more connected to God than to this world.

Question: What do you mean?

Rebecca: So many people try to be holy, to overcome their attachment to the physical. It was the opposite with Isaac. He had to make efforts to be engaged in the physical. Whenever he did engage in the physical world, it was only to bring blessing to it. His time was spent almost continually in prayer and meditation.

I, on the other hand, was more grounded, worldly, and more able to discern good from not good. I knew how to negotiate with the world and how to get things done. It was my job as his wife to protect Isaac so his connection to God would not be disturbed. His holiness should not and would not be tarnished by contact with evil or the mundane. Because Isaac was so holy, he only saw the good. He could not even see the wickedness that was in his son Esau. I did not think it was my place to tell him that his son Esau was deficient in morality.

Even though Esau treated his father with so much respect and pretended to be righteous in front of his father, the way Esau actually lived his life was so contrary to the ways of my husband. I could easily see through all Esau's pretenses because I had seen this kind of hypocrisy in my early childhood. I thought I had left that when I left my home. But it must be in my genes.

Question: Did you not love both your sons? It seemed like you did not love Esau and favored Jacob.

Rebecca: Both Isaac and I loved both our sons equally. It was not because I loved Esau less that I wanted Jacob to have his blessing. The blessing of the firstborn would not have been good for Esau. He would not have been willing to do what he needed to do. It actually would have backfired upon him and made his life worse. He was not capable of working together and sharing power with his brother Jacob. And with this blessing Esau would have been in a position to cause greater harm to the world as well.

Though the blessing of the firstborn offered many privileges, this blessing also required much responsibility and self-sacrifice. Esau did not show any evidence of his willingness to forsake the path of idolatry, murder, thievery, and everything else that he did that was in opposition to the values and ideals of my holy husband. In so many of his actions, Esau continually demonstrated that the material physical world was most important to him. Remember, he had previously sold his birthright for a pot of lentils. That clearly showed that he did not care to be engaged in the struggle that would be necessary to transform this world to a Godly place.

I saw clearly that Jacob was better suited for the work that needed to be done, even though I knew life would be hard for him, much more challenging having received the blessing intended for Esau as well as the one for himself. I also knew and trusted that this blessing would force him to grow in ways that would be good for him and in ways that would also bring blessing to the entire world. Because of the prophecy I had received during my pregnancy, I felt that it was necessary that I do whatever was needed to actualize what had been revealed to me. Jacob was the younger son so I knew that he had to receive the blessing of the firstborn to fulfill the prophecy I received.

Question: Is that why you encouraged Jacob to lie to his father? It would appear that he was initially reluctant to do so.

Rebecca: Yes. Jacob was so pure and good. He did not want to lie to his father. He was also fearful that there would be negative consequences to lying to his father as well. Perhaps he would be cursed rather than blessed. To persuade him to follow my instructions, I informed him of the prophecy I received when I was pregnant and assured him that I would protect him of negative consequences from his father Isaac. He listened to me and honored my request.

Question: Was Isaac upset by the deception?

Rebecca: Initially, yes, he was upset and startled. In a very short time, however, he realized that what happened was what was supposed to happen. It became also clear to him that I was behind the entire deception. Because he trusted me, he then trusted that this was the right way.

If he had not believed that this was a good thing to do, he would have and he could have nullified the blessing. He did not do so. He understood that the descendants of Jacob would need the protection of this blessing that he gave to Jacob.

Question: Do you think that it was right to deceive your husband? Is it good to lie?

Rebecca: Yes, I believe that it was right to deceive my husband in this particular situation. The world is based on truth, so in most instances it is important to be truthful. Honesty is the basis of trust and integrity. Nevertheless, there are extraordinary times like what I confronted when it is good to lie. It is even necessary to lie. To tell the truth in such circumstances is foolish.

Question: What do you mean? How can it ever be good to lie?

Rebecca: When one is confronted by evil, one must be cunning. If necessary, to fight evil, one may even be deceitful. If Esau had been prepared to be a worthy partner in continuing the transmission of YHVH, there would have been no need to take it away from him. But he was not, so rather than fight him directly, it was best to take the blessing away from him through deceit.

There is such a thing as holy lying. There is a difference between holy lying and ordinary lying. In holy lying, it is clear, after the deception, that it is the way it was supposed to be and that the outcome could not have been achieved another way. When the blessing is not revealed to a person or nation directly, one must go through the back door to receive it. That is what I did. It was necessary I do this to actualize the prophecy I received when they were both in the womb. Because this was a most holy matter of great importance, it had to be done through deception. The more refined and higher the light and blessing, the more it is hidden, and the more deception may be necessary to reveal it. That may seem counterintuitive, but that is how it is in matters of holiness.

One way to distinguish ordinary lying or deceit is that it is clear that the purpose of the lying was never noble. It was only self-serving and a person who engages in such acts loses dignity and connection to the Divine. That did not happen to me or Jacob at all. My purpose and that of Jacob was noble.

Question: If you look at biblical stories, women seem to engage in deception more than men. Why is that?

Rebecca: Yes, this is true. Women have a long lineage of holy lying and deception. A woman is inherently more attuned to what is hidden, inner, and holy, and is guided to reveal or actualize this dimension of reality when necessary by whatever means that are available to her. There are many examples of women throughout history engaging in deception for holy and noble purposes. For example, look at Tamar, who disguised herself as a prostitute to fulfill her prophecy, as well as Judith, who also disguised herself as a prostitute to seduce and murder the Greek general Holofernes. Rather than be criticized for doing what they did, they are honored. Similarly, I was not criticized for my actions as well. Many understand that my actions safeguarded the continuity of the Jewish people.

Question: In retrospect, do you have regrets in this regard for your actions?

Rebecca: I do not have regrets. I did what was necessary. If Esau had received the blessing of the firstborn, he would have been in a position to do more damage to the world than he had already done. In my mind, there was no other choice to do other than what I did.

Question: Was the blessing good for Jacob? Jacob's life was not easy. Was it even more difficult because of his stealing Esau's blessing?

Furthermore, the Jewish people, the descendants of Jacob, have been persecuted and murdered by the Christian nations, the descendants of Esau, for thousands of years. It seems like the struggle continues even to modern times. Was it worth it, after all?

Rebecca: Of course it was worth it. It is true Jacob's life was not easy, but his usurping this blessing was necessary to safeguard the sanctity and survival of the world. The Jewish people, the descendants of Jacob, have consequently had to carry an additional burden, requiring that they also demonstrate an enormous sacrifice. Until my son Esau and his descendants realize and accept that they must be subordinate to Jacob and his descendants and to the Creator of the world who has a special covenant with the Jewish people, there will not be peace. Be patient. In time they will.

Question: What does this really mean? Please explain your prophecy: "The older one will serve the younger one."

Rebecca: Please know that the fulfillment of my prophecy does not mean that the Jewish people will rule the world and laud their power over the other nations of the world. This is what the Christian-based nations of Esau have done throughout time. Jacob and his descendants are not interested in dominating the nations of the world. They are only interested in serving the Holy One and in sharing their knowledge and blessings with others so as to transform this world into a place of Godliness.

Question: How will this happen?

Rebecca: When the spiritual principles of faith, morality, and the belief in the oneness and unity of God that are at the core of the transmission of the Jewish people are accepted by the Christian nations, then and only then will there be peace and prosperity for all. This process of the acceptance of the principles of Judaism throughout the world has already begun. There is such a thing as democracy, due to Judaism. Christians are beginning to appreciate the Jewish roots of their faith as well.

Question: Still anti-Semitism is rampant in our modern time. What will it take for the Christian nations to not persecute the Jewish people? Sixty years ago they wanted to annihilate the Jewish people. Now they want to destroy the State of Israel as a Jewish state.

Rebecca: The power and protection of the Jewish people lies with their acceptance of and alignment with the covenantal relationship with God. When they seek the favor of the nations over that of God, they diminish themselves, they suffer and lose divine blessing. When the Jewish people align themselves with God, even non-Jews seek to support them as well.

Question: Do you have any concluding words for our readers?

Rebecca: Do not fret. Do not worry. The descendants of Esau will eventually realize the futility of war and domination and know that scapegoating and demonizing the Jewish people for their own moral failings does not help them but actually weakens them. In time, they will appreciate all the gifts and blessings that the descendants of Jacob have bestowed upon them and the entire world. They will even be grateful that they have received so many of the benefits and blessings without having to suffer and sacrifice in the same way that the Jewish people suffered to give them to them. There will come a time when Christians, the descendants of Esau, will ask for forgiveness from the Jewish people. And the Jewish people will forgive because they are a compassionate loving people.

Calling out to Mother Rebecca
(It is suggested that be be read out loud by reader or group)

"Mother Rebecca, you are such an inspiration to us. May your example guide us to give to others with the kind of generosity you demonstrated throughout your life. May we know directly that through giving we receive all that we need. You saw clearly at a very young age what was true and good and you were not afraid to act upon your own inner knowing. Courageously, you chose to leave all that you knew to go forward in life. You trusted your prophecy. It would have been easier for you to dismiss it, and not act upon it. You were even willing to deceive your husband and son, and absorb all the possible negative consequences because of it as well.

Help us to have your courage to trust ourselves and do whatever is necessary to actualize what we know as true in our hearts and souls. May we center ourselves in the truth that lies within the depths of our hearts so that we too live courageously. May we also be willing to go forward to make the changes we need to live more authentically. Like you did in your lifetime, may we each be willing to stand up to evil, to falsehood without fear, so we may do our part to pave a larger path for the light of the Shechinah to be revealed in our midst. Thank you again for your courage. We love you."

Prayer to the God of Mother Rebecca

Reader: *May the God of Rebecca guide me to discern what is true from what is false, what is good from what is evil, and empower me to live in accordance with my inner truth. Mother Rebecca lived in accordance with her inner truth, and so can I.*

What Quality of the Feminine Does Rebecca Demonstrate ?

Rebecca demonstrates all the beautiful feminine qualities exhibited by Eve and Sarah. This is understandable because Rebecca is considered a reincarnation of Sarah and Sarah was considered a reincarnation of Eve. Rebecca's commitment to her integrity, her courage, and her willingness for self-sacrifice is perhaps more remarkable because Rebecca is born in a place where duplicity, selfishness, and cowardice was so pervasive. Like Sarah, Rebecca demonstrates the ability of the feminine to remain true to her inner core regardless of what is happening around her. The feminine is naturally more intuitive and should allow herself to be guided more by what is internal, that which is found within her own heart and wisdom, than by what is external.

There are so many qualities of the feminine that Rebecca demonstrates that it is difficult to highlight one quality. Surely, Rebecca demonstrates courage and faith when she is willing to leave her parents at a very early age to marry a much older man whom she did not know. She also demonstrates the feminine quality of selfless giving when she gives water to the camels of Eliezer. However, when she takes the steps to actualize her prophetic vision, her willingness to engage in deception to accomplish what was necessary and even to sacrifice herself in this mission, this is what truly earns her the title of being a mother of the Community of Israel. Jacob is frightened initially to engage in deception. Rebecca then tells him: "Let any curse be on me, my son" (Genesis 27:13). In this instance and at many other times in her life, she models to all the willingness to take risks and even if necessary sacrifice oneself for the welfare of the Jewish people and the world. The love of a mother can know no bounds.

A Spiritual Practice Learned from Rebecca: Selfless Giving

Rebecca demonstrates abundant selfless giving in seeking water for Eliezer and his camels. It would have been generous for a young girl to provide water for the man but for the camels as well was an even greater display of giving. Furthermore, she did this on her own initiative and did not seek a reward for this action.

Selfless giving and charity are the gates to blessing and repentance. Consider several ways and projects through which you can pour unconditional abundant giving onto others. Pray and be mindful to give in as selfless a way as possible, so you are not considering what you would receive. If possible, keep this act anonymous. If it is helpful and supportive, discuss with others the importance and benefits of selfless giving as well as the different kinds of giving. Review the kinds of giving in your life currently and how you can purify yourself through giving in a more selfless way.

Questions for Reflection and Follow-up Discussion about Rebecca

1. Do you think that Rebecca was right in not revealing her prophecy to Isaac and in encouraging Jacob to lie and steal the blessing? Did this demonstrate a lack of faith on her part by taking the action that she did? Or rather, did she take the actions that were necessary to demonstrate faith in her personal prophecy?

2. Have there been times in your life where you have been guided to take an action reflective of a higher vision but was not savory or not true on a more superficial or external level? Is this action justifiable? How did you justify the action that you took?

3. What do you think about lying and deception for holy purposes? Have you ever engaged in holy lying?

Chapter Four

Rachel, Leah, Bilha, and Zilpa:

Wives of Jacob and Holy Mothers of the Jewish People

Women have been generally endowed with the gift of holy tears, tears of sadness, and tears of joy. A woman's heart typically is more sensitive than a man's so she is inclined to cry more easily and frequently. A woman should not be embarrassed for the tears that she authentically sheds. Rather than repress or suppress their weeping, a woman or a man in touch with the feminine should be encouraged to discover and explore the source of their crying at its spiritual root.

Rachel, Leah, Bilha, and Zilpa

Rachel and Leah, the daughters of Laban, along with their less known handmaidens Bilha and Zilpa, were the wives of Jacob and the mothers of the Twelve Tribes of Israel. Together they embody different aspects of the *Shechinah,* the Divine Feminine. Rachel and Leah are so important as archetypes of the *Shechinah* in Judaism that both are continually held in the meditation and prayers of Kabbalists who seek to reveal and foster connection between the two. Even today Kabbalists who I personally know actually wear burlap sack cloths, lie on the floor, and cry for the healing of Rachel and Leah in the middle of the night. Who are Rachel and Leah that they alone command such attention in Kabbalistic circles? What do they model and represent to women and men today? What do we learn from each of them individually and together? In addition to the featured interview with the women, please consult the material in the Kabbalistic commentary for a deeper response to these questions (see pages 235–241).

The first meeting between Jacob and Rachel, the beautiful, selfless, and beloved one, began with a kiss. The Bible tells us how Jacob moved the rock over the mouth of the well, watered the sheep of Laban, his mother's brother, then kissed Rachel and wept (Genesis 29: 10–12). It is told that he wept because he knew prophetically that he would not be buried next to her. The Bible goes on to tell us that he loved Rachel so much he worked seven years for her. Time flew by so quickly that it felt to him as if only a few days had passed. Usually one would think that to wait seven years to be with one's beloved would be challenging. The Tanya, the masterpiece of Hasidism written by Rabbi Schneur Zalman of Liadi, calls the kind of love based on need and desire "Love like flaming coals." Jacob's love for Rachel was a different kind of love, based on the sheer delight in the existence of the beloved, called in the Tanya "Love of delights," so even waiting to marry her was a joy. During Jacob's marriage to Rachel, he lived primarily in her tent. After much prayer and challenge, Rachel bore Jacob two children, dying in childbirth with the second one.

Leah was Rachel's twin sister, though slightly older than Rachel, and it is said that she was intended to marry Esau, who was Jacob's older twin. While Rachel was said to be beautiful in form, Leah in the Bible is known for her " tender" eyes, for it has been said that she was crying tears pleading that she not be forced to marry Esau.

As Rebecca and Laban were brother and sister, it had been agreed upon that their children would marry each other. Leah, as the slightly older sibling, was slated to marry Esau, the older one, as Rachel was to marry Jacob. Yet, when Leah heard that Esau was a wicked person, she prayed and she cried that she not be forced to marry Esau. Leah's prayers were indeed answered, for her father switched her for Rachel and forced her to stand in place of Rachel at the wedding *chuppah* (canopy). So as to not embarrass her, Rachel lovingly and selflessly gave her sister the secret signs that she and Jacob had agreed upon in the event that the possible switch would take place. It was so important to Leah to marry Jacob that she was willing to marry him even through deceit. Only in the morning after the wedding, after sexual relations had taken place, was Leah's true identity revealed to Jacob. By that time, she was already pregnant with her first son.

Leah was blessed to birth many children easily. When her first son was born, she named him Reuven and said, "God has 'seen' my affliction and now my husband will love me." Reuven comes from the verb "to see." When she birthed her second son, she said, "God has heard that I am the hated one, and he has therefore given me this one," and she called him

Simeon. Simeon comes from the verb "to hear." When Leah birthed her third son, she named him Levi and she said, "This time my husband will become attached to me, for I have born him three sons" (Genesis 29:34). The selection of these names shows how important it was for her to receive Jacob's love. With each child, she prayed that her husband would love her. When Leah finally birthed her fourth son, she named him Yehudah and said, "This time I thank God" (Genesis 29:35).

With the birth of her fourth son, Yehudah, Leah finally felt secure in her purpose, which was to build the nation and grow in her relationship with God. She no longer expressed her anguish and her hope for her husband's love as she previously did in the naming of her sons. Her fourth son, Yehudah, the son who symbolized her gratitude and love of God, was thus destined to become the leader of the Jewish people. Leah is credited as the first person in the Bible who expressed gratitude to Hashem (God). Leah is all about praising God and elevating everything up to the highest.

In comparison to Rachel, who was surely Jacob's beloved, Leah felt "hated," never receiving the love of her husband that she yearned for in this world. Quite different than the gentle sweet modest Rachel, Leah was assertive, sexual, intellectual, and even willing to challenge Jacob. Even though Leah birthed the majority of the tribes, Jacob never moved into her tent, even after the death of Rachel. Because building the nation of Israel was so prominent in the consciousness of Leah and Rachel, it is important to emphasize that both were willing to share their husband with their handmaidens, Bilha and Zilpa, when each was in a period of infertility. Pained by her own infertility, Rachel suggested that Jacob have sexual relations with Bilha when she finally accepted that she could not have children of her own. Leah saw the tremendous blessing occurring through Rachel's surrogacy with Bilha and decided to give her handmaiden Zilpa to Jacob in a similar fashion.

For more information about these women read about them in the Bible: Genesis 29-6 to Genesis 35-19

Invocation

For those seeking to participate in the birth of a new consciousness that expresses greater connectivity and oneness in the world, connect to the four mothers of the Jewish people who birthed all the tribes of Israel. Each of these holy women demonstrates the depth of love, selflessness, and sacrifice required to reveal the *Shechinah,* the Divine Feminine, in our midst. When faced with challenges in living one's life purpose, call out to our holy mothers for inspiration, vision, and blessing.

Mother Rachel inspires us to be so selfless that we can give ourselves wholeheartedly to love.

Mother Bilha teaches us how to be fulfilled and joyful through divine service.

Mother Leah inspires us with the strength to transform our burdens and challenges into blessings.

Mother Zilpa teaches us to reach joyfully to the highest places for divine revelation within us.

Interview with the Four Mothers

Question: There are no words to describe the overwhelming honor of being in the presence of the four of you at the same time. You are the mothers of the Jewish people. What an incredible debt of gratitude we owe each of you. I would like to speak to each of you individually and then have a conversation with all of you together. May I start with Leah? Leah, what is your message for women and men today?

Leah: I first want to convey my love and blessings to all women and men. My message to everyone is one of empowerment. Do not feel limited or resigned by what you imagine your destiny to be. If you seek to align yourself with divine will, you will be assisted on high. The main thing that I want to emphasize is the importance of being focused in one's life. We each come into this world with a mission and purpose. To fulfill one's life purpose requires much effort and blessing. My life was not easy and there were many challenges and obstacles as there are in everyone's life. Yet I was able to fulfill my destiny because I was clear and focused. I not only intensely prayed, I was willing to do what was necessary to fulfill my dreams. I took great risks. And I actually was able to even change my destiny. That is my message to you. What I did you can also do.

Question: Thank you for your inspiring and encouraging words. Is there anything more that you would like to add by way of introduction?

Leah: I also want to share with you a divine secret that is a key to everything good in life. Besides focus and determination, be grateful for all the blessings you do have in your life. Gratitude opens the gates of blessing for a person. Every day of my life, I never forgot the kindness and love I received from my sister Rachel and my other sister wives. I named my fourth son Yehudah and he became the leader of the Jewish people. Yehudah means "I praise God, I thank God," and that I do continuously.

Question: Would you please speak more directly about how you were able to change and fulfill your destiny?

Leah: It was my destiny to marry Esau but he was wicked. I did not want to have to be intimate with him nor bear children with him. Perhaps I might have been able to uplift and purify him, but I was not willing to make that kind of sacrifice or gamble. It was quite possible that he would have contaminated me and I would not be able to serve God in the way that I so much desired and knew that I could. So I cried and cried that my destiny be changed and that I be able to marry the righteous and holy Jacob. The Holy One had compassion on me as did my beautiful sister Rachel. When my father replaced Rachel with me on her wedding night and Rachel gave me the secret signs, I knew that all my tears were not in vain. It had been for this union that I prayed.

Question: How did it feel to deceive Jacob? It seems rather unbecoming of a mother of the Jewish people to be willing to be so dishonest.

Leah: It was clear to me that this was part of the divine plan so I was willing to do what was necessary to do my part. Jacob had "stolen" the blessings of Esau, so it was necessary that he marry me because I was the key to fulfilling those particular blessings. I told him that when he finally discovered that he had married me rather than his beloved Rachel. I said to him: "Just like you deceived your brother, so it was necessary that you be deceived. When you lied to your brother and to your father, you showed me that it is permissible to lie for a good cause. I am merely following your example."

He seemed to agree and accept my arguments. He could have divorced me after that first night when he discovered the deception but he did not. It is true that he never divided his time equally between me and Rachel. That was very painful and challenging for me as I really wanted his love and also validation that I had indeed done the right thing by deceiving him. As time passed and I was blessed with birthing many sons, I knew in my heart of hearts in time that my husband would recognize that I was also his soul mate in addition to Rachel. God had blessed me with vision and with children so I was patient.

Question: Will you please explain what you mean that you were blessed with vision?

Leah: It had been revealed to me prophetically that Jacob would have four wives and that there would be twelve sons who would form the Twelve Tribes that would compose the Jewish nation. With the birth of each of my first three sons, I prayed that my husband would love me and finally acknowledge to me that our marriage was part of the divine plan. When I gave birth to Yehudah, my fourth son, I experienced myself as greatly blessed, for I was given more than my fair share. This birth removed any doubt for me and confirmed to me that I had acted righteously in initially deceiving Jacob. After the birth of Yehudah, I knew for sure that Jacob would finally realize and accept me as his true soul mate. It was now easy for me to be patient.

When I was pregnant with my seventh child, I prayed that this baby be female, so as to not embarrass my sister Rachel. I reasoned that if I had another son, she would not be able to birth the number of tribes as even the handmaidens. She had been so kind to me, I could not bear that she would be humiliated in this way. My prayers were answered. The fetus within me changed to female and this child was called Dina. All in all, I was personally rewarded with six sons, and one daughter Dina, and two sons through my sister, Zilpa. I was fulfilled. I not only was blessed with such beautiful children, I experienced closeness with the Divine that healed me of any sadness or struggle I had felt previously. I finally knew in my heart that I had acted in a righteous manner, whether it was acknowledged by my husband or not.

Question: Did you ever feel loved by Jacob?

Leah: Yes, I did. My husband was given two names, Jacob and Israel. He was named Israel after his struggle with the angel of Esau. I was the true soul mate of Israel, while Rachel was the soul mate of Jacob. He needed both time and maturity to be able to see who I was and what I offered him. When he received his name Israel, he was finally on the level to see who I was. It was clear to each of us we loved each other but our love was not of this world. That knowledge made us both very joyful and fulfilled. Though he may not have lived with me when we both occupied physical bodies in your world, I am buried with Israel for eternity in the most holy burial place. I have been vindicated; I am fulfilled and deeply grateful.

Question: Do you have a final message for people today?

Leah: I pray that my life will model to you the power of holy tears. You can change your destiny. Come to my grave, pray to me, and I will help to give you the vision and the strength to bear your burdens and transform them to blessings. I am your spiritual mother for all time.

Question: Thank you Leah. I would very much like to hear from Rachel now. Rachel, do you have a message for people today?

Rachel: I also begin by extending my love and blessings to everyone. Please know that I serve also as an intermediary for you. Come to my grave, and cry to me, and I will bring your tears to the Holy One. I am with you in your darkest moments. I will comfort you. Your prayers will be answered.

Question: Thousands of people come each year to pray at your grave. How did your grave become one of the most special and beloved places for people to pray?

Rachel: I was buried on the road. My husband could have buried me in the family plot where I would have patiently waited for him to join me at the proper appointed time. But he was guided prophetically to bury me on the road into and out of Jerusalem, so I would be able to comfort the Jewish people when they were sent into exile from the Holy Land, and I would be able to be there to greet them on the road home when they return.

Question: Did you mind not being buried in the family plot?

Rachel: No. This was exactly what I wanted. This was the perfect place for me to reside to do the holy mothering that I always wanted to do. My exile from my proper resting place with my husband is symbolic of the exile of the Jewish people. When the Jewish people face challenges, when they are being persecuted, they come to me. I am there for the people who have not yet fully entered the Holy Land of Israel physically or spiritually. So many Jews do not have the home that they want or they find themselves feeling unfulfilled in the physical world. They need the blessing of marriage, children, livelihood, peace in the home, so they come to me. A mother is always ready to be there for her children wherever they are, so it is my joy to be there for people whenever they call.

Question: Your burial site has been the site of Molotov cocktails and other acts of terrorism in our time.

Rachel: Those who seek to destroy the Jewish people attack my grave because they know that I provide blessing to Israel. Do not fret. All their evil efforts will not be successful. My tomb will remain a center for prayer and blessing until the prophesied resurrection of the dead. This has been stated in our holy books as well.

Question: Why was this privilege and responsibility given to you?

Rachel: I was blessed personally with two holy beautiful sons, while my sister Leah was blessed with six sons and one daughter. Being a mother was so important to me. Even though I knew it might be dangerous for me to have children, I kept trying. I died giving birth to my second son, Benjamin.

Because my heart was so overflowing with love for this beautiful holy nation and I did not have my full share of children as a full wife of Jacob, I begged God that I be able to nurture and comfort the Jewish people even if and when I was not physically embodied. My prayers have been answered. More than anything in this world, I wanted to be a mother to the Jewish people. Because I showed so much compassion to my sister Leah, I gave her all the secret signs so she would not be embarrassed, and continually challenge God to be compassionate to the Jewish people. When I was flesh and blood, I told God I was not jealous of my sister, so God why would you be jealous of idols that the Jewish people worship due to their ignorance? I have been informed that my arguments resonate with the Holy One. Being buried on the road has given me the opportunity to be there for people who are wandering in this physical world. I am grateful.

Question: You were thirty-six years old when you left your physical body. Why did you die so young?

Rachel: When we were finally leaving Laban, after the birth of Joseph, on my own, without informing anyone, I took my father's favorite idols. When my father caught up to us, he was angry and threatening. To placate my father's wrath, Jacob issued a death curse on the person who took his idols, not knowing that I was the one who committed this theft. The words of a righteous person like my husband have spiritual power. It was not too long after this incident that I died. Because we were traveling and it was hard for me, I gave birth prematurely to my most precious son Benjamin. I named him Ben Oni, which means "son of my sorrow," but my husband changed it to Benjamin after my death.

Question: I am stunned! I have several questions in response to what you have just stated. First, why did you steal the idols? It is a sin to worship idols.

Rachel: Everyone must know that I did not steal these idols for my personal use, but only because I wanted to weaken my father's power of sorcery. His idols were his most precious possessions. Because my father had mistreated us for so long, admittedly, I also wanted to hurt him. I wanted him to be left with nothing, and be powerless to hurt us any longer. I was wrong not discussing this decision with my husband. At the time, I lacked sufficient trust in the God of my husband to fully protect us against my father's skilled wizardry. I kept the theft of the idols a secret because I did not want to reveal these feelings to my husband.

Question: Did you ever forgive your husband or God for your death?

Rachel: As you can well imagine, I was so deeply pained to be taken away so abruptly from my beautiful children, Joseph and Benjamin, especially when they were so young. After so many tears shed for too long and then to finally be granted the blessing of children, and suddenly my physical life was taken from me while giving birth, the whole experience was shattering to me. Because I left my physical body in childbirth, I missed all the wonderful opportunities to mother my baby, hold him, feed him, play with him, help him and my beautiful son Joseph to grow. Tragically they were also deprived of the kind of mothering that I would have offered them. Even though I remained connected to them from my heavenly station, it was not the same as being physically present. Because of this physical separation from my children, I was then and remain eternally heartbroken.

Because of my own personal heartbreak, I am deeply connected to all those who are also heartbroken in the physical world. Even though everything that happens in life is according to the divine plan, nevertheless, a person's pain is real. I know that personally so I can be there for others who also suffer. So, in answer to your question, I would have to say no, not totally, not yet. I have not totally forgiven my husband or Hashem. When the Jewish people are redeemed from exile and the Holy Temple is rebuilt, I will forgive and rejoice with my whole heart. Until then, I will do whatever I can to awaken divine mercy and compassion for the Jewish people through my own tears and by also being a messenger for your tears.

Question: Do you have a general message for the Jewish people?

Rachel: Come to my grave, pour out your heart, and cry to me, Mama Rachel, your spiritual mother. Please know that I was buried on the road only to let you, my beloved children, know that I am there for those who are also on the road. I am there for all those who have not yet found their place. My grave is a holy portal to the higher worlds. Your tears are holy and make a difference. Cry to the Holy One, the Creator of all.

The Jewish people have wandered through time, and they have been persecuted. It has not been fair, just as it was not fair I died so young. From my heavenly station, I want all to know with my full heart that is so filled with love for each of you that in the end the Jewish people will prevail and be victorious. Be strong and have faith. All our enemies will be destroyed or will simply vanish. Miracles are indeed happening in your time. Even though there is much strife, the Jewish people have returned to the Holy Land. More and more of the Jewish people will move to live in the Holy Land very soon. Additionally, those whose ancestors were forced to convert to other religions during this long exile from the Land of Israel will soon relinquish these shackles and return in earnest to the Jewish people. There will be more Jews living in the world than ever before. At the most auspicious time, the Jewish people will rebuild the Holy Temple on the land that had been designated to my son, Benjamin. There will be peace. Until that great day arrives, I am there for all. I will cry with you, and both guide and comfort all who come to my grave.

Question: Thank you Rachel. There is so much more that I want to ask you, but I would like to have a few words now with the *peligishim* Bilha and Zilpa. (*Peligishim* are women who have sexual relations with a man without a *ketubah,* marriage contract, but with an understanding of some sort.) Bilha, would you like to say anything to our readers? We do not know too much about you and Zilpa.

Bilha: Thank you. I have been blessed to be a handmaiden to this holy woman Rachel, a *peligish* wife to Jacob, and a mother to Dan and Naphtali.

Though I did not name my children—Rachel named them—my children were indeed full tribes composing the nation of Israel. I am so grateful and honored to be a mother of these tribes.

Question: Many might wonder why you agreed to be a surrogate mother for Rachel. Did you ever become jealous of her because she was the most beloved to Jacob?

Bilha: No, I loved Rachel. How could I be jealous of a person I both loved and adored? Rachel and I had grown up together. For my entire life, since I was a small child, I was given the responsibility of befriending and serving Rachel. There is nothing that I would not do for her. I lived to serve her and that was enough for me.

Question: What was your relationship with Jacob like?

Bilha: Jacob and I had a very special relationship. Because of my closeness with Rachel, he was particularly loving with me. He greatly appreciated all that I did to help his most beloved one Rachel. We shared a deep love of Rachel and that love brought us close to each other. We also enjoyed being together, always talking about serving God and the secrets of life, but also we spoke about him, his family, and his life purpose. He was very comfortable sharing with me, probably more than any of his wives, even Rachel.

I very much wanted to be a part of this holy mission. I felt extremely blessed and honored to bear children with him. When Rachel left her physical body, Jacob moved his tent to live with me. That was natural because we spent much time together in Rachel's tent and so much enjoyed being together. I was so sad after the loss of Rachel, so his presence was such a comfort and joy to me. We helped comfort each other. We also raised Rachel's son Benjamin together. When I lived with Jacob, I experienced the *Shechinah,* in a way that I had not before. I was truly blessed.

Question: Thank you. I would like to speak to Zilpa now. Would you tell us a little bit about who you are?

Zilpa: I was the maidservant of Holy Mother Leah. What an honor and joy to be close to her! I also was a wife to Jacob and mother to Gad and Asher. As was the case with Bilha, I also did not name my children, but they were full tribes within the House of Israel. My children added great joy to the House of Leah.

Question: What was your relationship like with Jacob?

Zilpa: Jacob did not spend much time at Leah's house, so I did not see him so much. That was fine with me. Leah and I used our time wisely to cultivate and strengthen our connection to the Creator of the universe. We had a deep spiritual and joyful life that we shared together. I did not feel the need of a man to fulfill me spiritually. I was, however, happy and honored that I could bear children with Jacob and such beautiful children as well. My son Asher was known to be the most beautiful tribe in all of Israel. And Gad—what good fortune he was.

Question: Thank you for such wonderful messages. I would like to open the floor for some discussion with all of you. What may be most of interest to our readers is the loving relationship between the four of you. There does not seem to be the level of jealousy that one may expect for four women to be married to the same man. Was there not competitiveness between you?

Leah: There was no significant competitiveness or jealousy between us. We were mostly united and the love between all of us was solid and unshakeable. We each had grown up in the household of Laban, so we knew from the very beginning of our lives that we needed and depended on each other for survival. The great love between us sustained us throughout our lives and even until today.

In my early years, I may have wanted my husband to love me more, and more importantly, more fully acknowledge that I was indeed his soul mate, but it was not because I was competitive with my beloved sister. How could I not wish the best for her at all times! She had protected me from marrying Esau. I owe her my life. I ached that she was not blessed with children as I had been. I prayed for her every day of my life.

Rachel: We each had our challenges but these challenges enabled us to grow and become more worthy of being the mothers of this holy nation. What helped to unify us was that we were always clear that our purpose and fulfillment lay in our capacity to birth the Jewish nation. It was true that Leah wanted more time with my husband and I wanted more children. In the end, we each received what we wanted. And we were each grateful for the role that we each played in birthing this nation. That was more than enough.

Bilha: I was born out of the concubine relationship that Laban had with my mother, so I had no aspirations of being a full wife myself. That I was a *peligish* to this holy man and my sons were considered full tribes in this emerging holy nation was more than I could have dreamed or wanted. I am eternally grateful for the friendship and love of my sisters, particularly the beautiful loving Rachel.

Zilpa: I was also born out of a concubine relationship that Laban had with my mother, so I had no aspirations of being a full wife myself. I really did not even want to be a *peligish*, but my beloved sister Leah requested me that I bear children with her husband so I did. I am happy that I was gifted with motherhood, but it never defined who I was. My relationship with Jacob/Israel was very limited. I had not the desire or the need for more.

Question: As a point of clarification, would one of you explain to our readers what the difference is between a *peligish* and a wife according to Jewish law?

Bilha: I would like to answer that because I was a *peligish* and the daughter of a *peligish*. Generally speaking, a wife has more status and privileges than a *peligish*. Rachel and Leah were full wives, and Zilpa and I were *peligishim*. We were both daughters of *peligishim*, as we said earlier. A man must provide for his wife with shelter, clothes, and conjugal relations. He is not obligated to do so with a *peligish*. A *peligish* does not have the same rights, privileges, and protection. There is no binding contract between a man and a *peligish* as a man has with his wife. A man can leave the *peligish* without offering her financial protection. Zilpa and I did not, however, worry about our welfare, because we knew that our protection was due to our relationships with Rachel and Leah, more than it was with Jacob. And of course when we had sons, we knew that we would be honored and cared for as well.

Question: Do you think that polygamy and *peligishim* is a good model for relationships for people in modern times? There are so many single women looking to be married and have children, would polygamy be an answer for them?

Leah: It is a good arrangement if the women are close to each other, love each other, and they are the ones who choose to enter into a polygamous marriage. Each woman who participates in polygamy must agree to this arrangement. It can never be forced upon her. The man must be able to love each of them, hopefully equally. We were all sisters—we grew up sharing everything with each other—so it was more natural for us to share a husband. Still it was not always easy for us either.

Rachel: Such a marriage may not be easy, but it is still good. In our case, it was necessary for us to realize the spiritual opportunity that was generously given to us by the Holy One. It was through our relationship with each other and Jacob that we birthed the Jewish people.

Question: Thank you. I would like to speak briefly about some of the traumatic events that happened in your life that were so important in defining the Jewish people. The most painful and prominent one might be the selling of Joseph into slavery. For so many years, everyone believed that Joseph was dead, killed by a wild animal. Later on, it was revealed that he had been sold into slavery by his brothers, the sons of Leah. I understand that you, Rachel, were not in a physical body at the time, but still you must have some thoughts and feelings about that as well.

Rachel: Unfortunately, my husband Jacob inspired jealousy among his sons by publicly demonstrating greater love to Joseph than to his other sons. He even gave Joseph a special coat and treated him as if he would be his sole heir. It was his way to stay connected to me. My most beautiful, precious, glorious son Joseph was surely a prophet, for he received visions and dreams of the future that were eventually realized. When he shared his prophetic dreams with his brothers prematurely that only added to their hatred of him and confirmed to them that Joseph also believed that he would be their leader and they would have to be subservient to him. That was more than they could bear. I am glad that I was not physically alive to witness this event.

Viewing this event from my heavenly domain, I knew, however, that all that took place was all part of the divine plan. Because my son was so holy and pure, he was sent on a mission that would take him to Egypt to free the souls who had been imprisoned by the impurity there. He was all the things that his dreams informed him he would be. I supported him as much as I could from my heavenly station. Though he faced great challenges in his life, my son Joseph was blessed and continues to be indeed a source of blessing to all. He became the ruler of Egypt. He saved not only his brothers in the time of famine, but all of Egypt. I am so proud of him. I am eternally honored and grateful to have been his mother.

Leah: I was so saddened to hear of Joseph's death. It was so hard to lose my beloved sister and then her most precious child. Jacob was inconsolable. I saw him even less than before. I was personally anguished and devastated for the role that I might have played in fostering jealousy among my sons for Joseph. Their actions were wrong, yet I have faith and I know that Hashem works in mysterious ways. Joseph being sent to Egypt was surely part of the divine plan because when he became the ruler of Egypt he was in a position to save our lives. Nevertheless, I am glad, however, that my sons in time had the opportunity to do *teshuva* for the terrible action of selling their brother into slavery. In the course of their lives, my sons each made mistakes but they also repented. I pray that they serve as models for all time that a person can do wrong but they can change and become better people than they were before.

Bilha: My sons, as well as Zilpa's, were not involved as this was really a battle between the sons of Leah and the sons of Rachel for supremacy.

Zilpa: There have been times throughout Jewish history when all the tribes were united. When there is unity, the nation of Israel is strong and divinely protected. When there is divisiveness among the tribes, the nation is weak and vulnerable to external enemies. It really is that simple and clear.

Concluding Response to our Mothers Rachel, Leah, Bilha and Zilpa

(It is suggested that this be read out loud by reader or group)

"We remain in great debt for the love and sacrifice you each made to be a mother of the Jewish nation. We stand today to acknowledge each of you as our spiritual mothers. Together you embodied different facets of the Shechinah, the Divine Feminine. We are inspired by each of you. Though your contribution has not adequately acknowledged in the tradition, we know that it was your love as the mothers of the tribes that imbued them with beauty and strength to carry out the mission prescribed for them. Most importantly, you together model to us an example of the kind of sisterhood that women can have. There is so much more that we can do when we are united with other women than we could ever do alone. As women, we are a powerful force for good in the world. As women, we bring more love into the world.

Help us to gather with and bond with other women so we can bring forth a new consciousness into the world that is more loving, gentle, and kind. May we do this in ways that are uniquely feminine, like you, our mothers did, so as to be able to draw down blessings to ourselves, our loved ones and the entire world. May we not be frightened. May we keep our hearts open. May our tears of love and tears of sorrow arose mercy and blessing in the world."

Prayer to the God of Mother Rachel, Leah, Bilha, and Zilpa

Reader: *May I be blessed to follow in the footsteps of my holy mothers Rachel, Leah, Bilha, and Zilpa to participate in the birth of a new consciousness that expresses greater connectivity and oneness in the world. May I be willing to undergo challenges in order to reveal the Shechinah in our midst. May the tears that I shed in my life be dedicated to this purpose.*

What Quality of the Feminine Do We Learn from These Four Mothers?

We must first learn from these four women the power and importance of sisterhood. Because these four women were bonded together in love, sacrifice, and dedication to the mission of birthing the Jewish people, they were able to fulfill their holy purpose together. On a more secular level, most women know the importance of female friendships. For many women, men may come and go in their lives, but friendships with other women endure throughout a lifetime and are often a source of unconditional love and support. There is a call in our time to strengthen the bonds between women. Interestingly enough, one of the reasons for the popularity of the television show *Sex and the City* was that it was more about the strong relationship between the four women who each embodied different archetypes of the feminine than it was about their affairs and relationships with men.

Female relationships provide a mirror for the personal and spiritual growth for a woman that is quite different than what she experiences with a man. Through relationships with other women, each woman is encouraged to more fully develop her particular archetype but also to express the other archetypes as well, and experience a greater sense of wholeness within herself.

The four mothers each demonstrate important qualities of the feminine that every woman must embrace. From the selfless love and goodness of Rachel, the willingness to serve and learn of Bilha, the vision and focus of Leah, and the mystical joy of Zilpa, women are invited to find dimensions within themselves to express the range of attributes embodied by these women. The following is a description of the four archetypes.

Which Archetype Are You?
The Rachel Archetype: A Moon-Identified Woman

Whether as wife, mother, or lover, women carrying the Rachel archetype in large part are defined and fulfilled by these relationships. Being a mother was so important to Rachel that she even cried to Jacob "Give me children or I will die" (Genesis 30:1). When Rachel gives birth to Joseph and becomes lover and mother, she then becomes the embodiment of the ultimate feminine energy and blessing.

Rachel is a model of holy selflessness and graciousness for all women. Archetypical Rachel women are generally married, traditional, and feminine. Because they are beautiful, they make everything and everyone around them feel beautiful as well. If a woman who embodies the Rachel archetype is married to a good man who can bring down the light of God, such a woman is unusually radiant and beautiful, no matter how old she is.

A woman is often compared to the moon. Generally speaking, many women have a special relationship with the moon because the time of her menses is often coordinated with the phases of the moon. A moon-identified woman like the Rachel archetype is beautiful and changeable, similar to the moon. Also, like the moon, she has no light of her own. A Rachel woman reflects the light of her husband, just as the moon reflects the light of the sun. Not having light of her own must not be seen as indicative of low self-esteem, spiritual deficiency, or a lack of intrinsic worthiness for Rachel archetypes. It is actually the opposite, for it is necessary for a person on the path of holiness to be able to surrender one's sense of self so as to reflect the light of God. Being able to surrender is quite different than being a doormat. A person needs a rather elevated ego to be able to know when to surrender and receive. A Rachel archetypical woman is beautiful and generous, and radiates a spiritual light through her that elevates all who are blessed to be in her orbit.

Leah Archetype

The archetype of Leah is of a woman whose soul ascends beyond attachments and relationships in this world since she can connect directly with God, the source of all love and light. Leah is the archetype of the independent woman, whether she is in relationship or not, who either works hard to cultivate her own direct connection with the light or who is naturally blessed with a more direct connection than most people have. On an ego level, she may still indeed want the love of a man to define her, but on a soul level, she finds this restrictive. Archetypical Leah women are the intellectual equals of men, and generally assertive sexually as well.

For example, we are told the story of how Leah purchased the sexual services of Jacob with a *dudaim* (fertility herbs). Leah often showed herself as dominant in comparison to Jacob. The archetypical Leah is that of an independent woman who will do what she feels necessary to actualize her higher vision. Archetypical Leah woman are strong, powerful and loving. Visionaries who see the larger picture, Leah women are willing to orchestrate changes to help move themselves and others forward in accordance with their vision.

Bilha Archetype

Bilha is *Ohr Makif* (the surrounding light) of Rachel and the intellectual, spiritual, and sexual consort to Jacob. Her relationship with Jacob is about learning Torah and otherwise receiving from the aspect of submission and dependence like Rachel. Archetypical Bilha women are loving, generous, and frequently are drawn to learn Torah with men whom they admire and view as more knowledgeable than themselves. Bilhas attend Torah classes regularly, read books, and listen to classes online.

In addition to learning, Bilha archetypical women love to serve. Bilhas thus are also the women who are active in organizations, spearheading and/or working devotedly for important causes because dedication to that which is higher and greater than oneself is meaningful to them. Bilhas enjoy being part of a community of like-minded people who share a common goal.

Zilpa Archetype

Women who embody the Zilpa archetype are those heavenly, beautiful, feminine, spiritual, free-spirited angelic souls who manifest all that is beautiful and holy seemingly effortlessly. Zilpas lift everyone up who is blessed to be around them. Zilpa archetypes offer the world a glimpse of the beauty and heart of the Divine Feminine. If you see a woman dedicated to a form of spiritual or mind/ body practice that embodies the feminine like yoga, dance, massage, or meditation, she is accessing Zilpa. Archetypical Zilpa women meditate, learn Kabbalah or other esoteric wisdom, and are joyful in themselves, happy to be in relationship with a man, and equally happy to not be. Characterized as the archetypal Goddess type, transcending all of Creation, Zilpa's light is above that of Jacob and she has no need of him. But in her role as *peligish,* Zilpa, as the *Ohr Makif* of Leah, is symbolic of the deep descent of the Divine into the natural world.

Know Your Particular Archetype and Embody Them All

A woman will be primarily either a Rachel (practical, modest, and grounded), a Leah (contemplative, mystical, and assertive), a Bilha (intellectual, submissive, and selfless), or a Zilpa (evolved, free-spirited, and detached) archetype. Even though most women embody aspects of several of the archetypes, knowing and accepting one's primary archetype as a woman is very helpful, healing, and even liberating. When a woman truly honors her primary archetype, she will be better able to appreciate the coherency of her life experiences. Simply stated, life makes more sense when you know your principal archetype and accept yourself as you are. All the material presented here is to help the reader identify her archetype or for the male reader to know the archetype of the women in his life.

Women are, however, multidimensional beings, so when a woman embraces, integrates, and expresses the other archetypes additionally she experiences wholeness and completion within herself. She completes the *tik-kun* (fixing) of the feminine for herself and the world. I have come to appreciate that throughout my life I have done just this. I actually even have four names that I use that correlate to the four spiritual worlds and the four archetypes. When a friend calls me by all my names, I feel seen for who I really am.

For example, for most of my life, but particularly when I was in my twenties and thirties, when I felt the pain of being single the most, I identified with Leah, the unloved one, or the one who is not as loved. Not being in a committed relationship with a loving man and having had a few heartbreaking broken engagements, like Leah, I was compelled to forge my own direct connection with the Divine. I even became a Jewish spiritual teacher, a guide, and an author to many so I could share the divine light and connection I had accessed. I celebrated my independence. I did not want to be economically or spiritually dependent on a man, though secretly in my heart of hearts, I confess for much of my life that I wanted to be a Rachel, the beloved, beautiful, and treasured one, much like Leah did in her lifetime.

When I have been blessed to be in a committed relationship with a man, I identify more with Rachel. I find myself spending more time beautifying myself physically, even getting my hair and nails done religiously each week. It is important that I look beautiful in the eyes of my beloved as well as my own. In my Rachel mode, I am willing to sit quietly beside or even behind the man and encourage him to shine. I seek my reflection in his love and deeply appreciate all the little gestures of caring he makes towards me. I still have to work hard, but my spiritual work is now more how to make myself smaller, and allow myself to open and to trust so as to receive the light and love from the man. Since we both understand that his work in the relationship is ultimately to bring pleasure to me, I want to build him up and elevate him so he can draw down more light to give to me, himself, and the world.

Though Rachel and Leah are the primary female archetypes, women also need to open to Bilha and Zilpa. I have embodied the Bilha archetype for most of my adult life as well. I have been blessed to almost continually be learning Kabbalah individually with men who are more knowledgeable than me. Some have been brilliant and teachers in their own right. Men seem to like learning Kabbalah with me because I offer a feminine perspective and am able to draw out deeper learning for them than they might access themselves. Furthermore, there is a kind of spiritual intimacy with a *hevruta* (study partner) that is unique. Sometimes, I have dated these men. When that happened, the relationship itself became a laboratory for Kabbalah learning and the learning was even more intense. And unfortunately, when the relationships ended, there were many tears for the lost opportunities for learning as well as for the loss of the relationship. When I am in my Bilha archetype, I serve my synagogue, the Jewish community as a whole, and my friends. In my early adult years, I used to spend almost ten to fifteen volunteer hours a week serving my synagogue and organizing *Shabbat* and synagogue activities for my primary teacher Rabbi Shlomo Carlebach of blessed memory.

Lastly, I am happiest when I am embodying the archetype of Zilpa. I am very much in my Zilpa when I am meditating and praying, especially in holy places in Israel. When I am teaching meditation, guiding myself and others to soar to great spiritual heights, I am accessing my Zilpa. When I am in my Zilpa, wherever I am, my soul is very expanded. My experience is that I barely exist, there is only God, and I experience myself as an expression of God. My Zilpa consciousness is more connected to the inner worlds that are revealed in meditation where there is no limitation or restriction, only love, joy, holiness, and truth. The *Shechinah* dwells within me and I experience myself as an embodiment of Her. I am not always living as an embodiment of Zilpa, but am grateful for the times when I do, as I imagine the people around me are as well.

What Spiritual Practice Do We Learn from Rachel and Leah?

Rachel and Leah were the masters of holy tears. From them, we as women or men in touch with the feminine within ourselves learn how to shed tears that are healing to ourselves and the world. With her tender eyes from crying, Leah changed her destiny and birthed six tribes to become a mother of the Jewish people. As a mother who cares for each of her children, Mother Rachel is said to cry her holy tears that offer protection and blessing to the Jewish people until they are all returned to the Land of Israel and there is peace. Jews go to the grave of Mother Rachel before *Rosh Hashanah* as well as throughout the year to beseech her to cry for their personal welfare as well as the welfare of the Jewish people.

Weeping is actually an important Jewish spiritual practice. The Zohar states that "there is no gate that tears cannot enter." Tears atone for sins, misdeeds, tears purify and open gates of blessing. If one weeps in prayer, one arouses divine mercy upon oneself and all of Israel. To weep in prayer is a sign of a vulnerable and open heart, not of weakness.

Unfortunately, many of us have grown up being told to not honor or feel the feelings that we do. Consequently, we learn at an early age how to defend ourselves against the feelings we do have. As a result, we avoid living our lives on a level of soul depth and connection that would be otherwise possible for us. We therefore cry less frequently or deeply.

Because we live in a world that is not entirely in resonance with our souls, most of us at some time in our lives will be forced to feel our painful sad feelings due to challenging inevitable life circumstances. All challenges must be seen as spiritual opportunities; however, many of us will not able to extract the spiritual gifts within our pain if we seek to distract or diminish our suffering with alcohol, television, sex, drugs, and food. At these times, we need to remember that it is natural and good to allow ourselves our feelings of sadness and grief when they are triggered and allow them be a springboard for healing and growth.

There are two types of crying. There is the unholy crying that comes from obsessing on negative thoughts. This crying often leaves one drained, exhausted, and feeling sorry for oneself. This kind of crying is actually an expression of anger turned inward that blocks the flow of healing and blessing to oneself. And then there is holy crying, that comes from deep in the soul. Holy tears purify, heal, and strengthen us. They may be viewed as a portable *mikvah* (ritual bath) that cleanses the soul. It is helpful to distinguish between these styles of crying so as to facilitate shift within oneself to holy tears that are redemptive and cleansing, releasing pain and opening the heart.

Women have been generally endowed with the gift of holy tears- tears of sadness, and tears of joy. A woman's heart typically is more sensitive than a man's so she is inclined to cry more easily and frequently. A woman should not be embarrassed for the tears that she authentically sheds. Rather than repress or suppress their weeping, a woman or a man in touch with the feminine should be encouraged to discover and explore the source of their crying at its spiritual root.

If we allow ourselves to honor our pain and venture deeply into the tears, we will discover that our tears are not essentially personal. Within every loss, trial, or betrayal are the tears for the lack of God's realization in the world. The true reason that we cry, our souls cry, is because God's Presence, the *Shechinah,* the Divine Feminine, is not fully revealed in this world. When our personal losses become a portal to weep for the *Shechinah,* our tears become holy. Within the tears of the woman are the tears of the *Shechinah* Herself.

As such, the tears of a woman must be honored and treasured rather than ridiculed or mocked. The tears of a woman have the awesome power to arouse a blessing of divine love and compassion and water the seeds for a fuller expression of beauty and balance in the world. When a woman cries for the *Shechinah* and allows the *Shechinah* to cry within and through her, her tears are healing to her and the world. A woman's tears can penetrate the heart of God and bring down blessings to the world. When women cry, they change reality, so a woman must be particularly careful not to use the power of her holy tears for personal manipulation. When we allow ourselves to feel the deep feelings within our own soul, to feel its grief, its sadness, its brokenness, paradoxically our pain is often lifted from us and we are made more whole. God heals the brokenhearted.

Questions for Reflection and Discussion

1. Discuss the ways you feel that Rachel showed herself to be the reincarnation of Eve (Chava) and how Leah could be seen as the reincarnation of Lilith. Can you find some of those qualities these women embodied within yourself?

2. How do Rachel and Leah heal the rift between Eve and Lilith in this incarnation?

3. Of the four mothers is there one who you identify with the most and why?

4. Can you find aspects within yourself that resonate with each of the four women? Explore and share that with others.

5. Look at your closest women friends, and consider what archetype they most embody. Do you tend to be friends with women who are similar to you? How would you have to expand yourself to befriend women who are principally of a different archetype? If you are a man reading this book, consider which of the archetypes of the feminine you are most attracted to. Which of the archetypes have you been in relationship with? What archetype is your mother?

6. What was the bond between the women that enabled them to be married to the same man? Could you be involved in a polygamous relationship? If so why and if not why not? Should polygamy be an option for men and women today?

Chapter Five

Dina the Heroine:

The Secrets of Overcoming Trials and Tribulations

Dina

"When good things happen in life, when bad things happen in life, one must use all of one's life experiences to deepen one's love, connection, and appreciation for God. In this way, a person reveals the Light of God in the midst of darkness and evil."

—*Dina*

Dina

Dina, the one daughter of Jacob and Leah, has no spoken words of her own in the Bible. She is acted upon; she is talked about; she seems passive and wounded. Almost invisible, the Bible does not even mention her when Jacob blessed his sons on his deathbed. The brief paragraphs in the Bible devoted to her life are filled with violence unparalleled anywhere else in the Bible.

Dina in the Bible is described in the Bible as "the daughter of Leah" because she went out to meet the young girls in the neighboring town. Just as Leah "went out" to initiate sexual relations with Jacob, her daughter Dina similarly "went out" to explore new horizons. Shechem, the prince of the neighboring town that was named after him, had already seen Dina and was so drawn to her that he hatched a plan to abduct her. He cleverly brought timbrel playing young girls within the hearing range of Dina and she was attracted to go out to hear the music and meet the young girls. Then Dina the first Jewish daughter born of a Jewish mother was kidnapped and raped!

After the act, Schechem tried to console her, appease her anger, and declared his desire to marry her. Only after the rape, does the Bible, interestingly enough, call Dina "the daughter of Jacob." After the rape, Chamor, the father of Shechem, traveled to Jacob and the brothers to request Dina's hand in marriage, offering a large amount of money along with a proposal that intermarriage take place between the two communities. The sons of

Jacob, Dina's brothers, then came up with the following scheme to avenge the honor of their sister as well as rescue her. Marriages could take place between the two communities if the men in Shechem would become circumcised. On the third day, when the men were the most weak, Simeon and Levi entered the town and rather than just kill Shechem and the men guarding Dina, they killed every man in this city and then they rescued Dina. They also looted the city because they had defiled their sister.

The actions that the brothers take to rescue Dina were troublesome to their father Jacob and are probably to many readers. It may, however, have been possible that the brothers originally only intended to kill Shechem so as to rescue Dina. The oral tradition tells us that Dina heard that there was a plot among the brothers of Shechem to slay Jacob's family after the circumcision and somehow she sent word to her brothers to warn them.

There are a few different accounts of what happened to Dina after the rape. In one account, she was so overcome with shame about what happened to her that she was reluctant to return to her family until her brother Shimeon persuaded her to return to live in his home as his wife. In another opinion, favored by Moshe Ben Maimon, known as Maimonides, the great Jewish thinker, she lived in Shimeon's house, not as his wife, but as a kind of widow. There is even another account that states that she married Job. I have mentioned the different *Midrashim,* and chose the one that resonates the most with me for the interview. Whether she married or she remained in Shimeon's home for the rest of her life is not central to our understanding the importance of Dina's story. From that night of rape, Dina became pregnant and bore a daughter named Osnat. The legend is that Osnat was adopted by Potiphar and was raised by the wife of Potiphar, the very same woman who tried to seduce Joseph. When Joseph refused the wife of Potiphar's sexual advances, she accused him of rape and he was sent to the dungeon for twelve years. Later when Joseph was freed and ruling Egypt, he married Osnat, her daughter and his niece.

For further Kabbalistic commentary on this chapter, see pages 241–245).

See Bible Genesis 30:21, Genesis 34:1-2

Invocation

If you seek comfort from pain afflicted upon you, let Mother Dina inspire you to grow and heal through your suffering. If you seek the courage to transmute whatever negativity you have experienced into good, connect with the God of Mother Dina.

No matter what has happened to you, you need not be a victim. You can overcome and bring light into the places that are filled with darkness. In small and large ways, we have each day an opportunity to choose light over darkness, unity over divisiveness, good over evil, so as to reveal the intrinsic beauty and unity of all life; that is the *Shechinah.*

Interview with Dina

Question: Dina, it is such an awesome honor to be in your presence. Do you have an initial message for women and men today?

Dina: Hashem is good, and is gracious to all of creation. Know this as a basic truth. Events may happen in your life and that of the world that seemingly do not look or feel good, but have faith, look beyond, look deeper, and you will find that it is all good. God is good and everything that takes place is all part of the divine plan. So it is all good.

Question: You were raped at a young age. Your child was taken from you by your father. How did you come to understand all of this in a positive light? How can that be good?

Dina: Of course, at the time when this incident took place, I was totally devastated and deeply ashamed of myself. Did I deserve this to happen to me? I wondered whether I was guilty of some crime from another lifetime. I was so young and had not done much in my life yet. I simply wandered off because I was lonely and wanted to play with some girls my own age. I had only older brothers. My biggest mistake was that I did not ask my family if I could go. I had not even told my family what I wanted to do. I just went.

That was wrong on my part. I did not realize how important I was to my family. My brothers did not abandon me; they rescued me, and assured me of my honor and value. My mother loved me. I was forgiven for wandering off the property of the Jewish people and chose to stay close to my family for the rest of my life. That was indeed a great blessing for me.

Question: Yet, how did you keep your faith in God through this incident? Many people also have terrible things happen to them, seemingly through no fault of their own. Do you have a message for them too?

Dina: As I grew older and more mature, I came to understand that all what happens in life is really divine providence. God is good and all that happens is good. This is a deep truth that everyone must internalize deeply into one's heart. When good things happen in life, when bad things happen in life, one must use all of one's life experience to deepen one's love, connection, and appreciation for God. In this way, a person reveals the light of God in the midst of darkness and evil. This is the essence of being a Jew. There is always good in everything, even though it may not be immediately clear. Remember that I am after all the daughter of Leah and Jacob so it was important for me and everyone that I demonstrate this truth for all to witness.

I also took responsibility for making a bad choice. For that, I suffered immediately. I quickly learned what I needed to learn, but that is not why this incident happened. I came to know that I was being used by God for a holy purpose, so this incident, even though it was unpleasant, became a blessing to me and to the Jewish people.

Question: What was the holy purpose?

Dina: As you can so clearly see, there is a war in the universe between the forces of good and evil. I was simply a soldier in one of the battles. After Shechem raped me, he thought he loved me and wanted to marry me. His father appealed to my father and brothers for my hand in marriage, as if the rape did not happen. Rape was so commonplace there, no apologies were offered, but for the Jewish people it is a horrible crime. My brothers wanting to avenge my honor and rescue me came up with a scheme that marriages between our peoples could take place when the men of Shechem were circumcised. Surprisingly, they quickly agreed to this painful procedure and converted to Judaism. Because of what happened to me, the souls of the people of Shechem reincarnated as Jews in their next life. So it was really blessing for them. Their power to cause future harm to God's world was mitigated, so that was very good too.

Question: But you were harmed, weren't you?

Dina: Shechem may have raped my body, but not my soul. Yes, I was initially harmed, I was emotionally devastated, but I was also spiritually transformed. Because of what happened to me, I understood at an early age that I am not limited to my physical body. I have a beautiful soul. That is what is most important in life. My soul was actually elevated by this event. This is true for all who have had a crime or an offense committed against them. Whatever negativity you may have gathered in your life, you have been actually greatly cleansed through the difficult experience you have endured. You did not consciously choose for terrible things to happen, but God had compassion on you and determined that this was the best way to remove blockages to your own soul.

Question: Is there anything more that you would like to say about yourself?

Dina: After the rape, I felt so ashamed and unworthy, and feared that I would be judged harshly by my family for leaving the family compound. My brother

Shimeon invited and persuaded me to live in his home after the rape. So grateful for his kindness, I lived out the rest of life within the confines of his tribe.

Question: Did you ever marry?

Dina: Because of what happened to me, I had no interest to marry and bear additional children of my own. I made that decision early in my life. Besides, I was busy with the extended family. Being an aunt to so many children was a great joy and yet it did not take up the same amount of time as having a child of my own. Not bearing children, I could devote more time in developing myself spiritually, so as to have the Divine Presence rest upon me. My mothers, Leah and Zilpa, my mother's handmaiden, instructed me on how to be strong, how to be holy, and how to embody the *Shechinah* in the most beautiful way.

Because of the love of my entire family, I felt blessed to simply be a Jewess. The *Shechinah* was such a source of love and comfort for me. To be the daughter of Leah and Jacob, I also had a certain responsibility to represent and embody the *Shechinah* for all to see. I pray that I did that well. I do not want people to feel sorry for me. I am not a victim. There are no victims in God's world.

Question: You, however, became pregnant from that one night of sexual relations with Shechem. Your daughter was taken away from you. Was that not difficult for you to bear?

Dina: Yes, that was very hard. Losing Osnat was a great loss. She was so beautiful and innocent. Because I was so young, my father determined that adoption would be the best option for a child born from a rape. He placed a special necklace with an inscription of the name of God upon it that later helped to identify her. At the time, I had no choice but to defer to his wishes and pray with all my heart that my child would be safe and protected. God must surely have a great plan for her. She was after all a Jewess, my daughter.

I was greatly blessed to meet her later in my life when the family immigrated to Egypt because of the famine. Can you imagine my delight after so many years to find that Joseph, my beloved brother, was ruling Egypt and had married my beautiful daughter. God is so good. What a beauty my daughter was! We loved each other instantly and completely. Through her, I was fulfilled and doubly blessed as she was blessed to bear two beautiful sons, Menasha and Ephraim, who became full-fledged tribes of Israel. It was then totally confirmed for me that everything that happened to me, to Joseph, to Osnat, was part of the divine plan. We were blessed to be a part of it all.

Question: You and your brother Joseph seem to have had a special bond. You were attacked in Shechem, and he is buried there. Could you offer some words to explain this?

Dina: As you remember, my mother Leah was pregnant with another son and prayed that the fetus become a girl so she would not embarrass her sister Rachel my aunt. My mother then gave birth to me and Rachel gave birth to Joseph. Joseph and I were twin souls. We had a common destiny. Even though I did not see him so much growing up, I have a special love and connection to him. My beautiful holy brother Joseph was able to transform Egypt and soften the divine judgments against them. He also graciously provided food for the entire Jewish people when it became necessary for us to travel to Egypt. Because of Joseph's stature, the Jewish people were given the finest land. When the Jewish people finally left Egypt, millions of Egyptians went with them and converted to Judaism. This is in part due to the merit of Joseph and all the good will he inspired among the Egyptian people. It is part of the divine plan that there always are windows of opportunity given to the people of the nations of the world to become Jews.

Just as it was the divine plan that I be raped in Shechem, it was also the divine plan that my beautiful holy brother was buried in Shechem. Joseph's body could have been brought to Jerusalem or another place, but he requested burial in Shechem. The city of Shechem is a vortex of evil in the world. Joseph's tomb has been violated by Moslems numerous times because they cannot tolerate the divine light that radiates from his tomb. Even murders of young Jews attempting to pray by his grave have occurred in your times. Joseph, such a *tzaddik* (a righteous person), continues to work in the spiritual realms to mitigate the evil that takes place in the physical world. That is why he is physically buried in Shechem. Without his blessing, life in Israel would be even more difficult.

Question: Do you have any final words for men and women today?

Dina: My heart is with all those who have suffered through no or little fault of their own as I did. Forgive yourself. Forgive others. Release any anger or guilt you are holding. It only hurts you. It is impossible to understand why bad things happen. Know that your soul has undergone a great soul correction through your affliction that is redemptive to you and to all of creation. May you be blessed to appreciate the spiritual gifts that have been given to you. Thank you for hearing my story. Love and blessings to all.

Prayer to the God of Mother Dina
(It is suggested that you read this out loud)

May the God of Mother Dina inspire me to grow and heal through the challenges I face in life. May the God of Mother Dina inspire me with the courage to transmute whatever negativity I have experienced into good. May I choose light over darkness, unity over divisiveness, good over evil, so as to reveal the Shechinah and the intrinsic beauty of life.

What Quality of the Feminine Does Dina Embody?

Dina embodies the wisdom and open-heartedness of the feminine that enables a person to find and experience light amidst the greatest darkness. Such a person is not contaminated or tainted by the evil perpetuated upon her. Just like the *Shechinah,* the Divine Feminine, dwelling in the midst of a world that seeks to deny Her very existence, such a person as Dina represents the *Shechinah,* who exhibits a beauty and dignity that is untouched by events on the earthly plane. She lives more internally than externally. Though Dina experienced an early trauma that did indeed leave scars on her life, she was not bitter, nor did she ever lose faith in the goodness of life. Dina reminds us that we too can overcome life challenges that may make us feel initially bitter or resentful. The name Dina actually means "judgment." Her mother Leah judged that she was given too much blessing in having a seventh son, so she prayed that the fetus be changed into a female. Dina carried a spiritual burden of being a male who had been changed into a female.

Though she may not have consciously chosen her destiny, Dina courageously embodied the aspect of divine judgment for herself and her people. Dina models to us how to rise above the limiting aspects of judgment to find divine mercy and compassion for ourselves as she did.

A Spiritual Practice Attributed to Dina

The rape of Dina is yet another expression of the violation of the Divine Feminine. So remember Dina, light a candle for her and for all women who have been violated and oppressed, and pray sincerely for the redemption of the *Shechinah* from Her exile. When you say a prayer or do a good deed, hold this intention as Jews do, that this act is done for the unification of The *Holy One Blessed be He* with the *Shechinah.* Pray that you should see the redemption of the Divine Feminine in your days.

Key Questions and Discussion around Dina

1. Does the story of Dina resonate with you? Write or share with another person about a "negative" experience that you have had and how it changed you. Have you come to terms with it? Or are you still holding on to feelings of hurt, anger, grief, etc.? If you are meeting with others, take turns sharing with each other. One person is the speaker; the other person just listens fully, without judgment or giving advice. "The story of Dina resonates with me because _____

2. If you were a " victim" of a crime or had and/or are currently experiencing a health challenge or another personal trial, and you still have questions about why it happened and what you could learn from this challenge, imagine that God can speak to you to comfort you right now. Take a few breaths to center yourself, and then take a sheet of paper and begin a sentence with the following words:

   "This is what I want to say to you" and keep on writing from your higher consciousness without editing too much from your mind. This is only for you, and you do not have to share it unless you want to do so.

3. Were the brothers right to murder all the men in the town of Shechem? Is it correct to do a preemptive strike against those who seek to kill you? Were the inhabitants guilty by association because they did not protest the prevalence of rape and murder in that society?

4. Rape is a crime about power, rather than passion, and yet women are often accused of instigating this crime. If a woman dresses immodestly, she may even be accused of asking to be raped. In a Moslem country, women may be jailed, punished and possibly even executed when they are raped. Why? Take time to discuss the power dimensions of this crime and how rape can be prevented.

5. Why do you think that Dina is called the daughter of Jacob only after the rape?

Chapter Six

Miriam's Faith

Seeing Life's Potential and Perfection

Miriam

"My dear sisters and brothers, do not feel limited by what appears in front of you. I never saw things as they appeared to be, but only as they would be in a more perfected state. Do not dwell on what is lacking in your life or in the world. Believe in your dreams, trust your passion, and pay attention to what makes you excited and enthusiastic. Say yes to life and claim your spiritual ticket to the new world that is unfolding before you."

—Miriam

Miriam

Prophetess and Visionary

More than any other women recorded in the Bible, Miriam, sister of Moses and Aaron, prophetess and visionary in her own right, emerges in modern times as a symbol of the rising of the feminine. Within the last decade, many books have been written about her. A cup of water in her honor has been added to the Passover Seder by feminists in the 1990s. For thousands of years, her legacy as a prophetess and spiritual leader of the Jewish people was relatively unknown and unacknowledged. Miriam speaks very few words in the Bible and very few words are written about her. As with many women in the past and in the present who have labored behind the scenes, Miriam's contribution has been largely hidden. Kabbalah, however, predicts that the legacy of Miriam, and the feminine that she embodied, will become the primary force for healing and redemption of the world.

When we learn about Miriam, it is important to keep in mind that Miriam demonstrated spiritual leadership as a woman. She did not imitate the masculine, as women often do when they move into positions of leadership. Throughout her life, Miriam embodied and demonstrated the intuition and the wisdom that is characteristic of the feminine. Her style and her message were radically different than that of Moses because she was a woman. In addition to being a prophetess and the spiritual leader for the women in Egypt and in the desert, she was also a mother, a wife, a sister-in-law, and aunt. Her relationships informed her work. As most women do, Miriam valued all her relationships. Miriam is the only women in the Torah said to have died with a kiss, which meant that the angel of death had no dominion over her soul. Her soul simply lovingly left her body.

Though the actual circumstances of her birth were not recorded, Miriam was born during the time when the Egyptians began to enslave the Jewish people. Her name Miriam comes from the Hebrew root *maroor*, which means "bitter," referencing the bitter hardship of the time in which she was born.

By the time Miriam was only five years old, her role as a prophetess, visionary, and a guiding light for the Jewish people was already revealed. According to the Jewish oral tradition, with courage, faith, and at risk of her own life, five-year-old Miriam and her mother disguised themselves as midwifes who defied Pharaoh's decree and birthed the male and female newborns. When brought in for questioning before Pharaoh as to why the male infants survived under their midwifery, Miriam and her mother stood up bravely and continued their holy work without concern for their personal safety. This act of civil disobedience on the part of these two brave females may have been the first recorded moral challenge to a tyrannical government.

Miriam was always the loving older sister and protector of her brother Moses. When her brother Moses was born, it was clear to all that this was the child Miriam had prophesied. The Bible simply tells us that this child was "good." Legends tell us that the entire house was filled with spiritual light upon his birth. When it was no longer possible to hide Moses, he was placed in a basket in the water and Miriam watched him from the shore. As soon as Pharaoh's daughter "drew" him from the water, Miriam was instantly there to help her. "Shall I go and summon a wet nurse from the Hebrew women who will nurse the boy for you?" Miriam inquired, never revealing that she was the sister of the child found in the water. Because of Miriam's intervention, Moses was nursed by his own mother who even received money to do so.

As Miriam grew, she became the spiritual leader of the women in Egypt and throughout the desert journey. Whenever the Jewish people traveled in the desert, they would not move unless Miriam, Moses, and Aaron were in front of them. There are many instances throughout the Torah that point to the spirituality and contribution on the part of the women that may be directly attributed to Miriam's leadership.

It is interesting to note that Miriam herself was not married until later in life. Said to be sickly looking with a green color to her complexion, she was passed over by the men looking for a mate, even though or perhaps because she was the sister of Moses and the leader of the women. Eventually, Miriam married a righteous man named Calev, who was said to be forty years her junior. Throughout her life, even when she was single, Miriam was a strong advocate for women and their right for martial relations. Her advocacy is most well known from the incident with Zipporah. When Miriam becomes aware that Zipporah, the wife of Moses, was hurt that Moses no longer engaged in sexual relations with her, Miriam advocates for her. In a conversation with her brother Aaron, she criticizes Moses for abstaining from sexual relations on religious grounds. "Has God only spoken to Moses? Hasn't He spoken to us and we continue normal marriages" (Numbers 12:1). For criticizing Moses, Miriam was afflicted with *tzara'as,* a kind of skin affliction resembling leprosy. From this episode with Miriam, the sages of Israel inserted in the daily and *Shabbat* prayer book a reminder of what happened to Miriam so as to encourage everyone to be mindful of their speech each day.

It is also important to note that when Miriam died, no mourning on the part of the Jewish people was recorded as was with her brother Aaron. With her death, however, the source of water that had accompanied and nourished the Jewish people as they wandered in the desert mysteriously dried up. The rabbis commented that because the Jewish people did not shed tears over the loss of Miriam, the water dried up. It was only then that the people realized that it was due to the merit of Miriam that there was water in the desert. As with many women, Miriam's contribution was not adequately appreciated until she was no longer living.

Throughout her life, Miriam was always connected to water. She stood by the water to watch her brother. She danced through the Red Sea.

And most importantly, the rock that magically produced water for the Jewish people through the desert was given in the merit of Miriam. The Lubavitcher Rebbe stated that learning about Miriam's well influences the entire week, bringing health spiritually and physically to a person (Sichos 5th Tammuz Parsha Chukas Balak).

For more information about Miriam, read the following chapters in the Bible: Exodus 15:20, Numbers 12:1-16.

Invocation

For those dreamers and visionaries who are ready to be ambassadors for a new order, commune with Sister Miriam. Align yourself with Sister Miriam for the world is undergoing a modern version of the Red Sea that we must each go through to enter the new order. Walk in Miriam's footsteps, dance in her circle dances, and let Miriam encourage and empower you to go forward in the way you have always longed for deep inside. Your dreams and your visions are beautiful, important, and provide direction for you. Sister Miriam will give you the love, the encouragement, and the faith to live your dreams.

Interview with Miriam

Question: It is such an honor to hear your wisdom and guidance Miriam. Do you have an initial message to people today?

Miriam: Dear ones, you live in most auspicious times. I am happy to share with you my wisdom and make myself energetically available to you. People in your time live with challenges and opportunities that are similar to when I lived in a physical body. Whether you know it or not, many of the souls inhabiting human bodies today are actually reincarnations of people who lived in my time as well who have volunteered to return to assist the world during this awesome time of transformation. Just as we were moved in the most radical way into a new reality at the time in which I physically lived, you are similarly on the edge of a new frontier of consciousness. Get your tambourines ready! I want you to know that there will be much to sing and dance about in your time.

Question: Would you please elucidate further on what you have said?

Miriam: Consider for a moment what an amazing period of time it was when I occupied a physical body. Through wondrous signs and many miracles, the Jewish people were brought out of the enslavement of Egypt. Prior to leaving Egypt, we lived through awesome plagues as recorded in the Bible. With every plague, physical reality crumbled before our eyes, yet it also brought forth a deeper revelation of Godliness that inspired faith on our part. Witnessing the ten plagues, seeing locusts appear, the Nile River turn bloody, and many other supernatural occurrences withered away our hold on reality as we knew it. There literally was nothing physical to hold on to. We had to put their trust in a God that we could not see or touch. This was quite new for many Jews who were assimilated and spiritually were not so different from the Egyptians. Many Jews who did not prepare their homes by pouring blood on their doorposts from the slaughter of the lamb perished during the last plague. Those deaths were so devastating to everyone who remained. We all lost loved ones. Then, very soon after, we had to leave Egypt and all that we knew to journey into the desert. We quickly baked matzah, which is what you eat even up to today during the holiday of Passover to remember this awesome glorious time.

Question: How is our time similar to your time?

Miriam: Your time is also awesome. People in your time whose consciousness is limited to a materialistic view of reality will have a very challenging time, as in my time. For those of faith, it will be a glorious time as it was for us. Please understand that there will be both hardship and spiritual opportunity as your world undergoes a time of transmutation. Floods, plagues, earthquakes, drought, war, and terrorism occurring in many places in your world will help awaken people to the deeper reality of how interconnected all of life is. Because of your technological advances, the world is informed quickly about what is happening everywhere. It will become increasingly difficult to dismiss the suffering of others that you see presented on television or read about in newspapers and on the Internet as not affecting you personally. People will more fully realize how interconnected they are.

I do not say this to alarm you but rather to help you prepare for the challenges before you. When the world is undergoing a major change and transformation, it will be natural to feel worried and frightened by all that is taking place. You may feel like life is out of control, but know that it is not. Divine order is being restored. Do not be afraid with the changes that occur around you. Find your peace within yourself and in your relationship with God.

Question: What do you predict for our time?

Miriam: That which you have longed for in the deepest recesses of your heart and soul will soon be upon you. You will see, feel, and experience God in a way that was not possible for you before. Lift your consciousness beyond what is happening on the physical plane of existence. Let go of materialism as a definition of your life. Cast away doubt and fear. Pray to God for protection, guidance, and wisdom. It is very easy in your time for everyone to turn to God, so be happy and grateful. Know that everything that is happening in your life and in the world is to prepare and purify you for a deeper revelation of God. You will also each learn firsthand as people did in my time that there is nothing in the world that can offer you protection but God. God is your deepest truth and reality. Rejoice for all you need is simple faith. With faith, you draw to you an angelic force field that will protect you. Your time is actually a very glorious time to be alive.

Question: Miriam, you were a prophetess. You were blessed with holy vision to know what was going to happen from the time you were a child. At the age of five, you persuaded your father, the leader of the Jewish people, to reverse a decree he had issued. Would you tell us more about this?

Miriam: My father had divorced my mother because of Pharaoh's decree that male infants be killed at the time of their birth. Because my father was the head of the Jewish people, all the Jewish men also divorced their wives so as to not have any children. I confronted my father. I told him that his decree was even worse than Pharaoh's because it was against the birth of all children, male and female. It was not right that my father, the leader of the Jewish people, should be afraid of Pharaoh. I also knew that my parents would birth the future redeemer of the Jewish people so it was necessary that they remarry and resume sexual relations. With holy chutzpah, when I was five years old, I told my father basically, "Do your part, trust, and God will do His." What happens to people as a result of the choices they make is in the hands of God. This is still my message to all. Do the right thing. Do what God wants you to do. Do not compromise yourself and make choices from a place of fear rather than faith and trust in God.

Question: How do we simple people develop faith?

Miriam: Faith is a part of every person, available and integral to the well-being of a person. Faith is not blind as people often say, but it is a higher level of knowing that is actually hardwired into the core of your being. Give yourself time to meditate and pray each day. Your consciousness will soon be refined and lifted upward to greater awareness of the *Shechinah.* When you experience God, you access the faith and the love that is your birthright. Sing and dance each day. Do kind deeds to people around you. Take time each day to receive guidance, wisdom, and direction from within. Be happy. You have each been given a soul compass to guide you. The more you listen and trust your intuition, the greater your capacity to receive accurate information and holy wisdom from the higher spiritual realms.

My dear sisters and brothers, do not feel limited by what appears in front of you. I never saw things as they appeared to be, but only as they would be in a more perfected state. Do not dwell on what is lacking in your life or in the world. Believe in your dreams, trust your passion, and pay attention to what makes you excited and enthusiastic. Say yes to life and claim your spiritual ticket to the new world that is unfolding before your very eyes.

Question: You have become a symbol for many women today seeking to claim their spiritual power as women. Would you speak about the role of women at this time?

Miriam: Since the beginning of time and until the end of time, women have always had and will always have a most important role and a special responsibility to guide humanity toward its highest good. For many women, this sacred role takes place primarily in the context of the family. As a mother, a woman is a child's greatest spiritual teacher, responsible for transmitting to her children, and even to her husband, the innermost secrets of the divinity of life. What an awesome and holy assignment the Holy One entrusted to women. For many women, the sacred role of care taking and soul guarding extends into the community and outward toward the entire world.

Everyone must know that it has always been and will always be the wisdom, the love, the intuition, the faith, and even the heroism of women throughout time that has sustained the humanity of all civilizations. The particular influence of Jewish women on safeguarding the purity of the nation of Israel is immeasurable. Quite simply, there would be no Jewish community if not for the courageous actions of the women. As a woman, you need to remember and claim this legacy as your own. The work of women in the past may have been more private than public, but just because these women were not validated publicly does not make their work less worthwhile or important. Besides, the most greatest spiritual work can only be performed in privacy.

Question: Today, many women are working outside of the home in addition to raising children.

Miriam: Your current world is quite unique for women for it is only in your time that the majority of women have entered into the general marketplace. Most women until recently were spared from having to enter the public arena, so they could better nurture and more fully develop feminine sensitivities in a more sheltered setting. The challenge for a woman in your time is to maintain access to the gifts and talents that have been given to her because she is a woman, even when she is in the world of work outside of the home. Women in your time must be quite careful to not confuse power with influence. Power for its own sake diminishes the sanctity of women. Who you are as a woman, as a representative of the Divine Feminine, wherever you are, impacts on others, more than you can ever know.

Question: As a woman, did you not feel marginalized by Moses? Many people suspect that there was a power struggle between the two of you.

Miriam: No, there was no power struggle between us. I always loved my brothers. Moses was chosen to be God's intermediary to the people. Most of the people were awed by Moses and did not find him approachable. Remember Moses had not lived with the people as Aaron and I had. Even when he was living in their midst, Moses was most of the time in meditation. Aaron and I were the indigenous leaders of the people who were intimately involved in their lives. I was responsible for the women from all the tribes. In many instances, recorded and not recorded, Moses clearly recognized that he could not on his own address the needs and concerns of the women. When Moses did not know what to do with the women, he either asked me or God and received an answer.

I was plenty busy caring for and advocating for the women. The women have much to be proud about, for it was the women who provided the stability and the support for the spiritual and physical sustenance of the entire people during the desert experience.

Question: What did the women do in the desert?

Miriam: There are so many examples of the holiness and righteousness of the women that there are too many to enumerate all of them with you now. What may be the most outstanding testimony to the greatness of the women was that the women did not participate in the sin of the Golden Calf. They withheld their jewelry, though sometimes it was taken from them against their will. Their lack of participation in the Golden Calf was not because they were stingy. You see how they contributed generously to the building of the *mishkon,* the tabernacle for the *Shechinah* in the desert.

There was a moral fiber within women during the desert experience that was unique to them. The women in the desert did not participate in the numerous rebellions against Moses' authority and often discouraged their husbands from participating as well. When the spies were sent to visit the Land of Israel prior to our entry into it, the women did not believe the negative reports about the land. It is generally accepted that it was due to the merit of the women that the Jewish people left Egypt and entered into the Land of Israel. Even the male commentaries written about this time testify to this fact. They also predict that it will once again be the merit of the women that will take the world forward in the times to come. I believe that as well. So it is important that women in your time understand this. Women are generally on a higher spiritual level than men so it is actually the women who must guide humanity forward. Women have always done this in the past and must also do so in the future.

Question: Why do you think that the women are on a higher spiritual level than the men?

Miriam: Women for the most part are more inwardly focused, intuitive, and naturally exhibit more faith than men. Every woman must know this about herself and claim the spiritual gifts of simply being blessed to be a woman. A woman's intuition is a real phenomenon and must be respected. A woman in touch with her feminine intuition is not limited or swayed by physical externalities as men may be prone. It is therefore appropriate that a woman be called upon to offer guidance and vision because she can see more clearly what is revealed in the heart but hidden to the human eye. She wisely seeks to improve herself first rather than change her circumstances.

As a general rule, a woman is more receptive to Godliness than a man. It is not because she is less than a man that she has fewer *mitzvot*, commandments or religious obligations. Actually, she needs fewer external obligations because she is inherently more pious than a man. Because a woman is heart-centered, she always seeks opportunities to love and embrace life and those around her wherever she is. Her deep yearning for love keeps her open and receptive to higher spiritual frequencies.

Question: But, did you not feel left out as a woman when the Torah was given on Mount Sinai to Moses?

Miriam: Before the Holy One gave the Torah to the Jewish people, God spoke separately to the women first and then to the men. This is coded in the Torah. The women are referred to as "the House of Israel." We women received all that we needed to be connected to God. It is true that I would have liked to be with Moses when he ascended the mountain, but I was not summoned. Only Moses, not even Aaron, was invited to ascend the mountain.

The Torah that you read in your time was channeled and written by Moses, so it primarily records what occurred through him. After the revelation at Sinai, Moses was responsible for recording the experiences of the desert and he did so from his vantage point. The subsequent commentaries on what Moses wrote were written by men primarily for men. This whole rabbinic tradition that emerged later in time is directed to men because there is greater need on the part of men for this kind of structure of laws and learning than for women. Men have written many books that they study continually because it is more of the masculine nature to stand outside of life, analyzing, attempting to understand and control life. It is the nature of the feminine to live in the fullness of life. You call it history and not her-story for a reason.

If you look only at the written accounts, it may look like my authority was limited, but that is not an accurate, or rather, a complete representation of what occurred. My teachings have not yet been written down and will never be. Words can never capture the depths of the heart of the feminine. The path of feminine spirituality was and is only transmitted orally from mother to daughter and found through communities of women celebrating, singing, and dancing together.

Question: What is the feminine path of spirituality about? What spiritual practices do you recommend to be on this path?

Miriam: The feminine path is all about the embodiment of Godliness within oneself and the revelation of Godliness within all of creation. Feminine spirituality is a celebration of the immanence of God. Said very simply, masculine spirituality is about how awesome and separate the Divine is. Feminine spirituality is about how intimate and close the Divine is.

One spiritual practice that I advocate for men and women is dancing. Pray to God and yet dance each day. When we were living in Sinai, we held drumming circles almost nightly and we danced all the time. It was such a glorious time being in the desert all together. Many people may trivialize dancing believing it to be inferior to serious study. But, is it really better for women to learn Gemara as men do? I do not think so. Dance offers a woman and a man in touch with his feminine a deeper connection to the Holy One than analytic study. To dance ecstatically before God is to live life fully. The deepest secrets of God are transmitted to the dancer who knows how to dance and be danced by the Divine Herself. You will learn all that you need to know through dance. You will learn to surrender, live authentically from the heart, and most importantly embody the *Shechinah*. It is one thing to talk about God and quite another to experience God within one's own body. Meditate and pray while you dance. Allow yourself to be moved from deep within. Create drumming and dance circles with each other and make dance your spiritual practice. Do not underestimate the power of dancing to bring joy, peace, and wisdom.

Question: You led the women in circle dances as they crossed the Red Sea. Why "circle dances"?

Miriam: The circle is the symbol of the feminine. A woman's body is full of circles for a reason. Have you not noticed that when women gather together they often form circles. Throughout time, there are always knitting circles, sewing circles, all kinds of women circles. Even when women gather in small groups to talk with each other, they naturally sit in the form of a circle. Women naturally feel most comfortable in circles. I guided the women to do circle dances when we crossed the Red Sea because I wanted to transmit to them then as well as for posterity the most direct experience of the *Shechinah,* the Divine Feminine, and Her wisdom that is only possible to receive when women are in a circle.

Question: Please explain more. What is so important about the circle?

Miriam: The circle has important spiritual properties that reveal much about the wisdom of the feminine. First, the circle has no beginning or end. There is no past and no future in the circle. The circle also reminds us that God is always the center and every point in the circle is equidistant from the center. While masculine energy is hierarchal and linear, feminine energy is circular, inclusive, and egalitarian. A woman in touch with the feminine does not look to others for spiritual direction but directly inward to the

God within her. Her circular vision enables her to see in all directions the oneness all around her. Through circle dances, a woman learns, embodies, and teaches the world that every person is equally important. Everyone is beloved. Without each person in the circle, there would be a hole. Dancing or sitting in a circle also reminds a woman ultimately to be a vessel and create holy vessels in her life as well. So, when we women danced in circles, it was to embody these deep teachings.

Question: The song you sang that is recorded in the Bible was a very succinct song in the present tense, while Moses' song was much longer and sung in the future tense.

Miriam: The song of Moses was prophetic, revealing what will take place in the time period known as "the End of Days." It is therefore sung in the future tense because this is the song that is to be sung for the time to come. What we experienced crossing the Red Sea was only a taste of the redemption that will come in the future when all evil will be obliterated and God is totally revealed through nature. My song was also prophetic, but it was more of a chant, brief, and sung in the present tense.

Question: Why was your song short and sung in the present tense?

Miriam: One does not need many words to reveal a deeper truth. Actually, the fewer the words, the deeper the truth. At the crossing of the Red Sea, the women through the short chant and circle dances were able to draw down, reveal, and even embody higher supernal lights than Moses was even singing about for a future time. Feminine spirituality is always present tense. In the deepest truth, there is only truly the now. The Divine Presence, the *Shechinah,* is only revealed in the present moment. Feminine spirituality is a perpetual celebration of the *Shechinah,* the Divine Presence, that is never based in what will be in the future, or what was in the past, but always in the present. The present is surely a present, by that I mean a gift.

Question: Thank you. That returns us full circle to what we were discussing earlier about feminine spirituality. Is there another practice besides dancing and chanting that you recommend for women?

Miriam: Yes, indeed. Because women are moved more by love than men, they must also create times for communing with their hearts and sharing with each other. Learning to speak from the heart and to listen from the heart is yet another important feminine spiritual practice that nourishes a woman's contact with her soul. Women are naturally intuitive and have been blessed with great internal inner knowing. Through the spiritual practice of sharing and communing with others, a woman will draw out of the spiritual wellsprings within her own very self the deepest secrets of God and creation that men can only read and study about in books. She has been blessed inherently with this profound inner knowing simply because she is a woman.

Question: Why then do women try to learn the Torah like men do?

Miriam: You live in a time when the feminine is devalued and not sufficiently appreciated. Too much emphasis in your technological culture has been given to the head rather than the heart or the body. The heart may be located below the head, but it is not lower in importance. With too much mental stimulation, a person can lose access to one's own soul. It is actually pointless to try to figure out life with one's mind, yet so many people think that is what they are supposed to do. The soul offers the highest guidance to a person. The heart and soul of a person are intertwined and must be honored as such.

Yes, I am quite dismayed when I see women valuing the masculine way over the feminine way. It does not make any sense to me. Why should a woman want to be equal to a man or like a man when she is superior to him in so many ways? When we lived in the desert, women were strong, united, and we celebrated ourselves as women, living our lives fully with our hearts and souls.

Question: More and more women today want to do the same work as men do. Is that good? Women want to be rabbis, doctors, lawyers, scientists, etc. They do not want to stay home and be housewives. To be home feels isolating to many women.

Miriam: It is okay for women to be out of the home as long as a woman remains in touch with her intuitive feminine wisdom. She can be whatever she wants to be, even the president of a country. I am simply concerned, however, that when women imitate men and abandon their own inner knowing of the feminine, the imbalance between the masculine and feminine in the world is increased. For thousands of years the world has been dominated by men in positions of power over other men and women. Just because women may be in these positions of power does not mean that they embody the feminine, and rectify the imbalance between the masculine and feminine in the world.

Question: Please tell us more about what you mean by the imbalance between the masculine and feminine.

Miriam: The world suffers due to this imbalance. Masculine energy has made tremendous accomplishments in the external world, for that it is the nature of masculine energy, it is always expanding. Unfortunately, these accomplishments have occurred at the cost of the feminine. For example, modern societies in your time have made great technological advances, but you lack intimate loving communities where people can be authentic, vulnerable, and caring with each other. It is the wisdom and the heart of the feminine that nurtures real intimacy between people. What good is technological advancement if more and more people are depressed, anxious, isolated, and unhappy because of the lack of meaningful relationships with other human beings? Societies pay dearly for the imbalance between the masculine and feminine. So if women become more like men, who will do the nurturing needed to make a person feel totally loved and validated?

Question: But what about women who have been terribly oppressed by patriarchal societies?

Miriam: I am deeply pained by the anguish, the torment, and even cruelty that many women have experienced. Yes, it is true, women have been oppressed by men and still carry a legacy of pain and inferiority that is often passed between mother and daughter. This is a most unfortunate burden that women have had to endure. It breaks my heart to have witnessed how men have dominated and oppressed women over time. It is not what God wants. When men are disconnected from God, they dominate and oppress women. Any man who is truly rooted in God honors and respects the wisdom of women. How a person treats a woman or women in general is a measuring stick of the Godliness of a person. The laws of Torah were made to safeguard and protect women from the aggressiveness that is inherent in the nature of man. Her sanctity as a woman must be protected. When the sanctity of women is violated, the society is in danger of losing its divine blessing for sustenance and even survival.

Question: What wisdom can you offer women who have been oppressed by men?

Miriam: Women, please do not see yourself through the lens of weak and insecure men who are actually afraid or jealous of your womanly power. As a woman, you are so beautiful and can be so radiant. You are an embodiment of the *Shechinah*. Never forget that. No one can take that away from you. You must know this as your deepest truth. I strongly recommend that each woman join or form a group with other women who will reflect back to you the beauty and wisdom of who you are as a woman. Your strength lies in community with other women. This was true for women when I lived in a body and it remains so for women for all time. Celebrate your blessings and gifts as women. You are more emotional than men but that is because you are more God connected. Too often your gifts as women are devalued by men and then you do not feel good about yourself. Do not define who you are from the feedback that you receive from men. When you need feedback and guidance, ask your women or girl friends who love you. The women in my time were deeply connected to each other. We had a vibrant spiritual and emotional life together.

Question: Many women today feel that Torah and Judaism are patriarchal and oppressive to women.

Miriam: I understand. If a woman only sees the externalities and is not in community with other women, it will look very much as if Judaism is totally patriarchal. But on the inside, in its true essence, Judaism is all about the feminine. First of all, the most basic thing everyone must know is that the Jewish religion is passed through the woman and not the man. If a woman marries a non-Jew, the offspring is a full-fledged Jew. It is not true if a Jewish man marries a non-Jewish woman. This is not a matter of biology, rather it is because the Torah recognizes the supreme influence that a woman has in raising a child. Similarly, an ill person is identified by his or her mother's name because it is the mother who is acknowledged as the one who can draw down blessings of healing more than the father.

Secondly, Judaism is rooted in the Torah. The Torah is a physical representation of the Divine Feminine. When you go to a modern-day synagogue in your time you see how the Torah is dressed in a beautiful velvet or silk cover and wears a crown. See how everyone kisses the Torah as she is paraded around the synagogue. She is adored and even worshipped. Then she is gently placed on the table, she is rolled open, and people read from her. A *yad*, Torah pointer, is used to read from her. After they read from the

Torah, they then roll the Torah scrolls up, dress her again, and shake each other's hands, because they just had contact with the Divine Feminine. The Torah is feminine. The Sabbath, *Shabbat,* is also feminine because this is a time when the *Shechinah* is most revealed. The essence of Judaism is all about the revelation of the Divine Feminine. Men are praying and learning all the time to even have a glimpse of the *Shechinah,* but a woman may intrinsically know how to even embody Her without much effort. Men study the written word of the Torah, but women know the white spaces in the Torah, what is beyond what is written.

Question: Then, why are women often relegated to be observers in much of Judaism, particularly in orthodox or Chasidic communities? Only recently have women been allowed to be rabbis and active participants in synagogue services.

Miriam: People have mistakenly accepted Rabbinic Judaism as the only expression of Torah and it is not. Because of this misunderstanding, women have wanted to become rabbis and know what men do so as to be able to have public recognition and influence in community life. But, remember that Rabbinic Judaism, the synagogue structure, prayers, learning, and many of the spiritual practices generally followed in your time, were created by men as a form of Judaism that is generally more suited to masculine sensibilities. Similarly, the rabbis emphasized analytical learning because that is in accordance with the nature of men. They also limited the participation of women in learning and services due to their own weaknesses.

The typical prayer service conducted in synagogues of all denominations is patriarchal. That does not make it bad, these services are beautiful, pleasing, and wonderful, but women must understand that they were written for men by men. Even though women today may participate and even lead synagogue prayer services, that does not change the basic structure or content. The synagogue has become the primary venue for Judaism for many people because men have defined it as such. It need not be and should not be. The home is actually the most important center for spiritual practice. What happens in the home really makes a difference in people's lives more than anywhere else. In every home, a woman must become a priestess, a prophetess, a visionary, a representative of the Divine Feminine for her husband and her children. Furthermore, as I emphasized earlier, it is essential women develop their own forms of worship that are better suited for their sensibilities that include meditation, dance, and sharing like we did in the desert. Spiritual community is important for every woman. In my time, women had a vibrant community of their own, independent of the men.

Question: Is there anything more that you will like to add on this important subject?

Miriam: Both feminine and masculine forms of spirituality are necessary because God is both transcendent and immanent, from the human perspective. It is the polarity between the two that gives vitality to services and to everything in life for us. Men tend to prefer the worship of the transcendence, the awesomeness of the Divine. They want to experience and have a relationship with The Holy One, Blessed be He, Who is beyond this world. Women, on the other hand, tend to want to experience, reveal and even embody the immanence of the Divine, the Shechinah, Who is hidden yet ever-present in the world. There is a difference between the two.

Question: Please explain this more clearly?

Miriam: People who favor feminine forms of spirituality want to meditate, sing, dance a lot so as to be uplifted to experience themselves as a part of God. If prayer services are solely masculine in style and content, without the feminine, prayers are said quickly without much feeling. Without the feminine, there is little vitality, for the feminine brings life and joy to everything. It is the " arousal from below of the feminine that brings down blessing. If prayer services are only feminine, there will be little outreach to the Holy One Blessed be He, who is beyond this world. Without the masculine, the feminine will lose her vitality. She literally dries up. To summarize, without the feminine, the masculine is lifeless. Without the masculine, the feminine dries up. There are men and women in this world for good reason. We both need each other.

Question: Before we conclude our time together, I would like to ask you about the unpleasant incident of *tzara'as* you were afflicted with that was recorded in the Bible. I heard in some Jewish circles that this affliction was a punishment for rebellion on your part against Moses.

Miriam: Contrary to what people may think, as I said earlier, there was no need or desire on my part to rebel against my brother Moses. I was afflicted with *tzara'as* that resembles leprosy because I spoke badly about Moses to my brother Aaron. I only did so because I was deeply pained by Moses' abandonment of his marital responsibilities toward his wife Zipporah. She cried to me about this and my heart went out to her. I know this pain all too well. For so long I was not married so I know what it is to be without a man's love. Everything that I know about sexual relations between a husband and a wife is that sex is holy. It is what God wants. We were created through sex and we create new life through sex. Our lovemaking is much more than procreation. It is a form of worship because we experience God so directly through sexual relations. As you can see, I am very passionate about this as I believe every woman should be.

Question: Is that why Judaism has not honored celibacy like other traditions do?

Miriam: Exactly, Judaism is not about celibacy but holy sexuality. We make unification between the Holy One (Divine Masculine) and the *Shechinah* (Divine Feminine) through sexual relations. We bring oneness and peace into the world through sexual relations. According to Torah, men have certain obligations to women sexually because sexual intimacy is very important to a woman. My well of water was used to prepare women for sexual relations with their husbands. Throughout my life, I continually encouraged women to have sexual relations with their husbands, no matter how challenging our external circumstances were.

So you must understand how terribly upset I was that my brother Moses refrained from sexual relations with his wife when she desired this intimacy with him. Why should any women be deprived of this experience, especially Zipporah, who is a convert, alone, and separate from her biological family? These were my thoughts and feelings. I was simply conferring with my brother Aaron to see if he shared my perspective about this issue. I am after all Moses' older sister and Aaron is his brother. I did not feel that there was anything wrong with my speaking to our brother about this matter. I found out differently. For the sin of *loshon hara,* speaking evil, I was quarantined for a seven-day period outside of the camp. I experienced firsthand how important it is to be mindful of one's speech. Everyone in the community of Israel also witnessed and learned from what happened to me.

Question: Why were you punished in this way?

Miriam: All punishments are metered out in proportion to the sin. Skin afflictions in the desert occurred with people who judged others superficially. Because they saw only the surface of a person, their skin, their surface, was afflicted. When I gossiped about my brother Moses and his private relationship with his wife, as if he was simply an ordinary man, I was punished. My brother was more of an angel than a man, so I had no right to judge him by my standards of what is appropriate for a man. Thankfully, Moses quickly prayed for me, so I was spared and did not die.

Question: What happened to you during this time of being quarantined from the rest of the people? It is said that you came back more radiant than you had ever been.

Miriam: I learned so much during this time of healing as anyone does when they experience an affliction or illness. In my case, it was clear to me and to everyone that mine came directly from God. This affliction brought me closer to God than I was before. It was truly a gift. It peeled away layers that had kept me separate from God. As an older sister and as a leader of the women, I had always taken care of others before myself. Now during the precious time when I was quarantined it was only me and God. Freed of my responsibilities to others, I went deeper in my experience of God. The *Shechinah* took residence within my body in a way that she did not do before. I never expected that my words about Moses would cause this affliction, but I learned so much about who my brother Moses was, who God is, and who I was, so I was deeply grateful.

At my request, my husband divorced me immediately as I left the camp so as to free me to be with myself without distractions and attachments. When I returned to the people, he remarried me. I was so happy, even happier than I had been when he married me the first time. Then I felt that Calev, who was such a righteous man, married me because I was alone and had compassion upon me. Now with the *Shechinah* shining and guiding me so fully, a greater and holier love and passion was awakened from my beloved Calev and this made me even happier than I had ever been before. From our joy, we birthed children, even in my old age. I had wanted children for so long, and after this tribulation and deeper prayer on my part, miracles occurred for me.

Question: Do you have any guidance to others who are healing from an illness and affliction?

Miriam: God is your healer. This illness or affliction has come to help you in the way that your soul wants. Peel away the fear, the anger, the judgments that have separated yourself from others, from God, and who you really are. Use this time of illness and affliction you have been given to grow spiritually. It is not random that you are challenged in this way. Examine your deeds carefully. I was fortunate that I knew what caused my illness. It is not always so clear for many. Always, remember that God is your healer. The Shechinah is with you always, but particularly when you are ill. It is very helpful that when you are sick that you give charity to others.

I offer all those who are suffering physically, emotionally, and spiritually my deepest blessings and love. May you heal quickly. And if it is not the will of the Shechinah that you fully recover physically, may you be blessed with Her love and peace. Always remember that this physical world is not the only world. The next world, the World to Come, is filled with great joy for those who have drawn close to the *Shechinah* when they were physically embodied.

Please make every moment count in your life while you live in a physical world. Your physical life is short, never for too long. You never know when your physical life will end. Remember that you cannot take your material possessions with you when you leave this physical world. You can, however, take with you your good deeds and your love of *Shechinah*. So, always make an effort wherever you are to give charity and do good deeds.

Question: Any final words to people before you depart?

Miriam: During this brief time on the earthly plane, do good deeds to others. Be kind. Be grateful. Open and give your heart away each day. Love God. Love yourself. Love others. And dance, always remember to dance and celebrate the gifts of life that you have been given. Connect with me and the women of the desert when you sing and dance with your full hearts. The same ecstatic joy that we experienced is there for you too. I love you.

Concluding Response to Sister Miriam
(It is suggested that this be read out loud alone or in a group.)

"Thank you for your words of love and inspiration. You are and will always be a powerful model for so many of us. Many of us are currently seeking new ways to express our love and help make this world a better place. Your words have reminded us of the unique role that women play in the world. We clearly know that we do not benefit ourselves or others by imitating men or envying their power. Admittedly, we have been shortsighted in honoring the masculine displays of power over the more subtle feminine forms of influence. We are grateful for the unique gifts and talents given to us by virtue of being women. As women, we are connected to the wholeness of life. When we share the love within our hearts, we open the hearts of those around us so healing can occur. Our words are powerful and transformative. Like the women who lived in the desert under your leadership, may we also embody the feminine spirit and help heal this world as women.

As you encouraged us so many times, we will seek to strengthen our community with other women. We will not be competitive with other women nor will we betray them. Our strength and healing comes through honoring ourselves and others. May we trust our feminine intuition. May we dance all the time. May we always have faith in the goodness of life. Amen."

Prayer to the God of Sister Miriam

May the God of Sister Miriam inspire me to trust what I know deep inside me as my truth. I can trust my intuition. May the God of Sister Miriam give me the courage to go forward in my life expressing my vision and truth.

What Qualities of the Feminine Does Miriam Demonstrate?

1. **Honor your feminine intuition as Miriam did:** Miriam is ultimately a visionary who inspires women and men with the faith to trust their intuition and not be limited to what they see happening in the physical world. There are still so many examples of Miriam's intuition that altered the destiny of the Jewish people that were not mentioned in the introduction and interview sections of this

chapter. For example, during the awesome time of departure of the Jewish people, Miriam "saw" the future and "knew" that a miracle was going to take place, so she persuaded the women to bring their tambourines when leaving Egypt. In place of taking other items that may have been practical and helpful for the journey, the women packed their tambourines as Miriam told them to do.

2. **Be in the present:** Do not put off living until a future time. God is only experienced in the present, not in the future or in the past. Miriam demonstrated how the Divine Presence is only revealed in the present moment. Being present is a gift of feminine wisdom.

3. **Dance:** Miriam taught the mysteries of the circle and feminine spirituality. When the Jewish people crossed the Red Sea, Miriam, the prophetess, the sister of Aaron, took the timbrel in her hand, and all the women went out after her with tambourines and with circle dances and Miriam answered them, "Sing to the Lord for he has triumphed gloriously; the horse and his rider has he thrown into the sea" (Exodus 15:20–21). Through her song and her simple circle dances, Miriam, ancient prophetess, heralded in a new paradigm of consciousness that embodied the power and vision of the feminine that is more revolutionary than the prophecy of Moses.

4. **Women's right to sexual intimacy:** A woman's right to sexual intimacy was important to Miriam as most clearly demonstrated when Miriam advocated for Zipporah. Miriam is also credited with inspiring and encouraging the women in Egypt to engage in sexual relations, even at times when it was difficult and dangerous for them to bear more children. Under Miriam's leadership and guidance, the Jewish women in Egypt would not only feed their exhausted husbands a hot meal after a day's work, they would beautify themselves so as to seduce the men to have sexual relations with them. We are told that the women would polish their copper mirrors and use them to beautify themselves

for their husbands. These holy mirrors traveled with the Jewish people and were lovingly donated by the women for the construction of the *mishkon,* the holy tabernacle for the indwelling presence of God, the *Shechinah.* By the way, Moses was initially reluctant to use the mirrors for they were an instrument for vanity, but he was told by God that these mirrors were holy and should be included in the *mishkon.* Even though the resources to feed additional people were limited, under Miriam's counsel, the women trusted that God would provide for all and another mouth would not burden God. It was the women who had the strength, courage, and faith to birth children, even at risk of their own lives.

What Spiritual Practice Do We Learn from Miriam?

In the interview section Miriam encourages women to dance. Many may think of dance as trivial, but Miriam explains that dance is a powerful spiritual practice for experiencing a revelation of Godliness within oneself. Every woman in touch with her feminine knows that singing and dancing give her faith, strength, and joy. It is one of the secrets of the feminine. Women need to remember to give themselves time to sing and dance with each other for it is there that they will find inspiration. If we can sing, dance, and play a tambourine and drum, in good times and challenging times, we can go forward in our lives.

Miriam also advocates that women allocate time for intimate sharing with each other. By intimate sharing with each other, women refine their capacities to listen, to be compassionate and loving. They receive the validation of these qualities of the feminine that they might not experience elsewhere. Women support groups help strengthen a woman's capacity to offer her feminine gifts to herself, her relationships, and the world at large. Talking to one's female friends from the heart and soul as is the nature of the feminine is in itself a spiritual practice. It is not a waste of time by any means.

Key Points for Reflection and Follow-up Discussion on Miriam

1. What traits did Miriam possess and what did she demonstrate in her life that may inspire you today?

2. How can you increase your awareness of Miriam, the qualities she embodied, and the spiritual practices she recommended?

3. Do you see Miriam as a feminist or as simply a strong woman? Is there a difference?

4. Should women have their own separate prayer and learning spaces, or is it best that in modern times men and women are fully integrated in prayer services and learning?

5. Do you imagine that Miriam was upset when Moses chose Yeshoushah to be his successor, rather than her husband Calev, who was younger and one of the spies who returned with a good report of the land? Would it not have been more appropriate to select Calev than Yeshoushah?

Chapter Seven

Batya's Rebellion

The Courage to Translate Vision into Reality

Batya

"I always prayed to live a life of truth, purity, and integrity, even if it was in conflict with everything I had known before. Living a meaningful and purposeful life was always my greatest goal. I knew that such life offered to me the greatest riches, more than all the gold that I had in the palace."

— *Batya*

Batya

Batya, the firstborn and adopted daughter of Amenhotep III, Pharaoh of Egypt, was acknowledged as the mother of Moses, the redeemer of the Jewish people. Though Moses was not her biological son, Batya named him and raised him as her own. Batya was said to be one of only nine people recorded to have entered into Paradise, the Garden of Eden, with full consciousness. Indicating that her soul had reached total perfection, capable of basking in the full radiance of the Divine Presence, she was considered free of the necessity of reincarnation. She did not die in the manner of most people. Her consciousness simply left her physical body at the time of her choosing.

As the princess of Egypt, Batya was a mystical adapt with full entry into the esoteric knowledge, sorcery, and spiritual practices of Egypt. Over time, on her own, she came to realize the falsehood of polytheism and idolatry prominent in ancient Egypt. Within her own soul stirred the awakening of a revelation of the One God. Willing to forsake all comfort, all honor, all pretenses for the truth of this revelation, she sought to free herself and also her country from the influence of idolatry.

When her father, the Pharaoh, had issued a decree requiring that all Jewish male children be killed at birth, so as to prevent the fulfillment of a prediction that a Jewish male would live to redeem the Jewish people, she defied him. Batya not only rescued the child who would be the redeemer from the Nile but raised him as a prince of Egypt. Without Batya, there would not have been a Moses. A spiritual warrior for the Divine Feminine, Batya sought to transform the entire Egyptian empire from within its own palace.

Batya knew from divine inspiration that the prophesied and much awaited Jewish redeemer would be raised through her. She courageously accepted this responsibility. Every morning and evening, Batya would bathe in the cool waters of the Nile River to ease her discomfort from a horrible skin affliction that she and most of the Egyptian people had been suffering. While she was there, she would stroll around, keeping her eyes open for the fulfillment of her prophecy. One day she saw a basket carrying a male Hebrew child in the bulrushes.

There is a legend that Batya's arm miraculously extended to become long enough to reach the basket in the river. It has been said in the merit of Batya, "Stretch your arm and God will do the rest." When Batya saw this child, she knew that he was the one she was waiting for. It was not only because there was a spiritual radiance to this child, but legend says that when she touched the basket containing this infant, the boils and scabs all over her body immediately vanished. She was miraculously cured. The Egyptian sorcerers had forecasted the redeemer of the Jewish people would perish in the water. After Moses had been cast into the water, they no longer saw the sign and the decree was cancelled.

Pharaoh's daughter, Batya, named this child Moses, derived from the word *masha,* "to draw something from water." It should have been *mashuy,* meaning "drawn" in the past tense, as he was drawn out of the water. Batya, however, knew that Moses would "draw" the Jewish people out of Egypt so Batya named him in the present tense of the verb. There were many different names for Moses by his family members. But the Torah only reports the name given to him by Pharaoh's daughter.

In turn, Pharaoh's daughter was named Batya, which means "daughter of God." The Talmud records God saying to Pharaoh's daughter, "Although Moses was not your son, you raised him as your very own. I will make you my daughter. You shall be known as Batya,' God's daughter.'" Her reward was that she was allowed to enter Paradise while she was still alive.

She raised her sons, Moses and Ikhanaton, with the belief in One God. Moses was twenty-six years old when Pharaoh died. Ikhanaton, who had been raised with Moses as a child, known as Amenhotep IV, became the next Pharaoh. Moses was eighteen years old when he left the palace and was out of Egypt during the reign of Ikhanaton. When Moses returned, the Pharaoh was Horemheb, who was not of royal birth. An Egyptian general, Horemheb overthrew Ikhanaton's successor and abolished the cult of Aton, established by Ikhanaton. Even though she was the firstborn of Pharaoh, she was spared during the plague that killed the firstborn of Egypt. She left with the Jewish people out of Egypt as well.

Invocation

For those who seek the courage to discover, to stand and to act for the truth revealed within one's soul, no matter what the environment around you dictates who you should be and what you should do, connect with the God of Batya. She will guide you and help you to strengthen your contact with the deeper inner knowing that is you.

Interview with Batya

Question: What is your message to our readers?

Batya: It is my prayer and my blessing that every woman and man discover within themselves the unique role that each may play in revealing the Divine in their lives and that of others. When a man and woman choose to live purposefully and meaningfully, he or she will be protected and supported in the most miraculous of ways. I encourage all to live wisely. Live courageously. Live outrageously, and dedicate your life to the noble purpose your Creator instilled within you.

Question: Please share about your journey to the awakening of your life purpose.

Batya: Early on, even as a child, I recognized that I was raised as the daughter of Pharaoh not for a life of privilege but for one of responsibility. It would have been quite easy for me to live a life of luxury and riches, but that would not be the truth of who I was and what I came into this world to accomplish. I always knew that I had an important task to accomplish and did not know exactly what it was. I prayed each day that it would become clear to me and that I would be worthy of fulfilling what I came to earth to do.

Through my initiation and training in Egyptian magic and sorcery, I developed certain powers and abilities to manipulate the forces of reality for desired outcomes. Yet with all my knowledge and skill, the deeper yearnings within my soul were not satisfied. Even though I was a princess, I experienced myself as a stranger in my own culture. All the honor and the riches that were given to me because of the position I occupied seemed meaningless and empty to me because they were not based in the deeper truth of reality. Only the truth was important to me. Idolatry became hollow to me.

Question: You lived in the most polytheistic and richest culture in the world at that time. Your father was considered a god and you were considered a goddess. How did you come to discard that and embrace monotheism?

Batya: Every morning when I would bathe in the Nile, I would immerse myself fully in its cooling waters with the prayer that I be cleansed of all impurity and idolatry. I prayed that I be worthy of receiving the grace of a direct revelation of the One God along with the courage and strength to fulfill the will of the Only One, the True Reality. Through this simple practice, all that I needed to know was revealed to me. This spiritual practice that I later came to know as *mikvah* is a practice that I would like to recommend for everyone.

Question: Would you speak about *mikvah,* what it is, how we can do it, and how it helped you to fulfill your purpose?

Batya: *Mikvah* is a most powerful practice of purification and soul empowerment. A *mikvah* is the practice of immersion in a natural body of water with intention and purpose. In your time there are special facilities that are built to contain rain water. I used the Nile. It is fine to use any lake, river, or even the ocean. It is customary for a woman to go to *mikvah* to prepare herself for sexual relations. It is also done to convert a person to become a Jew. I knew all of this intuitively, for the Holy One graciously reveals knowledge to all who sincerely desire to know and serve all of creation.

It is good and healing for everyone to go to *mikvah. Mikvah* purifies a person on the level of thought, heart, and action. When people think, feel, and act in ways that are self-serving, and not in accordance with divine will, they become energetically blocked and unable to receive information from the higher realms. *Mikvah* cleanses them, renews, and offers them a new start in life. *Mikvah* is marvelously simple; that is, what I like about it.

Question: How did you have the courage to rescue a Hebrew male child when your father ordered them to be murdered?

Batya: I always prayed to live a life of truth, purity, and integrity, even if it was in conflict with everything I had known before. Living a meaningful and purposeful life was always my greatest goal. I knew that such a life offered to me the greatest riches, more than all the gold that I had in the palace. All external riches were temporary in my eyes, only valuable to the extent that they served this greater truth. When my consciousness was finally awakened to behold the majesty of the One God, the creator of all of life, I was wholeheartedly dedicated to living from this deeper truth and transmitting it to others. That depth of commitment brought me courage along with a faith and trust in God.

When my father became so obsessed with fear that he was willing to murder innocent male children to protect himself, I hated him for being so self-serving. He was unworthy of being Pharaoh, ruler of the greatest land in the world. If he was a god, why did he fear a child? Once again, all too clearly, I saw the emptiness of idolatry for it surely did not provide my father with the courage needed to rule and care beneficently for his people as a leader must. My father was not necessarily an evil man, but a fearful pathetic one. His advisors had knowledge but lacked truth. I vowed that I would not follow in the path of my father. I would change Egyptian society from within, slowly and gently. I could not be a part of the perpetuation of evil that I witnessed all around me.

Question: How did you plan to effect change in Egypt?

Batya: As a woman, it was not my way to fight, but to wait to be guided by the Holy One for whom all life emanates and all change comes. I prayed deeply and I trusted that my life be used as an instrument for the greater divine plan. Much before I discovered Moses, it was revealed to me in meditation that I would raise as my own son the Hebrew child designated to be the redeemer. Together we would redeem both the Jewish people from slavery and cleanse Egypt of idolatry, making it a holy kingdom in the eyes of the Creator. I would educate and train this child for this role that he was designated to perform by the Holy One. As his mother, I would transmit to him the secrets to the deepest mysteries and knowledge that I had been privileged to receive. I trained all my children in the belief of the One God.

My other son Ikhanaton who succeeded my father as Pharaoh established the religion of Aton, the belief in One God for all of Egypt. During his reign, Egypt was purified and became more spiritually refined until the reign of my beloved son was overthrown by an evil man who sought power for himself.

Question: How did you recognize this particular child Moses when you named him as the redeemer?

Batya: It was easy and clear as it came directly from the Creator of the universe. When one day I beheld the shining countenance of an infant in the water, I hoped that this child was the one I long awaited. When I was healed from this dreadful skin affliction as I touched the basket that carried him in the water, I knew for certain that I had indeed found my precious son. The divine plan that had been transmitted to me in my meditation was now to be actualized. This infant was also so radiant and beautiful, I loved him instantly. I arranged to have him nursed by his biological mother so he would receive the foundation of love and support by her. After his weaning, he would be returned to me and I would raise him as my son.

Question: Why do you feel it was important for Moses to be raised as an Egyptian?

Batya: I knew that it was part of the divine plan that the redeemer of the Jewish people be raised in the palace. Here he would not only learn and acquire mastery of all that Egyptian magic and occult had to offer, but he would be trained to be a royal leader, a prince of Egypt. He would not have a slave mentality, fearful and ashamed, but he would be strong, confident, and fearless. I personally taught him about how to summon the angelic forces to connect with the One God and receive guidance and knowledge. I always reminded him that he was a Jew and that he had an important role and responsibility to the Jewish people, to me, and to the Holy One. It was our secret.

Question: What is your understanding of what happened in Egypt when you and Moses lived?

Batya: When the Jewish people entered into Egypt, the Divine Feminine, the *Shechinah*, was with them. I saw this clearly in my meditation. Their presence in the land of Egypt brought blessing to Egypt. It was revealed to me that the Jewish people came into Egypt because it was the will of the Creator. It did not happen by chance, or even by the conscious choosing of the Jewish people.

They thought they were coming to Egypt for food, but rather it was to feed Egypt spiritually. That is the real reason that they came. In the infinite mercy of the Holy One, when the Jewish people were in our land, Egypt was given a chance to attach herself to the Holy One and reject the path of the serpent. You might recall Egypt's fascination with serpents. Men even shaved their heads to better resemble the snake. The magicians of Egypt had gained tremendous spiritual power through the manipulation of the demonic forces. We used divination; we communed with the spirits of the deceased; we consulted ghosts and disembodied entities. We were master sorcerers and astrologers.

Over time I along with many others realized that the power of Egypt was sourced in impurity and fear and not in faith or connection with the source of truth and goodness. I did all I could to educate and spread the belief in One God among Egyptians. When it became clear Egypt could not change from within for evil had permeated its very fiber, many Egyptians, the best of Egypt, chose to leave Egypt with the Jewish people and follow Moses and the path of faith that he taught. This act took great courage. Ultimately, those Egyptians who left assimilated into the Jewish people, forgetting that they were once Egyptians. Many of them were once the master sorcerers and magicians, the elite of Egypt.

Question: Do you have any final words for people living today?

Batya: I am sad to announce to people in your time that the power of the serpent still lives. It may not be clear to modern people today who and what the serpent is. Know that in your time the serpent is the power of illusion and of falsehood. First, to combat the evil of the serpent, you must know that the serpent thrives on fear. It becomes more powerful when you are afraid. It has no real power except what you give it. So do not let fear stop you.

Today, as in my time, each person must chose to follow the path of the truth and goodness and reject the serpent whose life force energy is based on what is unreal and false. When people are connected to the truth, the power of the serpent is vanquished. When enough people give up their inner truth, because they are frightened, the power of evil increases.

Question: What should people do?

Batya: Firstly, attach yourself to the Creator of life and you are unstoppable. There is no obstacle that you cannot overcome. Live your life with confidence and joy. Be willing to break out of your comfort zone. Your true self is deeper than your fear-based conditional self. You came into this life for a purpose.It is not to accumulate wealth that you cannot take with you when you leave your physical body.

To discover what this purpose is for you, each of you must also go out of Egypt, that place of bondage, from the belief in what is false, to walk in truth and faith. Until you make this exodus for yourself with the help of the Divine, you will find yourself in bondage. May you be blessed to bring yourself and help bring others from darkness to light, from bondage to freedom.

Concluding Response to Mother Batya
(It is suggested that this be recited out loud alone or by group)

"Mother Batya, you are such an inspiration to us. You were truly worthy of being the mother of Moses, the redeemer of the Jewish people. You model to us a person who was courageous enough to trust her inner knowing and act upon it. We want to be more like you. We want to have your courage. We will listen and honor what is revealed to us in the deep recesses of our soul like you did. Too often we betray our own inner knowing to please other people. We seek to be comfortable rather than authentic. We play it safe, rather than speak and act in ways that honor God and what we know as the truth in our heart and soul. Admittedly, we have been selfish, shortsighted and impatient. With you as our example, we affirm right now that we will live more courageously and selflessly. Only by being selfless and courageous like you were will we know the true vitality of life. Our life is a divine gift that we treasure. In this very moment, we make a deep choice to devote ourselves more wholeheartedly to the discovery of our holy purpose for being created on the earth at this time. We affirm now that we do trust ourselves to live more fully from our deep inner knowing. We affirm that we will honor the Shechinah in all that we are and do."

Prayer to the God of Mother Batya

May the God of Mother Batya empower me to live the truth that is revealed within my own soul no matter what the environment dictates what I should do and who I should be.

What Quality of the Feminine Does Batya Demonstrate?

Batya demonstrates the courage and power of a woman in touch with the feminine to trust inner knowing, and not be defined by externalities. The Egyptians worshipped the Nile as a god. Batya in her feminine wisdom realized the falsehood of this idolatry. She chose to not give away her inner power and inner knowing as a woman to serve what was false. She defied her father, the Pharaoh. When she saw the basket containing Moses in the water, she had compassion, totally aware that it probably contained one of the Hebrew male infants that her father wanted killed. She raised this son as her own, right in the palace of her father. She left Egypt with the Jewish people.

What Spiritual Practice Do We Learn from Batya?

In the body of the interview, Batya speaks about the spiritual practice of *mikvah*. *Mikvah* is the immersion in a natural body of water for purposes of purification. Most Jewish communities maintain a public *mikvah* that may be used. An ocean, river, or lake is also acceptable. *Mikvah* is done by a woman to resume sexual relations after menstruation and to convert a person to Judaism. *Mikvah* is also done for spiritual purposes, to release negativity and open oneself to greater revelation of Godliness.

Mikvah Meditation

(To Be Done Solely as a Meditation or as Preparation for Actual Mikvah Experience)

When you go to *mikvah,* prior to immersion, make a strong intention that by this act, or through this meditation, you will indeed be cleansed and purified. Your intention is always so important. In your imagination or in actuality prior to the real mikva experience, remove all your garments. In addition to disrobing your clothes, let go of all the roles you have to play in your life. Take a few moments to meditate. You are not what you do. You are not the roles you play. Experience yourself as totally naked, deeply alone, and gloriously vulnerable. Allow the deep inward yearning to be whole, to be pure, to simply become stronger as you prepare for immersion. When you finally enter into the water in actuality or in your imagination, let the water surround your entire body. When you are in the *mikvah,* it is like you are returning to the womb and you can imagine that now you are on the inside of God. The walls of separation are removed between you and God. The love, compassion, and strength of the Creator of the universe surround you, embrace you, and permeate you.

Open to divine love. You are unconditionally loved for that is the nature of love of the Creator. You are loved for simply being you. Open to this feeling, affirm it, and know it as a primary truth. When you are under the water, this is the most auspicious time to ask for anything that you want. Immerse yourself several times in the *mikvah,* take note of the experience of being fully immersed in the water, and then prepare to leave the *mikvah* and take a moment to be with any openings that occurred through this experience or visualization.

Key Points for Reflection and Follow-up Discussion around Batya

1. Do you think that Batya has been sufficiently appreciated in Judaism? Without Batya, would there have been a Moses? How might we call greater attention to the important role that she played?

2. Batya demonstrated the power of the feminine to both discern and remain faithful to her inner truth. In the midst of an idolatrous country, she was a Jew. How is Batya a meaningful model for you in your personal life?

Chapter Eight

Chana's Prayer

Secrets of Getting Prayers Answered

Chana

"It is so important that a person not give up and continue to turn to God daily in prayer, because it is principally through prayer that a person grows and is transformed. Do not be afraid to make yourself vulnerable before God. You cannot do life on your own. When you stand before God in prayer, it is essential that you be authentic. God is close to all who call sincerely, from the heart. When your heart is open, you will experience God and know firsthand that your words will make a difference. God loves you more than you can fathom."

—*Mother Chana*

Chana

Mother and Prophetess

Chana, esteemed as one of the seven ancient prophetesses, is regarded as the role model for prayer for both men and women for all times. From Chana, the Jewish guidelines and laws of prayer are formulated. Each *Rosh Hashanah,* one of the holiest days in the Jewish calendar, the story of Chana and her prophetic song are read. Not only because her prayers to bear a son were answered on that day, but also because her words and her life story itself inspire us to call out in prayer more powerfully and authentically on this most auspicious day of blessing.

Many women like Chana throughout the ages have been challenged with infertility. Even biblical women like Sarah, Rebecca, Rachel, and Miriam prayed as they each confronted this challenge. Chana's challenge of infertility is recorded in depth in the Bible, not just for the particular child she bore out of her prayer, but because the way in which she prayed for this son was unique. No one had ever prayed like this before.

As with biblical women before her, Chana's prayers for a child were not answered immediately. When Chana had been infertile for more than ten years of marriage, her husband Elkanah, at Chana's suggestion, married a second wife, Peninah, who quickly bore him ten sons in eight years. Rather than being grateful to Chana, Peninah ridiculed her for her barrenness.

Chana lived in the time period before the Holy Temple in Jerusalem was built. At the time, it was customary to journey to Shiloh to make sacrificial offerings where the tabernacle that held the *Shechinah* during the desert was maintained. Chana would journey regularly with her husband annually to pray for a child there. It was in Shiloh that Chana's prayers were finally answered. Upon witnessing one of her prayer sessions, Eli the Prophet accused her of being drunk because she moved her lips in her pleading with God. Apparently, Chana was praying in a way that was not commonly done before. To this very day, however, people emulate Chana in their prayer by moving their lips and speaking in a whisper. Chana is also credited with revealing for the first time in her prayer the Divine Name of *Adonai Tzva'ot,* Lord of Hosts. This name attached to the *Sephira* of *Netzach,* a particular divine emanation, is the name of God that provides victory over obstacles.

When Chana finally offered her child to God and said, "Hashem, Master of Legions, if You do not forget your maidservant and You remember me and give Your maidservant male offspring, then I shall give to Hashem all the days of his life" (Samuel, 1:11), her prayers were answered. When Samuel, her son, finished nursing, Chana brought him to Eli to raise and teach to be a prophet. As she surrendered her beloved child, Chana joyously uttered a most profound and awesome song that transmitted the highest spiritual teachings and prophecies for the future. Through this song, it is clear that Chana personally attained the most elevated consciousness of the Divine. There are many songs that have been recorded in the Bible. Miriam sings at the Red Sea, Devorah sings before battle, Moses also sings, but the Zohar (3:19b) testifies that Chana's song was beyond any song or praise ever uttered by a man or woman before.

We know from her song that Chana knew prophetically that her son Samuel would be the principal prophet in the Land of Israel in the days when Israel would be miraculously saved from the Philistines. Samuel indeed became one of the primary Jewish prophets for all times, even compared in prophecy to the stature of Moses. He ruled as a prophet in Israel for ten years on his own, then for two years with Saul, and seven years with David in Hebron. After bearing Samuel, Chana was blessed to birth five more sons.

In the book of Samuel, Chana 's song is recorded. It is written "A barren woman bore seven" (Samuel 1, 2:5). This prophecy was literally fulfilled.

Chana lived to see the two sons of Samuel and these two grandsons were considered like sons for her. It is also said in the oral tradition that when Chana would birth a son, Peninah would bury two sons. When Peninah had already buried eight sons, and Chana was expecting her fifth son, Peninah went to Chana and said the following: "I know that I have sinned against you. Please forgive me so that my two sons I have left will live." Chana prayed for them; they lived and were also considered as sons of Chana. But seven is indicative of the seven *Sephirot*, the seventh being *Malkut*, which refers to the revelation of the *Shechinah*, the Divine Feminine. Not only having seven sons indicated the completion of Chana's work and her fulfillment, Chana was considered as an embodiment of the *Shechinah* in her lifetime.

Invocation

When you feel bereft and despair is knocking at your door, because you have not yet been able to receive the desires of your heart, connect with Mother Chana for the strength to continue to pray and live your life joyfully with the faith that your prayers will indeed be answered in the right time.

Interview with Chana

Question: It is such an honor to be with you today. Do you have a message for people today?

Chana: Prayer is potent. Even though your prayers may not be answered quickly, never give up. Every person has something important to bring into this world. You must pray unceasingly to be capable of fulfilling what you came into this world to do. The more lofty your soul mission is, the greater the challenges you will confront. If you feel guided to bring forth something positive in the world, you must pray continually, do all that you can, and have faith that your prayers will be answered. Do not give up.

Question: As we look at your life, we can truly witness the power of prayer. Yet, why was it necessary for you to suffer so much before your prayers were finally answered? The deeper underlying question is, "Why do good people like you and like so many of our readers have to suffer?" Do you have a message for them?

Chana: On one hand, it is really heartbreaking that people have to suffer in this world, but please know that suffering is the primary means by which a person is refined and cleansed. Suffering is actually a divine gift of love, offering an opportunity to come closer to the Holy One, enabling a person to grow spiritually to fulfill his or her potential. There are all kinds of challenges. Every person will suffer pain and suffering at some time in life. Some people will have health challenges; some people will have financial challenges; others will have love challenges. Ultimately, all pain and suffering is a blessing. How a person suffers holds the keys to the particular soul correction needed for them to fulfill their soul mission. Most people complain to others about suffering rather than cry out to the Only One who can transform their suffering into blessing. Suffering becomes a gift when it is a springboard for prayer.

If you are strong, have faith, determination, and maintain your focus, you will be victorious and reap the spiritual rewards from your toil and tribulation. In time, you will be grateful for the challenges you have been divinely given, for they have been the fertile soil upon which access to your own holy soul deepened and grew.

Question: How does this important teaching apply in your life?

Chana: When I saw that Hashem had closed my womb and did not allow me to bear children, I knew that I had to pray for a child from the depths of my heart. When my prayers were still not answered, I told my husband to take another wife. Perhaps I could have children through her like Rachel and Leah had children through their handmaidens. And so it was that Peninah, the second wife, was blessed with children so easily while I remained barren. But Peninah and I were not sisters or friends as I had hoped we would be. She was unwilling to allow me to play any role in her children's lives. She lauded being a mother over me all the time and continually taunted me for not having children. For example, she would rise early and taunt me, "Aren't you going to get up and wash your children's faces so they can go to school?" and continue throughout each day with these kinds of insensitive remarks. Her cruelty made my plight of childlessness even more painful but it also made me even more determined than ever to storm the gates of heaven with prayer.

Question: What do you mean by storming the gates of heaven?

Chana: I did not pray quietly for a child nor did I surrender gracefully to my fate. Rather, I channeled the negative emotions of anger, bitterness, and even jealousy that I was experiencing to strengthen and deepen my connection with the Holy One. I not only supplicated myself before God, I debated God. I bargained with God and I even demanded that God give me what I wanted. I was bold and audacious in prayer and in life. I never stopped praying because in my heart of hearts I knew that God loved me. It would just be a matter of time and my prayers would be answered.

Question: What do you mean by being bold in prayer? Can you give some examples?

Chana: I challenged God and declared "Nothing that you create is superfluous. So what are my breasts that You placed on my heart if not for nursing? Give me a son!" I even threatened to play the adulterous woman. When a woman in my time was suspected of adultery, she would be brought to the priests and ordered to drink a special potion. If she was guilty, she would die instantly a painful death. If she was innocent, she would be blessed with a child. I continued with so many arguments. I did not relent.

When I finally made a "deal" with Hashem, that I would give my son to Eli to raise as his own, my prayers were answered. I named my son Samuel, which means "I have requested him from Hashem."

Question: Why do you feel your prayers were finally answered?

Chana: I believe that my prayers were finally answered when I became sufficiently cleansed, purified, and spiritually worthy of bearing a holy son who would be the savior for God's holy people. Through my soul wrestling, inner work, and deep prayer, I grew in my understanding of what it is to be a true mother. To be a mother is such a privilege.

I was angry with God because I had not experienced being a mother. My anger caused within me a sense of feeling separate from God. Feeling separate and abandoned by God is very painful. In my heart of hearts, I came to know that it was the closeness with God that I deeply desired, more than anything in the world. I realized that my desire for this child was not for my personal glorification, but rather it was a way of my coming close to God. When I was able to make the most supreme gift of offering this son to God, only then were my prayers answered. This child was holy! There was a golden light that surrounded him and seemed to emanate and radiate from him. When I gave my son to Eli to be raised as a prophet, I experienced a closeness with God much greater than I had ever experienced before. After birthing this extraordinary child, I was truly fulfilled.

This particular child was the answer to my prayers. The love and training he would receive from Eli would enable him to fulfill his soul mission better than I could ever have done. After the birth of Samuel, I was even blessed with additional children. Hashem is so awesome and generous.

Question: How did you have the strength to keep on praying for so many years?

Chana: From my prayer and meditation, it had been revealed to me that I was destined to give birth to a prophet who would guide and save the Jewish people. I had reason to keep praying. Because my son was such a lofty soul, I understood that it would be very hard for me to bear him. As long as I had breath in my body, I would never give up praying for this particular son.

Question: Do you have any guidance for others about prayer?

Chana: Never give up! Never give up! Throughout my entire life, I never gave up praying for this son. My husband would try to comfort me by telling me that he loved me more than ten sons. He so much wanted me to be happy with my lot, but I would not be appeased. I would not give up.

Question: How does a person begin to pray?

Chana: Speak to Hashem the words of your heart and soul. Be real and be authentic. Do not waste time praying for what is superficial but pray only for what you need from the core of your soul. First, it is important to ascertain that what you want must be attuned to what you would imagine God would want for you as well. For example, my soul told me to keep praying, because God wanted this child to be born. When you do this, you are not simply praying for yourself, but also for God. At the root and core of your personal prayers must be the prayer for a greater revelation of the *Shechinah* in this world.

After personal reflection, then open your mouth, and speak out loud from the depths of your heart, yet also allow the words to flow through you. Make your case, present your arguments, and convince Hashem of the worthiness of your prayers. God loves when you debate. Most importantly, tell God how you will be able to love and serve more if your prayers are fulfilled.

Question: Do you have particular advice for people whose prayers are not answered quickly?

Chana: Remember this! People are often deprived of what they want because Hashem wants their prayers to help them forge a deeper bond with Him. For example, the snake in the Garden of Eden story was cursed to eat dust. At first glance, it looks like the snake was blessed because everything he needed was readily available for him. The truth is that this was a curse, as the Bible records, because he did not have to pray for what he needed. Recognizing your need for prayer is a spiritual gift and an opportunity if the challenges you are confronting energize your prayer life. When you know directly that you need God, you cannot do what you want on your own, you are indeed blessed. It is the lack, the deficiency that you are experiencing, that actually helps to forge a more dynamic and meaningful bond with God. You grow through challenge in ways that are not possible any other way. It may not feel good, but that is because you do not at the time when you are experiencing a lack or deficiency in your life have the whole picture to be able to appreciate the blessing that is contained within the challenge you are confronting.

Question: Can you offer us some tips to making our prayers more effective?

Chana: With delight, I went through so much, so I have something to teach others regarding prayer. I want to reveal an important secret to having your prayers answered. Whenever you pray for something in particular, foremost, be sure to include in your meditation and prayers your personal yearning for closeness with Hashem. Always take time to express your gratitude for all the blessings in your life. Gratitude opens the gates of blessing and answering prayers. If it is difficult for you to be thankful because you are angry or hurt, it is also good for you to express those feelings as well. God wants your heart, so be real and honest.

If your prayers are not answered immediately, as mine were not, and yet you continue to pour out your heart to God, like I did, not recoiling in anger or surrendering in defeat, you will ultimately be victorious. By your faith and the sincere intensity of your prayer, you will draw down infinite blessings and a profound inner joy to you, whether your prayers for something specific are answered or not. Hashem, *Yud-Hay-Vav-Hay,* the God of the Jewish people and of the entire world, is a God of awesome mercy and infinite love for you and all of creation. The greatest gift that you will receive from prayer is the deepening of your relationship with God.

Question: Would you please further instruct us on how to pray? Are there any more secrets?

Chana: I would like to share a few more secrets for having your prayers answered. Firstly, even though you may be praying for your own needs, be sure to also pray for the others as well. Most importantly, pray for the Jewish people, and pray for peace in Jerusalem. If you do this, you will be more greatly blessed even more than if you pray just for your own welfare or benefit. People who pray for the Jewish people and for Jerusalem even gain a spiritual radiance that makes them shine for all the world to see.

God is the ultimate giver, so to be close to God is to become a giver in your life. Seek opportunities to give to others and to God alone. It may be a little secret, but whenever you make a sincere offering to God, to do something for God, God rewards you beyond your wildest dreams and hopes. You must however be careful that when you give to God that you are not attempting to bribe God. Give not to simply receive but give so as to become closer to God. By giving you will naturally become a greater vessel worthy of receiving additional blessings in your life. When we are willing to truly give something of ourselves, we become more worthy.

For example, when I expressed my willingness to give my beloved son to Eli the Prophet to raise as his spiritual son, my prayers to have a son were quickly answered. Not only did my son become the most awesome prophet,

I was personally rewarded with a profound revelation of the *Shechinah*. Thousands of women and men recite the very words of my song to this very day and this song lifts them up to the highest levels of consciousness. What a gift this revelation was for me and also to the world. I have been greatly blessed. That is how the Divine works. Whenever we give to others and to God, we are blessed. Look always for opportunities to give to others.

Question: If prayer is so wonderful, why do people stop praying?

Chana: Many people envision God as a man on a throne or even as sugar daddy who will fulfill their hopes and dreams. In the act of prayer, they attempt to bargain or bribe God to have their hopes and wishes fulfilled. If God does not respond accordingly in the time period that they deem appropriate, these people often stop praying. If life is harsh, they also stop praying. It would appear that they want God on their terms. If they do not get what they want, when they want it, they become angry at God. They may cry that God has abandoned or rejected them, but it is they who have abandoned and rejected God. It is they who terminate a relationship with God, not God. This is most unfortunate. They do not realize that the Holy One by not answering their prayers has given them an even greater opportunity to grow, to be cleansed and purified and become a better person. Hashem always does good. It is we who must lift up our eyes and heart to see the blessings even in the challenges we confront and grow from them.

It is so important that a person not give up and continue to turn to God daily in prayer. It is principally through prayer that a person grows and is transformed. Do not be afraid to make yourself vulnerable before God. You cannot do life on your own. When you stand before God in prayer, it is essential that you be authentic. God is close to all who call sincerely, from the heart. When your heart is open, you will experience God and know firsthand that your words will make a difference. God loves you more than you can fathom.

Question: Thank you. I have come to understand now that it is the relationship with God established through prayer that is even more important than having one's prayers answered. I would like to conclude our interview with reciting your most beautiful song for our readers and ask you to comment on it. Here it is, as written in our holy books:

"My heart rejoices in God, my glory is raised by God, my mouth derides my enemies because I rejoice in your salvation.

"Do not talk so very proudly, let not arrogance come from your mouth. For God is a Lord of knowledge and by him actions are weighted.

"The bows of the mighty men are broken, while those who stumbled are girded with strength.

"Those who had plenty have hired themselves out for bread, while those who were hungry are at ease. The barren has borne seven and she who had many children is desolate.

"God causes death and brings to life. God brings down to the grave and raises up.

"God makes poor and makes rich. God brings low and lifts up.

"God lifts the poor from the dust and raises the beggar from the rubbish. To be seated among princes and inherit a seat of honor. For the pillars of the earth are God's and God has set the world on them.

"God will guard the feet of his saints and the wicked will perish in darkness, for no man will prevail by strength.

"God's foes will be crushed, God will thunder in heaven against them. God will judge the ends of the earth. God will give strength to his king and exalt the power of his anointed."

Chana: Recite my song each day, study the verses, internalize them into your heart, and a person will be transformed. Everything that I know about life is contained within these words.

Question: Do you have any further concluding words for men and women?

Chana: Always talk to God in your own words each day. Express your honest and deepest feelings to the Holy One, the Only One, who can help you, heal you, and answer your prayers. Be strong in faith. Never give up. This is my blessing to all.

Prayer to the God of Mother Chana
(It is suggested that this be read out loud by reader or group)

May the God of Mother Chana empower me to pray unceasingly for my needs, for the needs of others, for the welfare of the Jewish people, and the peace of Jerusalem. May I never give up praying for what is good and what I truly need to fulfill my soul purpose. May I be strong, courageous, and grow through prayer.

What Quality of the Feminine Does Chana Demonstrate?

The Jewish oral tradition recorded in the body of knowledge known as the Gemara tells us that women have been given the gift of speech. We only have to look around us and can easily note that women generally like to talk more than men. Heart-centered communication is also more important to women because women are more attuned to their emotions and feel more deeply. Therefore, we are told that when a woman directs her heartfelt words in prayer to God, she can truly bring down blessings. A man must similarly access the feminine within him to draw down blessings as well.

Women are generally more internal and find their connection to God internally more than externally. Wherever a woman prays, the *Shechinah* is present. There is no need for a quorum of ten for a woman. A woman is a priestess with a direct connection to the Divine. Though a woman may enjoy communal prayer services and participate in them, there is no spiritual obligation as there is for a man. According to Jewish law, a woman is not obligated to attend synagogue or pray communally except for a few days in a year. Individual prayer such as talking to God in her own words, meditation, and heartfelt sharing in intimate woman circles may be more powerful for women than traditional services. Men need to be obligated for public worship as a way to bond with other men. A woman does not need to be required to bond with others. She will naturally bond with other women because that is her nature to do so. Because men are more externally oriented, as a general rule, they also need to be honored with being called up to the Torah and even parading around with the Torah a few times a week. Women do not have this need in the same measure as men.

It is somewhat ironic that laws of Jewish prayer for men and women are derived from Chana, for a woman does not have the same requirements for prayer that men do. Men and women, however, do move their lips and speak in a quiet voice because of Chana. Speaking out loud was an innovative form of prayer that was not done prior to Chana.

What Meditative and Spiritual Practice Do We Learn from Chana?

Chana boldly opens the gates of prayer for all people in a new way. Because of Chana, people are encouraged to talk to God authentically, debate, and even argue with God if necessary to have their prayers answered. Chana also demonstrated vulnerability as well as fortitude and strength in her prayer life. She prayed as a woman and models to men and women a new way to pray.

A person is advised to talk directly to God in one's own words every day. Many great teachers in the Jewish tradition like Rabbi Nachman of Breslov advocated the simple and powerful practice of talking out loud to God each day. During this time period, a person should feel free to pour out their hearts to God, express all the pain, troubles, regrets, needs, and desires as well as make requests. If necessary, a person should scream and shout either aloud or silently.

Questions and Follow-up Discussion on Chana

1. Do you think it is right or best to pray specifically for something you want and argue like Chana did, as opposed to praying for acceptance of divine will? Is one approach better than the other?

2. Doesn't God know what we want? If it was divine will that we should have something, would we not have it? Why do we have to pray for what we want? Should we not simply attune ourselves to divine will and accept our lot in life with gratitude?

3. When you pray, do you include requests for your personal needs? Have you ever cried, argued, and even debated God like Chana? How did that make you feel about God, especially when your prayers are not answered the way you wanted them to be? Or perhaps they were answered, and your life became even more difficult. Have you ever been angry at God?

4. What about the role of personal responsibility in creating the life that you want? Should we have to pray for what we can do ourselves or should we take responsibility to do what we can do to make what we want happen in our lives? How do you reconcile personal responsibility with Divine will ?

Chapter Nine

Queen Esther

The Secret of Her Power and Beauty

Esther

" What was so miraculous in my time was that the Jewish people who were so divided among ourselves became unified because we woke up to see clearly that we shared the same fate as Jews. I pray that unity comes easily for Jews and all people who seek goodness in your time. Unfortunately, there may have to be additional wake-up calls in your time to remove the blinders of delusion to help people see clearly what is really taking place. In the interim do what you can to strengthen spiritual community and offer shelter to others. "

—*Esther*

Esther

Prophetess and Savior of the Jewish People

If you are female, and grew up with even minimal connection to Judaism, you probably at one time of your life wore the costume of Queen Esther during a celebration of Purim. At the time, you most likely did not know very much about Queen Esther, other than she was a heroine, she saved the Jewish people, and was very beautiful. As you smiled for the camera on Purim, you most likely felt very pretty and proud to be wearing a gold paper or plastic crown of some sort on your head, red lipstick and ruby cheeks, and a cute dress. I know that I did when I was dressed up as Queen Esther for Purim.

Purim was a happy day for me as a child. Many people even consider it a children's holiday, not such an important one. Kabbalah, however, states that in the time of the messiah, only the holiday of Purim will remain. This teaching provides a hint of the importance of Purim and lets us know that something more is happening with this story than we might think on the surface level. Kabbalah predicted thousands of years ago that the last battle prior to the Messianic Era will be with Persia, now called Iran, so the story of Esther is important for today.

Who Was Esther?

Esther, cited as one of the seven prophetesses within Judaism, was also considered to be one of the four most beautiful women who ever lived.

Sarah, Avigail, and Rachav are the other most beautiful women cited in the Talmud. Esther lived in Persia (now Iran) in the time period after the destruction of the first Holy Temple in Jerusalem. Along with her uncle/ husband Mordecai, Esther is accredited for saving the Jewish people living in the 127 provinces ruled by Persia at the time. An annual community reading of her book, the Megillah of Esther, a retelling of the story of her life and the events surrounding the miracle that occurred in her time, is considered mandatory throughout the worldwide Jewish community. Furthermore, it is required that everyone hear every single word of this writing.

Esther, given the name Hadassah (meaning "myrtle") at birth, was called Esther when she became queen of Persia. The nations of the world called her Istahar, meaning "beautiful like the moon." Her name was also said to be derived from *satar,* in Hebrew meaning "secret," or *histera,* in Hebrew meaning "hidden," because Esther kept her identity secret.

Esther was an orphan. Her father died at the time of her conception and her mother at her birth. She was raised by her uncle Mordecai, though Esther was also said to be the daughter of Mordecai's uncle. There are many who say that Mordecai married her when she was of marriageable age. Her status is unclear. Esther is a mystery.

The megillah tells us that "Esther would find grace in the eyes of all who saw her" (Esther 2:15). Everyone who saw her thought she was a member of his nation (Megillah 13a). It was more than her beauty and unique spiritual radiance that made her so appealing and attractive to everyone she met. She was the most rare kind of person who mirrored back to others their own beauty. Seemingly selfless, she did not need to prove or validate herself through her contact with others, but rather she could be whoever a person wanted her to be. She was exceedingly humble, almost self-effacing, but in the most gracious, elegant, and dignified way. To be in her presence was to feel elevated, validated, and charmed. Esther, actually a descendent of King Saul, was true royalty from the House of Israel. She always knew who she was, but her true identity was hidden from the world.

King Asherverous, a commoner, had seized the throne of the empire of Persia and married Vashti, who was a Babylonian princess, as a way to legitimize his claim to the throne. When he felt secure enough in his reign, after three years, he held a week-long feast to celebrate his reign and invited everyone to attend, even the Jews. When he was drunk enough on one of the nights, he sought to debase his wife by demanding that she dance naked before him and everyone at the party.

"You are worse than the stable boy of my father; he could at least hold his liquor. You can't." According to the Gemara, Vashti retorted these very words to this request. For her insubordination and refusal to follow his commands, King Asherverous had her murdered to demonstrate to all of his subjects that he was independent of her. Because Vashti stood up to her husband, she is celebrated in some feminist circles. According to Jewish teachings, Vashti was however known for her arrogance and cruelty particularly with the young Jewish maidservants who she would make work naked on the *Sabbath,* knowing that it was against what they believed. It is said that a person is treated measure for measure. Vashti's refusal to dance naked at the party resulted in her death. Chided on by his advisor Haman, after the death of Vashti, King Asherverous issued a rather ridiculous decree proclaiming throughout all the provinces that every man should be the ruler of his own home.

In his search for a new queen, all girls of a certain age were ordered to appear before the officials for consideration. Eventually Esther was selected to be the queen and was placed in a position where she was able to save the Jewish people from an edict calling for their annihilation. Much of the story is told in the subsequent interview with her.

On the thirteenth of Adar, the Fast of Esther is observed in memory of the fast that Esther observed and asked the Jewish people to observe. On the fourteenth of the month of Adar, the holiday of Purim commemorating the miracle is celebrated with the reading of the Esther's megillah in its entirety, followed up with parties, concerts, spoofs, and a tremendous feeling of joy. In Jerusalem, the holiday of Purim is extended to the fifteenth of Adar, Shushan Purim.

In the Purim story, God's deliverance comes through a woman in the midst of feasting, drinking, and sexual intrigue, revealing a most important teaching that God is everywhere and in everything. People, adults, and children alike reenact the story of Purim and dress up in all kinds of costumes. The celebration of Purim is not complete without eating *hamantashen*, those delicious three-cornered pastries filled with prunes and jelly, supposedly reminding us of the hat worn by Haman. It is a rather silly custom, but the celebration of Purim is all about fun.

Read the Megilat of Esther for the entire story of Esther..

For additional Kabbalistic commentary on Esther, see pages 245–250).

Invocation

When faced with seemingly insurmountable challenges, connect with Queen Esther, the savior of the Jewish people in the story of Purim. She will empower you with the courage, the faith, and creative intelligence to do what is difficult. Through her guidance and your meditations, you will discover that you already have all the resources required to transform your life in the way that is needed at this time.

Interview with Esther

Question: It is such an honor to be with you. You have been such an inspiration to so many men and women. Would you introduce yourself to our readers and share with us something about your life?

Esther: First, I send my love and blessings to all. The main thing that I want you to know about me is that my life was blessed. It was clear to me that I was where I was supposed to be. I was privileged to be in a position as queen of Persia where I could help save the Jewish people and rebuild the Holy Temple through my son. My life had meaning and purpose so I was happy.

Question: How did you become the queen of Persia, one of the capitals of the world at the time when you lived?

Esther: I was forced to enter a beauty contest after King Asherverous murdered his wife for refusing to dance naked before him and others at a party celebrating the destruction of the Holy Temple in Jerusalem. Soon after that, the king began looking for a replacement wife. All girls of a certain age were ordered to appear before the government officials for consideration. After I was selected to be one of the girls who would appear before the king for the final selection by him personally, I had to undergo a year of beauty preparation, six months soaking with the oil of myrrh and six months with perfumes and cosmetics. I had no desire to marry this evil man, but it would appear that my being queen was part of the divine plan as I learned much later. Even though I had not requested anything special to beautify myself as all the other girls had done prior to their appearance before the king; nevertheless, when he saw me, he placed the royal crown on my head.

Question: You said earlier that your life was blessed. But what about your personal happiness? You had to stay married to King Asherverous for the rest of your life. There are even some people who say that you were married to Mordecai when you were kidnapped by the king and forced to enter the beauty contest. If that was true, how much more difficult it must have been for you to stay married to the king, knowing that your beloved one was so close by but you could no longer be together with him as a married couple. No one talks enough about this tremendous sacrifice that you made to save the Jewish people.

Esther: I learned very early in my life to accept life and divine will graciously. Because my parents died before I was born, I grew up very aware of the spiritual world. As I did not know my parents physically, they were not limited physically to me. As far back as I can remember, I always felt enveloped with their love and God's love as well. My life was never limited to the physical sphere. When I lived in a body known as Esther, I accepted life as it was, because I experienced whatever was happening in life as an expression of divine will. My life was not easy nor was Mordecai's but together and individually we surrendered to what was and always sought to align ourselves with the Holy One's will.

Knowing that there was no other choice for me, I understood that it was divine will that I stay married to this king. Over time, I grew in compassion for the king and that helped to refine and uplift him. Being queen of a large empire also provided me with the privilege of uplifting and caring for so many people. I am grateful for the opportunities given to me to serve and give. And of course my son Darius was my joy, my hope and inspiration.

Question: Please tell us more about the circumstances that resulted in the holiday of Purim. What was your role in helping to save the Jewish people?

Esther: When Mordecai refused to bow to Haman, the king, convinced by Haman issued an order calling for the extermination of the Jewish people on a particular day in the month of Adar. The Jewish people were such a small minority within the empire, yet we were perceived as a threat. The king was all too happy to eliminate the Jewish people because he also feared their spiritual power. Though this evil decree was a secret, Mordecai overheard a few guards discussing it. He quickly informed me of this decree and challenged me to plead for the welfare of the Jewish people before the king. I was initially resistant, because to appear before the king uninvited meant death to anyone who tried before to do so.

Previously I had been passive in my relationship with the king. I was distressed that Mordecai was now asking me to initiate a relationship with the king. I did not want to do this at all! Mordecai then reminded me of the most important teaching. I remember his very words to this day: "Do not imagine that you will be able to escape in the king's palace any more than the rest of the Jews. If you persist in keeping silent at a time like this, relief and deliverance will come to the Jewish people from some other place, while you and your father's house will perish. Who knows whether it was just for such a time as this that you attained the royal position."

From his words, I clearly saw that my being in the palace as queen was part of the divine plan. I was in this position because I had been given the privilege to serve the Jewish people and make a difference. If I did not do what God wanted me to do, someone else would do it instead of me.

Question: What did you then do?

Esther: Because I needed spiritual fortitude to do what I must do, I immediately asked the entire Jewish people in Shushan to pray and even to fast for me for three days. I intuitively knew that it was only because the Jewish people are divided among ourselves that we have enemies. When the Jewish people are unified, we will be victorious. The Jewish people at the time must have known this as well, because quite miraculously they were willing to undertake this arduous fast. My maidens and I also prayed and fasted incessantly for three days. Though the fast may have weakened me physically, it strengthened me spiritually. Because I was unified with the Jewish people, I contacted the strength and faith needed to carry out my mission. On the third day of the fast, I received *Ruach Hakodesh,* the Holy Spirit.

Question: What did you then do?

Esther: To speak to the king, I had to walk down a very long corridor to the king's office. Admittedly, I was frightened. This long walk felt like eternity to me. As I walked down the corridor, I was confronted with all the idols of the country that adorned the hall as well as the palace courtiers who tried to intimidate me the whole time with many terrible threats. Though I was fearful, I kept on walking, finding the faith and trust deep within me that I would be protected and successful in carrying out my mission. When the king finally saw me, he seemed defenseless. He told me that I appeared to him as an angel and that his soul left him for a moment. He then offered me "up to half of my kingdom, your petition should be granted." Surely God was at work.

Even though the king was very loving toward me in that moment, I intuitively knew that pleading or sexual seduction alone would not be effective. The king would need to see clearly for himself the evil of Haman to rescind his terrible decree. I knew that I simply needed to create doubt in the king's mind about the trustworthiness of Haman. As a woman I could do that best by inspiring jealousy within the king. I invited the king and Haman to a party. I trusted that the perfect opportunity would present itself at a party for me to reveal my true identity and turn the king against Haman. I recorded all the events in my scroll that is read annually throughout the Jewish world for those who would like more details.

At the first festivity, I placed my couch next to Haman and gave him my goblet, so as to arouse jealousy. It worked. The king saw this and was jealous and annoyed. No opportunity, however, presented itself for me to reveal my true identity at the first party, so I invited the king and Haman to another party the next evening.

I learned at the second party the king had been unable to sleep the night before so he reviewed his records and discovered that Mordecai had done him a great favor that was not rewarded. The next day, he asked Haman what he should do to show favor to someone. Haman described all kinds of wonderful honors, thinking that he was the one the king wanted to favor. How surprised and visibly shaken he was to discover that it was Mordecai and not he whom the king wanted to honor.

The king then asked me what I wanted. "What is your request Queen Esther, it shall be granted to you, even if it be up to half the kingdom." At this moment, I clearly knew that this was indeed my opening. I seized the moment, revealed my true identity as a Jew, and informed the king that Haman wanted to kill me and my people.

The king quickly rose from the wine fest, and angrily left the room briefly. When he returned he saw Haman prostrated on my couch. It must have looked like Haman was going to assault me. Furious, the king then ordered that Haman hang on the very gallows that Haman had prepared to hang Mordecai on for failing to bow to him.

Question: What then happened?

Esther: The king gave the estate of Haman to me and the signet ring that the king had removed from Haman he gave to Mordecai. Mordecai left the king's office in royal apparel with a large gold crown on his head. Though the king was unable to rescind his first decree, he issued an edict that the Jews may defend themselves. There was a war, but the Jews were victorious and celebrated their victory on the fourteenth of Adar. The fighting continued in the walled city of Shushan until the fifteenth of the month, so that became the date of Shushan Purim.

Question: What a story! Everything seemed to be going one way and then it was miraculously turned around to be the opposite. Haman was hung on the very same gallows he had prepared to hang Mordecai upon.

Eve: Yes, that is what often happens. Life can change in a moment.

Question: This also seems true for you as well. When you were selected to be queen, you were said to be a shy and almost self-effacing woman. At the end of your story, you are bold and even telling the sages in Sanhedrin what to do.

Esther: After the war, I petitioned the sages of the Sanhedrin that the scroll I wrote recording the events of my day be read by the Jewish people for eternity in a celebration honoring the miracle of the deliverance of the Jewish people in my time. "Establish my story for all generations" as it says in my scroll. Initially the sages refused me, but I prevailed and my request was approved.

Question: How did you change from being meek to becoming assertive and even bold? Do you have any guidance on how women can be similarly empowered?

Esther: Quite simply, I did what was necessary. I was empowered because there was a need to be met and I was in the best position to meet that need. I also knew how to use my power as a woman. When I unified my heart with that of the Jewish people during the fast, I was purified and spiritually empowered to carry out this important mission of saving the Jewish people. Any person in my position would have done what I had to do. Similarly, any woman who becomes aware of the needs of people around her and realizes that she is in the best position to meet these needs will be also divinely empowered. Like me, she must also pray and purify herself so that she receives divine assistance. We are all conduits of blessing in God's plan. If we do not do what should be done, someone else will do it. Unfortunately, we will then miss out on the privilege of being a blessing.

Question: But, isn't it unusual for a scroll to be written by a woman?

Esther: Yes, that is true. It is unusual for a woman to write a scroll. You must first know that it was not for my personal glory that I recorded these events in a scroll and asked that they be canonized within the holy books of the Jewish people. I did so because there was so much to learn from these events around this story. Most importantly this Purim story has relevance for future times. It was primarily for this reason that I requested that my scroll be read every year. The fact that deliverance came through me, a woman, is also very significant for the future as well. It will be the women who will help usher in the final redemption. I simply served as a model for what women must do in the future.

Question: When Asherverous first issued that terrible decree against the Jewish people in your time, you did not record any outcry of opposition from the non- Jews. Was there an outcry? If not, did their silence surprise you? So many Jews had assimilated. Surely they must have had working and personal relationships with their non-Jewish neighbors who would have protested this decree.

Esther: No, silence on the part of the non-Jewish world did unfortunately not surprise me. The Jewish people have a long history of living in other countries, other than their own, of contributing greatly to the benefit of the host country, only to find themselves at a later time discriminated against, persecuted, and even cast out of the country for no logical reason. Throughout time, we have lived in our homeland and been cast into exile from our homeland, only to find ourselves once again then rejected from the places we were forced initially to reside. This story has repeated itself so many times throughout history.

Question: Why does that happen?

Esther: The are so many reasons for this mysterious phenomena. It has to do with our worthiness to live in the land of Israel according to divine will as well as the mission of the Jewish people to heal, uplift and perfect the rest of the world as well as ourselves by living in the midst of different host countries. Because the Jewish people have been charged with an important task of revealing the *Shechinah*, wherever they find themselves, they have been scattered all over the world. When the Jewish people do their job correctly, the nations are uplifted through them and receive much physical and spiritual blessing. Evil is diminished. The Jewish people may not know this about themselves, but the enemy does and is spiritually threatened by the goodness, the universality, and freedom within the message of the Jewish people. Leaders of these countries who seek to rule for their own nefarious reasons are threatened by the very existence of the Jewish people, so they are driven to destroy or oppress them. This is what happened in my time. The Jewish people were such a small minority in the Persian empire, they lived peacefully with their neighbors, and yet they were singled out for annihilation.

Question: In the last generation the same thing happened. Under the leadership of Adolph Hitler and the Nazi party, Germany tried to annihilate the Jewish people who lived within its country and who also lived in much of Europe for centuries. Today, Iran and other Moslem nations and terrorist groups announce publicly their intentions to destroy the homeland of the Jewish people and annihilate the Jewish people once again. They continually engage in war and acts of terrorism against our homeland and spread many lies against Israel.

Esther: This is an ancient battle. Nations that are particularly rooted in Edom like Germany and much of Europe or in Ishmael like Iran and many countries in the Arab world at a certain point quite simply cannot tolerate the Godly light of the Jewish people. They are jealous, but it is even more than that. The very existence of the Jewish people is perceived as a direct challenge to the religions practiced in these countries as well as to the rulers who seek to dominate the world for their own selfish purposes. The Jewish people are the conscience for the world and reflect back to evil dictators the ugliness of their deeds. Rather than change and become better people, the rulers in these nations scapegoat their moral, political and economical failures onto the Jewish people. If the rulers can mobilize their people to hate the Jewish people, they will not be held accountable for the ways they have exploited and harmed their own people. This tactic has been successful for the people direct their frustrations towards the Jewish people instead of their rulers who tyrannize them.

Question: It does seem odd that the countries that seek the destruction of the Jewish people are also terribly oppressive to their own people. It would appear that these rulers do not seem to care if their people suffer and even die in their effort to murder Jews. Their hatred of the Jewish people seems greater than their love for their own people.

Esther: That is one of the biggest clues to identify a certain kind of primordial evil in the world. The Jewish people call this evil Amalek named after the sworn enemy of the Jewish people in biblical time. Even though the Jewish people posed no threat to Amalek and the Jewish people were not even traveling near their territory, Amalek, a tribe of descendants of Esau, went out of its way to fight the Jewish people after their exodus from Egypt.

Question: Is Amalek alive today? How can we identify Amalek?

Esther: Yes, Amalek is alive in your times once again. One of the ways to identify Amalek is that Amalek is an entity, either a country, group or person, that cannot tolerate the relationship that the Jewish people have with God. Amalek is also so bent on destruction of the spiritual entity and integrity of the Jewish people, even if its proponents receive no real benefit from Israel's destruction. Their hatred is not logical and cannot be placated with bribes such as land for peace. This is important to remember when dealing with Amalek. There is no bribing Amalek. That is why the Jewish people read the Torah portion about Amalek every year so they will remember what they must do when confronting Amalek. In my time, Haman was Amalek and was even a direct descendent from the actual tribe of Amalek.

Question: If we look at history, it would appear that there have been so many countries that do not want the Jewish people to live in their midst nor do they want them to live in their homeland. What are the Jewish people supposed to do? Today Israel is surrounded by twenty two Moslem countries, enormous in size in comparison to her. These nations treat their citizens so poorly and women even worse than men, yet much of the world considers Israel a terrible occupier and oppressor. Why is that?

Esther: You must understand that the enemies of the Jewish state of Israel are not just against the Jewish people, they are against God and all that is good. Remember, this is a most ancient battle. True God-believers love all of creation, especially the Jewish people. People who truly believe in God are not jealous of the faith of another, because they know deeply that God is one. Many non-believers in God are simply jealous of the special relationship that the Jewish people have with God and the gift of the Land of Israel to the Jewish people. It is really quite simple.

Question: I am worried by the rise of anti-Semitism in the world.

Esther: Do not worry, all will be good. Trust in the Holy One, and you will be protected. In time, evil will be exposed for what it truly is and its power to mesmerize and seduce people will be greatly diminished. The prophecies about the Jewish people, the rebuilding of the Holy Temple, and the messianic time, will be fulfilled. That is the truth, no matter what the enemies of the Jewish people may say.

Question: Israel is such a small country, yet it has made remarkable and even miraculous achievements that have benefited the entire world within the short time of its existence, in spite of having to defend herself in so many wars and acts of terrorism. It does not seem to matter what good Israel does. Israel continues to be demonized by so many. Israel is the one democracy in the region and even offers health, education and voting rights to the Moslems who live in her midst, yet Israel receives more proclamations against her in the United Nations than any other country.

Esther: Israel is indeed the most beautiful and God-centered country in the world, so no one should believe all the lies that are said about her. In time, it will be very clear for all to see that Israel, such a miniature country, is blessed and is a source of blessing for the entire world. Though many want to occupy this country and claim it as their own, they do not yet realize that Israel only blossoms when the Jewish people live in it. Look what she has accomplished in such a short time, under so many challenging conditions. If another people would live in this holy land, they would not be prosperous.

Question: There are many leaders and politicians from several countries, even the United States, who think that peace will come to the region if Jerusalem is divided between the Moslems and the Jews. What do you see from your heavenly station?

Esther: Dividing Jerusalem will not bring peace, but only more war. Everyone knows that in their heart of hearts. No good for Moslem or Jew alike will come from dividing Jerusalem. Those who want to divide Jerusalem do not seek peace, but only to weaken Israel so as to destroy her. They fear the power of a unified Jerusalem upon the world. Jerusalem, the heart of the world, is that place in the future where God will fulfill and reveal the divine purpose for all of creation and rebuild the Holy Temple on the Temple Mount. It is for that reason that the world does not want the Jewish people to rebuild the Holy Temple in Jerusalem.

Because of their intrinsic selfishness and jealousy, the nations of the world, even Jews who are disconnected from Judaism, do not see the importance of the rebuilding of the Holy Temple in Jerusalem. Jerusalem and the Holy Temple are a source of blessing for the entire world, not just the Jewish people. I instilled this within my son, so when he became king, he worked hard to liberate Jerusalem and rebuild the Holy Temple. It was his first accomplishment when he began his reign as king.

Question: I pray that the readers and you, Queen Esther will not mind indulging me a little more. I have such deep concern and am confused about what is happening today. Please forgive me for being so political. For so many years, the United States has tried diligently to be fair in brokering a peaceful settlement between Israel and the Arab peoples who seek to destroy her. Besides placing so much pressure upon Israel to give up land, the United States also gives these Moslem countries billions of dollars, trains the armies, and even sells advanced weaponry to sworn enemies of the Jewish people. It would appear that the United States thinks that with enough bribery there will be peace. What do you think?

Esther: If the United States of America does not align itself with Israel and willingly even abandons the security of Israel in efforts to be " fair", they will sadly enough lose the divine blessings that have been bestowed upon them. This is most unfortunate for them. America in the hearts of its founding fathers was envisioned as a new Israel with a covenantal relationship with God modeled after that of the Jewish people. Because of this spiritual foundation, America became a very prosperous nation and a source of blessing to all. However, as the United States becomes increasingly secular, and is no longer governed by the highest moral values, it will no longer feel its primary affinity with Israel.

Question: What about the fate of Israel if the United States does not support her? In addition to Iran, the surrounding countries have secured advanced missiles that can target any point in the land of Israel. As I speak to you now, the former official leadership in many of these countries is being overthrown and replaced with leaders who are Islamic fundamentalists who are more anti-Israel than the previous ones.

Esther: Do not worry that God's beloved country, the holy land of Israel, has very few friends, if any at all, among the nations of the world. This was true in my time and it will be true until the End of Days. Do not be dismayed. Israel does have the Holy One, the creator of the universe, on her side, if and when the Jewish people honor their love and covenant with the Holy One, and that is more than enough. This is an ancient love affair that will soon be consummated. God is faithful. The people of Israel must not look to other nations for help, but realize that they have all that they need to be victorious. When they are aligned with Divine Will, they are protected.

Question: Do you have a particular message for people today?

Esther: You live in extraordinary times. There is a great battle between good and evil underway once again in the world. When I lived, Persia was a great empire occupying 127 provinces. In your time, Persia, now called Iran, is quickly spreading its tentacles to once again dominate the world for its own nefarious purposes. Battle lines are being drawn. This last battle will not be easy, but there is much blessing for those who are called to fight. "Not by power, not by might, but by the spirit of the Lord" says the prophet Zechariah. This last battle is primarily a spiritual war. Unlike previous wars, there are ultimately no political or military solutions for the conflicts amidst the world in your time. The stage is being set for a divine revelation. So rejoice.

Question: What should people do today?

Esther: Even though the world may seem hopeless at times, and the challenges people face are so very great, the first and most important thing is to have faith and believe in the goodness of God. Trust that God will help you and fight this battle through you. Nevertheless, you still must do your part. Everyone's contribution is needed because this battle is to be fought on many fronts. External enemies seeking to dominate and destroy others must be defeated externally. Internal enemies within each person such as doubt, hate, greed and fear must also be overcome. Most people will not be called to battle the enemy physically, but still each must fight the battle against the evil inclination within themselves.

Question: Many people are not alarmed about what is happening in the world. They just want to have a good time.

Esther: What perhaps is most dangerous in your time is that many people prefer to live in the illusionary comfort of denial and fantasy. They have not yet recognized that there is a current battle for the soul of the world. Closing one's eyes does not make the danger disappear. What was so miraculous in my time was that the Jewish people who were so divided among ourselves became unified because we woke up to see clearly that we shared the same fate as Jews. I pray that unity comes easily for Jews and all people who seek goodness in your time. Unfortunately, there may have to be additional wake-up calls in your time to remove the blinders of delusion to help people see clearly what is really taking place. In the interim do what you can to strengthen spiritual community and offer shelter to others.

Question: What should we do?

Esther: There is power in community. I encourage everyone to join and support the Jewish people in continuing the holy work of eradicating evil externally and internally. Be part of a community dedicated to love and goodness whatever that may be. There is great power in unity. That is something that must be learned from the Purim story. When the Jewish people and good people all over the world are unified, they can accomplish much. Everyone has all the resources needed to do what each can do to defeat evil. I needed to learn that, and so do many of you. If the situation worsens, organize fasts with prayer for the people. Fasting arouses greater divine compassion and averts an evil decree. That is what I did and it worked. You can and must all be soldiers now. This battle must be fought on many fronts, internally and externally. Your prayers make a difference. Faith is your protection. Joy and love are your spiritual weapons. You are not powerless.

Question: Do you have any particular guidance for the Jewish people?

Esther: The protection and strength of the Jewish people comes from their unity with each other and commitment to their covenant with God. The Jewish people become more vulnerable to evil when they are divided among themselves. When the Jews are united together in love and service, their enemies, who are truly God's enemies, will be destroyed. Miracles and blessing will be commonplace for them.

In my time, as I said earlier, the Jews were divided as they are in your time. There were primarily two groups: the Jews who attended the orgies of the king, who ate un-kosher food, who assimilated with the general culture and were even willing to desecrate the vessels from the Holy Temple that were used at official parties, and there were the Jews who refused to attend these affairs, and kept to themselves, occupying themselves with living a life devoted to Torah. These groups were very separate from each other and did not respect the choices of the other.

Haman saw these divisions clearly and tried to exploit them. The enemy of the Jewish people will always exploit the disunity within the Jewish community. When the Jews are divided, they are surely weakened and vulnerable as a people. This is true in all times. Ultimately, as I said earlier, the Jewish people in my time were victorious because we overcame our differences and understood that we all shared the same fate as Jews. It was clear to everyone that there was no point in further ingratiating ourselves with our enemies anymore. That kind of clarity will happen in your time; God willing, it will be sooner rather than later.

Question: How do we create unity within the Jewish people? There seems to be much divisiveness among us.

Esther: Giving creates bonding. It is important for Jews as well as for all people in the world to give to others, for no other reason than to express love and unity with them. Every person must overcome the selfish desire to receive for oneself alone by sharing with others. Only by sharing and giving to others can one draw blessings into the world. As a general rule, if you want to be connected to people, give to them. Life is all about sharing and giving. The quality of a person's life is enhanced greatly by acts of giving to others. When we give to others, not for what we will receive, but simply for the sake of giving, we become close to God, we internalize God, and we ourselves are filled with the Divine Spirit. It is for this reason that I instructed people to give gifts of food to each other and invite poor people to their homes for a Purim celebratory meal.

Question: Do you have some final words to people?

Esther: Though you may not be placed to be in the kind of extraordinary situation that I was, everyone has opportunities in small and large ways to reveal and redeem the *Shechinah* and thereby bring redemption to oneself and others. Like me, you never know when you will be called upon to do something absolutely amazing. You can never fully appreciate the effect of all the good that you do. Let my story inspire and empower you with the courage and the faith to do what is difficult if it is the right thing to do, even what seems impossible, if it is necessary.

I send my love and blessings to you. May you take time to receive all the blessings generously bestowed upon you each day. May you be a blessing to others.

Responding to Queen Esther

(It is suggested that this be recited out loud alone or by group)

"Queen Esther, thank you for your inspiring words. You model to us the beauty, the heart and the power of the feminine. We can never thank you enough for the role you played in your lifetime to save the Jewish people.

We honor you for your willingness to sacrifice your personal happiness for this cause as well as your courage to do what was difficult for you. Thank you for reminding us to make small and large gestures to create unity between people. We will do our share to create and strengthen community. May we also be empowered to validate and uplift others around us, like you did, with our love and innate joy."

Prayer to the God of Queen Esther

May the God of Queen Esther empower me with the courage, faith, and creative intelligence to do what is difficult if asked and to know that all the resources needed to respond to any challenge before me are already within me. May I align myself with divine will and go forward in my life with trust and faith.

What Quality of the Feminine Does Esther Demonstrate?

Esther like Sarah was considered to be one of the most beautiful women in the world ever. This natural beauty radiated from her because of her alignment with the *Shechinah*. Besides being beautiful inside and out, she used her beauty for holy purposes. Esther modeled this power of the feminine in the most elevated way. For example, in her preparation to see King Asherverous she fasted and prayed, rather than take that time to beautify herself physically with all kinds of skin and makeup preparations. Even though she clearly understood that it was her sexual appeal as a woman that gave her some power over the king, she also knew that her power as a woman depended even more on how she embodied the *Shechinah* than how she physically looked.

Like Esther, any woman, regardless of her physical appearance, aligned with the *Shechinah* has a natural beautiful radiance that will make her attractive and appealing to men and therefore she will have some power over many men. The question before all women is whether they will use their inherent gifts and blessings of being feminine for noble holy purposes like Esther or primarily for their own benefit or gratification.

Another quality of the feminine that made Esther particularly beautiful was that she mirrored the beauty within others back to them. Everyone felt validated and elevated by Esther. To connect more with how Esther embodied the Divine Feminine, and to be more of an embodiment of the Divine Feminine yourself, make particular efforts each day and every week to acknowledge the beauty within others. How many people can you acknowledge and validate today or this week? Make a special effort to validate people in your immediate family. Sometimes these are the people we take for granted. Refrain from criticism of yourself and others. Loving and accepting yourself is the foundation for all the good you radiate to others.

What Meditative Practice Do We Learn from Esther?

The name Esther means "hidden" and the hidden is the domain of the feminine. In seeking to attune to Esther or the feminine, we need to meditate and pray each day to find that place within us that is hidden, that is private, that is holy. Let go of what is external and come into the sacredness of life that lies deep within oneself. In this space of holy intimacy, there is only you and God. Surrender your ego self, your small self, and allow yourself to be permeated with the light of *Shechinah* until you identify with Her. From this place, you can draw down the strength to bring forth miracles in your life.

Remember that wherever you are, God is. You may embody the *Shechinah* wherever you are. Know that you are in the place that you are intended to be. God is with you. Nothing is by accident.

What Spiritual Practices Do We Learn from Esther?

In the celebration of the holiday of Purim that commemorates the miracles of Esther's time, there is a custom of giving gifts to friends that is called *mishloach manot,* or shortened to *shalach manot.* These gifts are simple offerings of fruit, nuts, wine, and cake that are distributed widely to friends, acquaintances, and even strangers. It can be just two items. Usually, these gifts are delivered through a third party, so it feels that God is giving to the person.

Additionally, giving to the poor is encouraged at all times, but especially on Purim. "It is preferable to increase gifts to the poor rather than increasing *mishloach manot*" (Kitzur Shulchan Aruch on the laws of *mishloach manot*).

Each day you are given opportunities to give to people in small or large ways. When we give to others in any way for any reason or for no reason at all, we are uplifted. Giving to others helps us to feel close to people.

Fast for Esther

In honor of Esther, make a spiritual connection with her on her fast day, the day preceding the holiday of Purim. Look at the Jewish calendar for what day it will be. Make efforts to fast, at least part of the day, and spiritually connect with the Jewish people. Dedicate your fast and prayer toward your own purification and the elimination of evil in the world. Join with Jews all over the world who pray that the consciousness of the wicked be turned to the Divine.

Follow-up Questions and Discussion on Esther

1. How does Esther's story inspire you to make your life better? What ways can you make this world better and defeat evil, even if it is just in your immediate circle?

2. Esther is considered in Kabbalah as a reincarnation of Eve and Sarah. Explore the connections between these women, their accomplishments, and how Esther completes the journey of the feminine that began with Eve.

3. How can you emulate Queen Esther? Can you emulate her speech pattern? Esther means hidden. What is the hidden part within you that is the Esther within you?

4. How does this story of Esther help you to understand the role you can play to fight evil and selfishness and reveal more light and love in your personal life and in the world at large?

5. Many Jewish women view Vashti as a feminist because she refused to disrobe before the king. Young girls today are even dressing up as Vashti for Purim, even more than Queen Esther in some communities. Considering all the *midrashim,* teachings in the oral Torah, regarding her cruelty, do you feel that Vashti should be regarded as a model to young girls today? How do you understand this recent phenomena?

Chapter Ten

Prayers to the God of the Mothers

Prayers to the God of the Mothers

(It is suggested that you light a candle, take a few breaths to prepare yourself, stand or sit and recite these prayers every day for forty days. It is more powerful if you say these verses out loud in a group. Take time to meditate between verses.)

May the God of Mother Eve grant me the vision, the courage, the strength to enter into places of darkness, so as to heal and redeem what is wounded, what is hidden within myself, others, and the world. May I be blessed to help restore all that I encounter to a greater light, openness, and love.

May the God of Mother Sarah guide me to make the choices that serve the highest good. May the God of Mother Sarah empower me with the strength to remain true to my vision, even though it may not be what others would want of me.

May the God of Mother Rebecca guide me to discern what is true from what is false, what is good from what is evil, and empower me to live in accordance with my inner truth.

May I be blessed to follow in the footsteps of my holy mothers Rachel, Leah, Bilha, and Zilpa to participate in the birth of a new consciousness that expresses greater connectivity and unity in the world. May I be willing to undergo whatever challenges that present themselves in order to reveal the *Shechinah* in our midst. May the tears that I shed for any reason be dictated to this holy purpose.

May the God of Mother Dina inspire me to grow and heal through the challenges I face in life. May the God of Mother Dina inspire me with the courage to transmute whatever negativity I have experienced into good. May I choose light over darkness, unity over divisiveness, good over evil, so as to reveal the *Shechinah* and the intrinsic beauty and unity of life.

May the God of Sister Miriam inspire me to trust what I know deep inside of me as my truth. May the God of Sister Miriam give me the courage to go forward in my life expressing my vision and my truth. May the God of Sister Miriam help me to inspire others to live more joyful and purposeful lives.

May the God of Mother Batya empower me to live the truth that is revealed within my own soul no matter what the environment dictates what I should do and who I should be.

May the God of Mother Chana empower me to prayer unceasingly for my needs, for the needs of others, for the welfare of the Jewish people, and for the peace of Jerusalem, the holy city.

May the God of Queen Esther empower me with the courage, faith, and creative intelligence to do what is difficult if asked and to know that all the resources needed to respond to any challenge before me are already within me. May I align myself with divine will and go forward in my life with trust and faith.

Chapter Eleven

Kabbalistic and Midrashic Commentary

on Biblical Women

Eve

Mother of All Life

Adam and Eve Were Initially a Single Nonphysical Being!

"Let us make man in our image, after our likeness.... So God created man in his image, in the image of God he created him, male and female he created them" (Genesis 1: 26). The first thing that the Bible tells us that we need to be mindful of in our understanding of this story is that Eve and Adam were originally one being that was called "Adam."

In this biblical verse about the creation of Adam, the Bible also hints to us that God is both male and female. "... in the image of God ..., male and female he created them" (Genesis 1: 26). What is below is a reflection of what is above, a general Kabbalistic principle. God is often portrayed as masculine, but there is a lesser known feminine expression of the Divine that is articulated prominently in Kabbalah. It is this feminine expression known as the Divine Mother (*Binah*) and the *Shechinah* (*Nukva* or *Malkut*) that is still relatively unknown outside of Kabbalistic circles.

God, according to the Bible, consults with others to participate in the creation of Adam. God is not autocratic, a reminder that neither should we be. Do you wonder to whom is God talking when saying in the Bible "Let *us* make man ..."? Some commentators say it was the angels. The oral tradition says that the angels had some reservations about the creation of man that had to be addressed by God. And yes, angels and even demons are a part of Judaism and actually play a prominent role in this story.

The Zohar, the Kabbalistic commentary on the Bible, however, explains that it was the Divine Mother (*Binah*) who was, so to speak, invited to be a co-creator. Since there is only one God, how can this be? The Zohar is not saying that there are two creators, one male and one female, but rather that the initial act of creation was one of insemination, pregnancy, and birth, which involved both the masculine and feminine aspects of the one creator. The original stage of creation was the Divine Father's (*Chochma's*) dissemination, or emanation of His Infinite Light, which had to be received, nurtured, and birthed by the Divine Mother (*Binah*) in order for something "other than God" to exist. Thus, one of the feminine names for God (*Elohim*) is used in the first sentence of the Bible to denote the Divine Feminine aspect of God that was involved in the final act, the birthing of Heaven and Earth. The name *Elohim* is associated with the feminine *Sephira* (divine emanation) of *Gevurah,* which means "strength, restriction, and setting boundaries," and is used in the first sentence of the Bible describing the act of creation. It is important to understand that creation was not a revelation of something new, but rather a restriction of Infinite Light that allowed something new to be formed within it. The word *Elohim,* interestingly enough, has the same numerical value as the Hebrew term for nature, *HaTeva.*

Adam was initially not a physical being as we know physical. Adam was a body of light, or a thought form, a being who resided in a spiritual, non-physical dimension of reality. The Zohar tells us that when Adam was created, the sun and moon saw him and their light was dimmed, the heels of the foot of Adam darkened their light. Adam's light was darkened only when he ate of the Tree. Adam and Eve "fell" only to become physical after eating from the forbidden Tree of Knowledge. Once physical, they needed to be clothed. This is what is meant when it is said in the Bible that God clothed them. The Hebrew word for light is pronounced *Ohr* and the Hebrew word for skin is also pronounced *Ohr.* The Hebrew letter *aleph* is present in the word for light and the letter *ayin* is present in the word for skin. Rather than continue to exist in their light bodies, Adam and Eve were clothed with skin resembling the snake after the sin of eating from the Tree of Good and Evil. There are others who say that Adam was physical before eating of the Tree yet translucent, and was much larger than man's current height. Adam was initially said to be so lofty and so radiant that even the angels wanted to worship him.

The first instructions to this bi-gendered being known as Adam were to be fruitful, multiply, and rule over the fish, the birds, and every living thing (Genesis 1: 28). When Adam received these instructions, Adam was a singular being, male and female, so it would appear that Adam could reproduce asexually. Adam was originally placed outside of the Garden of Eden and then was taken and placed within the Garden to work and guard it (Genesis 2: 15). Adam was then instructed to freely eat of all the trees except the fruit of the Tree of Knowledge of Good and Evil, for if he were to eat of this fruit, he would die (Genesis 2:17).

"It is not good to be alone," God says later (Genesis 2:18). It is interesting to note that the name for God that is used in this verse is both YHVH and *Elohim* for the very first time. According to Jewish law, it is forbidden to pronounce the name YHVH, since it is a concept of God that is so high and holy that it completely transcends even the use of divine names. It is more of a code than an actual name. Nonetheless, it is important to note that YHVH is the divine name associated with compassion.

The Creation of Eve and Lilith

"I will make him a helper, opposite him" (Genesis 2:18). Adam requires a mate like all the other creatures. The oral tradition informs us that God brought all the animals before Adam and asked Adam to give each a name. To name the animals, Adam had to know the essence of each creature. Though he tried to mate with each one, Adam could not find a soul mate with any of them. None had the consciousness that Adam possessed. Naming the animals only awakened a greater sense of isolation within Adam, for the animals all had mates and Adam was alone.

To help Adam overcome his feelings of isolation, Lilith was first given to him, according to Jewish legends. Lilith is not mentioned in the Bible, but is prominent in Kabbalah and *Midrashic* (orally transmitted) sources. She also appears as the dark feminine in ancient Sumerian mythology as well as in other surrounding ancient cultures. Lilith was created separately from Adam and never assumed bodily form like Adam did after the "fall." The legend is that Lilith insisted on full equality and consequently abandoned Adam because Adam was unwilling to yield to her demands. With the use of the ineffable name, Lilith flew to the Red Sea, away from Adam. Lilith is said to be spurned by Adam and is still overcome with jealousy of humankind, and capable of injuring babies. Even to this day, people secure amulets to protect infants from her. Also, according to legends, Lilith arouses men to commit the sin of wasting seed, a terrible sin that is said to cut off a man from the experience of the *Shechinah*. It is believed that it is principally through Lilith that Satan gains hold of a man.

Lilith represents the dark force of unloving feminine sexual seduction residing as a potential within each woman. Most women at some time in their lives realize how vulnerable men are to the sexual seduction of the feminine. It is for that reason that much attention is given to modesty in traditional Jewish spiritual practice, to combat the Lilith-like potential to use sexual attractiveness purely for the sake of attaining power, money, or ego gratification.

So afraid of her sexual seductive power, Kabbalists consider Lilith to be the feminine expression of the *nahash* (serpent, Satan), so dangerous, that my Kabbalistic study partners do not want to even mention her name. We simply refer to her as L. It is said that even after Eve was created, Adam copulated with Lilith and produced demons through these acts. Lilith was not the partner that Adam needed, but she was the one that he both feared and desired.

According to the Bible, the best helpmate that Adam needed would not be separate from Adam but would come directly from him. This woman was always there, they were one being, they were adjoined back to back, and she was not even noticed. Now she was to be separated from the body of Adam. It was part of the divine plan from the beginning that they would be separated, but it was important that they first share the memory of being part of one being. This deep connection did not work with Lilith because she did not share a common root with Adam.

"Hashem (God) cast a deep sleep upon Adam and took one of his sides" (Genesis 11:21). And man said, *"This time* it is bone of my bones and flesh of my flesh. This shall be called woman, for from man was she taken"(Genesis 11: 24). Now man and woman stood separate from each other, face to face, so as to now be able to help and challenge each other to grow. According to Kabbalah, the conscious portions of this original bi-gendered being became known as man (Adam) and the unconscious parts were now known as woman (*Isha*). Here, woman is considered a more perfected being than her male counterpart, with greater intuition, because she is connected to the depths of the unconscious, making a woman more intuitive. She came from Adam rather than like him just from the dust. Adam called woman *Isha*, meaning "woman," after she was created. The woman, however, had no name, no personal identity in the beginning other than *Isha*. According to the Zohar, the name *Isha* is derived from the Hebrew word for fire (Aish) with the Hebrew letter *hay* added to it. The woman contains within her judgement from the fire and mercy from the letter *hay*.

Woman Gains a Name!

Woman only gains a personal name only after the Sin of Eating of the Tree of the Knowledge of Good and Evil. "The man called his wife's name Eve, because she had become the mother of all living" (Genesis 3:20). Rashi, the biblical commentator, tells us that the Hebrew name Chavah, translated as Eve, is similar to Haya, which means "living." The *Midrash* says that the name Chavah is a play on the Aramaic name *Chivya*, serpent. It is said that she was like a snake to Adam. She seduced him like the snake seduced her. We also use this descriptive word "sneaky" or "snake-like" in our language to refer to a person who is cunning, seductive, or even unethical. Women, perhaps more than men, have been seen as being seductive, cunning, and have often resorted to meet their needs in underhanded or indirect ways.

The Deeper Meanings of the Story of Adam and Eve

The serpent at the time of this story was said to have stood erect. He was cunning and had a beautiful human-like appearance. The serpent was possessed by the spirit of Samael, the angel who also came to be known as Satan. The oral tradition tells us that just as Lilith was jealous of Chava, Samael was jealous of Adam. According to the Zohar, the serpent wanted Eve to eat the Tree of the Knowledge of Good and Evil because he really wanted to marry her and usurp Adam's authority and role as progenitor of humankind. He was certain that Adam would be punished and excommunicated for eating the forbidden fruit, but he did not think Eve would similarly be punished because she had not heard directly the prohibition against eating of the Tree.

The serpent said, "God knows that on the day you eat from it, your eyes will be opened and you will know God, knowing good and evil" (Genesis 3:4). The *Midrash* and Gemara, the second part of the Talmud consisting primarily of commentary on the *Midrash,* consider these words as the first act of *loshon hara,* or evil speech, against Hashem, as the serpent portrayed God as a jealous tyrant who did not want Adam and Eve to become like God. It is a falsehood and unseemly to ascribe jealousy to God's motives for prohibiting eating of the Tree of Good and Evil. The Gemara learns from this story that the *nahash* (the serpent) symbolizes the person who speaks *loshon hara,* because just as a snake bites without deriving any benefit from the bite, so a person who speaks *loshon hara* causes damage with his mouth without deriving any personal benefit from it. *Loshon hara* may be one of the ways that we can identify the power of evil.

We generally consider *loshon hara* a falsehood but it is not necessarily so. *Loshon hara* can be the truth but said for evil intent. The serpent did not tell lies to Eve, but rather he beguiled her with possibilities for increased wisdom by saying that "you will know God" (Genesis 3:4). To know something in Judaism is to become one with it. To know God is to be intimate with God. Eve wanted to unite with God and saw that "eating of the tree was a means for wisdom" (Genesis 3: 6). Eating of the Tree of Good and

Evil would indeed offer wisdom to her. The serpent did, however, confuse her when he pushed her against the Tree and nothing happened to her. She did not consciously retain the knowledge of hearing the divine prohibition against eating. God commanded Adam not to eat from the Tree. The biblical story then has Eve quoting Adam that she should not eat nor even touch the Tree. Why did Adam add an extra prohibition? Perhaps it was an indication that Adam did not trust her or perhaps he simply wanted to protect her.

When Eve did touch the tree and nothing occurred, she did not know whether she should or could believe Adam. She then ate the outside of the fruit and when seeing that nothing happened to her, she ate the entire fruit. When Eve completed her eating of the fruit of the Tree of the Knowledge of Good and Evil, her consciousness was indeed tremendously altered. She saw the angel of death. She was now truly alone, radically different in consciousness than Adam. There was a great and painful separation between the two of them. She then gave it to Adam so they could be united in this different dimension of reality. I have heard it said that Eve pleaded with Adam to eat the fruit and I have also heard it said that Adam couldn't bear the separation from his wife so he willingly ate it.

As soon as they ate of the Tree, they realized that they were naked and covered themselves. The divine call to Adam "Where are you?" (Genesis 3:9) offered Adam an opportunity to do *teshuva*; that is, to repent for this act of disobedience. When God then questions whether he ate of the Tree that he was commanded not to eat (Genesis 3:11), Adam is given yet another opportunity to confess. Adam's response was "The woman whom you gave to be with me, she gave me of the Tree and I ate" (Genesis 3: 6). Adam blames Eve and even implies in his response that he would not have sinned on his own. What Adam said was the truth. He did eat because Eve gave the fruit to him. Nevertheless, in answering as he did, Adam failed to take responsibility for his own action. Furthermore, he displayed his ingratitude to God. Eve was a gift to him from God.

Eve is similarly confronted and given an opportunity to confess and repent. She also fails to take responsibility for her actions and blames the serpent. Because both of them are unwilling to express their regret for what they did, they were punished and cast out of the garden. They were both given opportunities to repent. They might have been forgiven if they had repented. We will never know for sure.

The Even Deeper Meanings

Kabbalists teach that there were seven worlds that were created and destroyed prior to this one. These seven worlds are in the world of chaos (called *Tohu* in Hebrew). *Tohu* was a primordial form of existence that was created in order to be destroyed and rebuilt in a more perfected form. This is referred to in the Bible as "kings who reigned in the land of Edom before there was a king of Israel." The destruction that resulted in the succession of the kings refers to the concept known in Hebrew as *Shevirat HaKelim,* the breaking of the vessels. In *Shevirat HaKelim,* the divine sparks of light ascended upward and the vessels descended or collapsed into greater density that resulted in a disconnection between the light and the vessel. A residue of the original divine sparks remains, however, within the fallen vessels because nothing exists without the divine spark within it that enlivens it. *Shevirat HaKelim* is the kabbalistic explanation for the origin of evil.

Because of the fall, the divine sparks were covered, imprisoned, and disconnected from a total absorption in the source of light. Kabbalistically, the covering of the light is referred to as husks or shells, called in Hebrew *klippot.* The spiritual mission of the Jewish people is to reconnect these fallen sparks to their source and transform this world into a dwelling place for the *Shechinah.* Originally, as stated earlier, Adam and Eve were pure light emanations that fell into physicality after eating of the forbidden tree.

After the shattering of the vessels, a form resembling Adam and Eve was created from the remnants of the vessels and sparks of divine light. Kabbalists call this *Adam Beliya'al,* which literally means "a man without a yoke." *Adam Beliya'al* is comprised of nations of the world that experience separation from the One Creator. Rabbi Yitzhak Luria described the crown of *Adam Beliya'al* as Egypt, Babylon is the head, Medea and Persia are the two arms, the torso is Greece, and the two legs are Edom and Ishmael. In her book *Israel and the Seventy Dimensions of the World*, Nadborny-Burgman beautifully outlines the seven exiles of the Jewish people in teachings and paintings. It is into the belly of these very nations that the Jewish people, who represent the *Shechinah,* enter to liberate the fallen divine sparks that have been imprisoned in the *klippot,* so as to connect and restore these nations, which constitute the fragmented pieces of the original soul of Adam and Eve, to the Divine Creator. This is the mission of the Jewish people whether they accept or know it or not. As Burgman writes in her book, "Our souls are splintered pieces of the once unified soul of Adam and Eve, which became intermixed with the *klippot* of *Adam Beliya'al....* Adam's consciousness was transformed into the kaleidoscopic consciousness of the seventy archetypal nations.... When Israel rises to her potential, she extracts the light of the reality of the creator from the limbs of *Adam Beliya'al*. When Israel sins, the reality of the creator becomes obscured for all humankind, causing all souls to enter more deeply into the *klippot*." It is generally understood in kabbalistic thought that the actions of the Jewish people impact directly upon the well being of the nations of the world. By the way, the Jewish people and the world are currently completing the exile of Edom (the Christian nations) and entering into the exile of Ishmael, considered one of the most terrible and difficult exiles, because Ishmael also carries the blessing of Abraham.

Eating of the Tree of the Knowledge of Good and Evil brought evil into the world yet the words of Isaiah (45:7) tell us " I am Hashem, there is no other. I am the One who forms light and creates darkness; Who makes peace and creates evil; I am Hashem, Maker of all these." These words are repeated in daily prayers. It would appear that evil was part of the divine plan. Evil had to exist, the vessels had to shatter, but in the beginning evil was outside of man. Though evil was encapsulated within the Tree of Good and Evil, if they did not eat it, it would not have been part of them. Adam's only instruction and responsibility was to rectify the Tree by refraining from partaking of it until *Shabbat.* It was not out of jealousy that God prohibited eating of the Tree but out of love. Eating of the Tree before they had matured sufficiently to be able to digest the experience was harmful to them.

When Adam and Eve did indeed eat of the Tree prior to *Shabbat,* the evil that was formerly outside of them was now incorporated into their very being. As a result, everything in the world now, as within man and women, would contain a mixture of good and evil within, making it no longer so easy to distinguish good from evil. Because of this challenge, Adam and Eve were now endowed with the burden and privilege of free will.

Free will, the ability to make meaningful choices, becomes possible only because of the lack of clarity between good and evil. If the good is totally revealed, there is really no real choice to do evil, because it would be clear that evil will only bring chaos, pain, and suffering. Why would we choose that over all that is good and true and that which will bring joy and peace unless we are bent on seeking death rather than life. Because good and evil are not so clear for most of us, we have to make choices. Through our choices, we gain meaning and definition for ourselves. It is a burden, a challenge and a privilege to discern the good from the not so good to make choices that support the good in our lives.

What is good and evil? How do we distinguish between them? Evil in Kabbalah has been defined as the desire to receive for oneself alone. This is a definition of selfishness and egoism. Good is the desire to receive only to share. Simply stated, good creates unity, sharing and love and evil creates divisiveness, anger and jealousy.

What Eve did may actually have been good because she wanted to share with Adam and give him the gift of free will as Eve explained in her interview. By eating of the Tree, Adam would now become an active participant in creation and be able to draw down more light for himself, for her, and for the world. Free will, the ability to choose, to not simply be a recipient but to be a creator with the Divine, offers humanity greater meaning and purpose. This is what Eve wanted for Adam. Eve ate of the Tree not to bring evil into the world, but to bring free will into the world. Was this really evil? Was it naive? Eve explained her motivations in the interview so you will have to decide how they resonate with you. Did Eve bring evil into the world as she is frequently blamed? Or rather did Eve demonstrate both leadership and courage to usher into the world the opportunity for humanity to live responsibly and purposely?

What was the Tree of the Knowledge of Good and Evil anyway? Many envision it as a tree in a literal sense. Some say that it was an apple, but there is no basis for this idea. Others say that it was a fig tree, because they covered themselves with the leaves from the fig tree. Interesting, the fig is associated with the Torah, for it is a fruit that is totally edible. The Zohar considers it a grape. That is why juice of the grape or wine is used for *Kiddush,* so as to sanctify and lift up the grape that participated in the downfall of man.

This story begs us, however, to understand it metaphorically. For example, we say that in our Jewish prayers, "Torah is a tree of life to those who cling to it. Her ways are ways of pleasantness and all her paths are peace." We do not mean that the Torah is a literal tree. Torah resembles a tree, for within Torah are the roots, the branches, the leaves, and the flowers of life.

Kabbalah teaches us that God created the world through what are called *Sephirot,* which are the ten foundational attributes or virtues present in God, women, and men. In total, these ten attributes are referred to as the Tree of Life, but this tree actually includes what in the creation story are called the Tree of Life and the Tree of Knowledge of Good and Evil. In the story of Adam and Eve, the Tree of Life specifically refers to the lower seven *Sephirot* that have both masculine and feminine aspects. The six divine emanations that comprise the lower masculine Divine Personality called *Zeir Anpin* (small countenance) are *Hesed* (love), *Gevurah* (strength), *Tiferet* (compassion), *Netzach* (endurance), *Hod* (humility), and the lower feminine Divine Personality called *Malkut* (kingship), the lower of seven

Sephirot. The Tree of Life and the Tree of Good and Evil are not to be taken literally, nor are the *Sephirot* to be taken as separate divine entities.

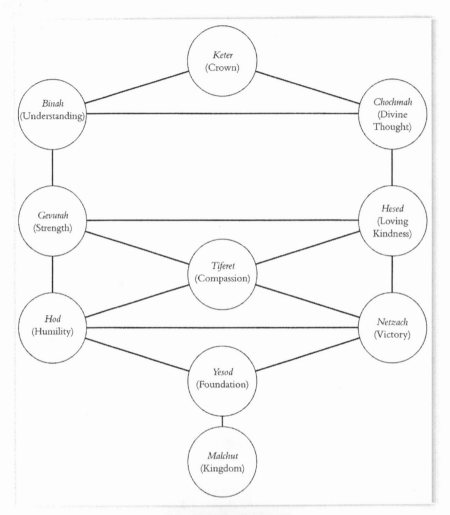

The Tree of Life

Look at the chart of the *Sephirot* referred to as the Tree of Life. The three top *Sephirot* are *Chokmah,* the higher Divine Masculine, known as *Abba* (Father); *Binah,* known as *Ima,* Mother; and a connective *Sephira* called *Da'at* (knowledge), which is a channel connecting the Divine Masculine and the

Divine Feminine to the lower *Sephirot*. These top *Sephirot* hold the keys to creation, to miracles, to infinite love and bliss. The six lower *Sephirot*, or divine emanations, constitute what is referred to as *Zeir Anpin* (small countenance), also known as *Ha-Kodesh Boruch Hu*, the Divine Masculine. This is the Face of the Divine that primarily interacts with this world.

Creation occurs through an "arousal from below," that is, through a stimulation within the Divine Feminine, known as the *Shechinah*. In Kabbalah, it is understood that the lower Divine Feminine (*Malkut* or *Nukva*) first stimulates the higher Divine Masculine, known as *Abba*, or Father, who then inseminates *Binah*, the higher Divine Feminine, with the flow of the Infinite Divine Love, Light (*Ohr Ein Sof*). In other words, all creation in this world occurs as *Chokmah*/wisdom, also known as *Abba*, the Divine Father, transmits the Divine Love, Light to *Binah*/understanding/the Divine Mother, who then goes through a period of "pregnancy" and " birth," both creating and sharing the Infinite Love and Light with *Zeir Anpin*/the son, the prince, also known as "The Holy One Blessed be He," who in turn inseminates the daughter/princess (*Malkut*), who is also known as the *Shechinah*. It is the Shechinah who initiates and is also the ultimate recipient of the flow of Infinite Love and Light (*Ohr Ein Sof*).

It is important to highlight and acknowledge that it is through the agency of the feminine that creation begins and culminates. Because *Malkut*, the ultimate vessel, is empty with no light of her own, she yearns to know and be filled with the highest light. Though *Malkut* is the recipient of *Zeir Anpin*, she is also a reflection of *Binah* and is unified with *Binah*. What happens in the higher spiritual worlds is reflected in the lower worlds. This is a most important point to understand.

In the creation story, Eve represents *Malkut*, the *Shechinah*, and wants both Adam and herself to receive the highest light, so she reaches out for this higher wisdom of the top *Sephirot*. The desire itself was good, the timing was not, for neither Adam nor Eve had the vessels to incorporate this highest light. The action was premature. Deep within every woman is Eve's desire for the higher wisdom along with the experience of the higher face of the feminine, known as *Binah,* the Divine Mother.

The Story of Adam and Eve Is All about Sexuality.

According to Kabbalah, the eating of the tree was ultimately all about sexuality. When the Hebrew word "to know" is used, it is usually a coded reference to intimacy and sexuality. The prohibition of the Eating of the Tree of the Knowledge of Good and Evil really meant that Adam was to wait to cohabit with Eve until *Shabbat.* The Sabbath would offer such a revelation of the *Shechinah* (Divine Feminine) that would grant Adam and Eve the spiritual power needed to transform the world to the perfection and goodness that was intended through their sexual relations. *Shabbat* is indicative of the time when their consciousness would have matured sufficiently so that they would be able to eat of the Tree, digest its fruit, extract the divine sparks from the *klipot,* and lift them up and return them to the source. That was the divine plan. Adam and Eve would have done a *tikkun* on what was before, restored harmony to their world, and eliminated evil from their midst. This desire to lift up fallen sparks, to do the *tikkun,* was explored in the interview with Eve.

However, Eve's contact with the serpent awakened the force of sexuality within her. She was not patient. Eve saw Adam's sexual attraction to Lilith and wanted to attract Adam to herself, so as to use the force of their sexual union not as an end in itself, but for the healing and transformation of the world. Sexuality, according to Kabbalah, has the power to take us to the highest levels of knowing God when done with proper intention. If done without love or connection to God, sex is an animalistic act and can take us to the lowest depths. According to a Kabbalist friend in the Old City in Jerusalem, the *nahash,* or serpent, in the story is in large part a phallic metaphor. (The penis does kind of look like a snake, doesn't it ?) He also told me that according to some Kabbalistic sources Eve and Lilith were really one woman. As I understand it as well, every woman contains within her the energy of Eve and Lilith.

The divine plan was that the erotic force of sexuality that was awakened within Adam and Eve and the love force of the soul would be unified on *Shabbat*. Love and sexuality were intended to be a unified force through which one would experience God in the most direct way. Eating before *Shabbat* symbolized that these two forces remained separate, not fully unified. When these forces are unified, we experience God directly, we reveal the *Shechinah*, the Divine Feminine, on earth and bring peace to ourselves and the world. But, when we use our sexuality purely for our own physical pleasure, without love, we create chaos, and separation from the Divine. According to the Zohar, the exile and suffering of the Jewish people is attributed to transgressions in sexual behavior.

Therefore, it can be said that the real sin of Adam and Eve was impatience. They only had to wait until *Shabbat,* but alas, they did not wait. And so often we do not wait. Adam and Eve ate of the Tree before they were mature enough to digest it. People are still working on bringing these two basic forces of life into balance. One of my beloved teachers of blessed memory Rabbi Yitzchok Kirzner taught that one of the indicators of the *yetza hara*, the evil inclination, is impatience. Since Adam and Eve contain within them all souls, we today continue to suffer from the effects of their actions. Patience continues to be an important quality to both acquire and demonstrate in life.

The Need for Tikkun

In messianic times, according to Rabbi Isaac Luria, the great and holy medieval Kabbalist, the feminine will rise, be healed, and the rift between Eve and Lilith, the two wives of Adam, will disappear. Lilith will no longer be a murderess, seductive, promiscuous demon, full of anger and jealousy, and Eve will no longer be the simple, practical, submissive, and chaste virginal wife. They will be blended and unified in a single woman. That seems to be what is taking place in our time. According to Rabbi Isaac Luria, known as the Arizel, the soul of Lilith must undergo a great transformation and rehabilitation. Lilith reincarnates much later as Leah, her daughter Dina, Zipporah, the wife of Moses, Orphah, the sister-in-law of Ruth (Lilith is even in Ruth to a lesser extent), and much later as Rabbi Akiva's second nameless wife, who converted to Judaism, previously married to a wicked man Turnus Rufus. Eve also reincarnates many times for soul correction as well in Sarah, Rebecca, Rachel, and Esther. Kabbalah gives much particular attention to the Lilith/Eve incarnation of Leah and Rachel.

Sarah

Sarah is the only woman who has a chapter in the Bible named after her. The Zohar, the Kabbalistic commentary on the Bible, in its chapter *Chaya Sarah* reminds us "Of Sarah alone among all women do we find recorded the number of days and years and length of her life and the place where she was buried. This was to show that there was none like Sarah among all the women of the world." Sarah was considered sinless. Some Kabbalists say that she was a reincarnation of Eve, correcting the sins of the first women. Unlike the first woman, Eve, who was intimate with the serpent, who injected his impurity into her, Sarah was considered pure and untouched by the power of the serpent. She entered Egypt and left Egypt untouched by the contact with impurity there. The Zohar says that because Sarah did not cling to the "other side," Sarah earned supernal life for herself, her husband, and her son after her.

The chapter in the Bible named after her is "The Life of Sarah," for it is said that Sarah attached herself to life and made her life on her own. This biblical chapter, however, begins with a report of her death in an unusual way. Rather than saying that Sarah was twenty-seven years when she died, the Bible says, "The life of Sarah was 100 years and twenty years and seven years." Her life is divided into three periods of time, marking the three stages of life and three very different kinds of divine beauty whose perfection exists in each stage. Seven years of age represents childhood and the beauty of innocence, twenty years of age represents young womanhood and the beauty of healthy physicality and sexuality, and 100 years represents the beauty of wisdom and the sum of good deeds achieved in life. Leading rabbis such as Rashi, the preeminent medieval rabbinical commentator on the Bible, and Rabbi Samson Raphael Hirsch, a modern-day rabbinical commentator, explain that the Torah wants to tell us that Sarah was as beautiful when she was 100 years old as when she was twenty and she was as pure and innocent at twenty as when she was seven years. They also emphasize that the description of Sarah in this way is to express that Sarah loved life and lived fully and vibrantly in all these periods of her life. She remained true and consistent. Her righteousness and the different manifestations of her beauty were unchanged throughout her life. Interestingly enough, as an aside, Sarah had three names for these three different periods of her life, Yiscah, Sarai, and Sarah.

The Zohar, in its chapter on *Chaya Sarah*, offers a Kabbalistic explanation for why Sarah's life was introduced in the way that it was. A translation of the actual Hebrew written in the first verse about the life of Sarah states the two integers of time, 100 year and twenty year, are given in the singular, rather than the plural, as it is translated into English, while the final account of the seven years of her life are presented in the plural. The Torah does this to offer a code to indicate that Sarah lived in a very different, almost supernatural way. Most of her life was beyond this world, connected to a place of unity and blessing that is not said about anyone else.

Sarah's birth name was *Yiscah*, which comes from the Hebrew *socar*, "to gaze." Eve was considered very beautiful, but Sarah was deemed even more beautiful. People would gather around her to simply gaze at her to have their hearts opened and be filled with love and light. She was also called *Yiscah* because she was a prophetess, a seer who could see things through divine inspiration. At the time of her marriage to Abraham, her name was changed by him to *Sarai*, which means "my princess" and she became a princess to her people. Her marriage to Abraham indicated her willingness to join Abraham in his mission to perfect the world. Later in her life, her name was later changed to Sarah, without the restrictive "my" by God to signify that she was now princess to all the nations. The addition of the letter *hay* to her name expanded her status and fate. It is taught that a change in name brings about a change in fate. Sarai could not bear a child with Abraham, but Sarah can. After a visitation of three angels, Sarah does indeed give birth to Isaac at the age of ninety years when she had no longer been menstruating. It was not exactly Immaculate Conception, but it was a miraculous birth nevertheless. Sarah's youth and beauty were restored to her.

The Zohar tells us that Sarah reached such a high spiritual level that all of life depended spiritually upon her. Known as a holy seer from the time of her childhood, Sarah was said to have reached a level of prophecy greater than other prophetesses for the Divine spoke directly to her. Her prophecy was even considered greater than Abraham, her husband. When Sarah was alive, according to many commentaries, the success of the people around her was attributed to her.

Both Abraham and Sarah laughed at the news that their son would be born. The name Yitzchok (Isaac) means "laughter." When Isaac was born, the world around them also laughed with joy. The oral tradition testifies that when Sarah conceived, many barren women also conceived. There was such a blessing in the world that hearing was bestowed upon many people who were deaf and sight to people who were blind, all attributed to the blessing of Sarah.

Sarah, the mother of the Jewish people, died alone in Hebron. Her husband Abraham had sent her away to Hebron prior to carrying out his plan of sacrificing Isaac. This act was between him and God. It was the greatest of the ten tests Abraham underwent, the supreme test through which he could express his full devotion to God. Abraham could not, however, hide what was happening from Sarah for Sarah was a prophetess.

The Bible tells us how old Sarah was when she died, but avoids telling us directly how she died. The Bible, however, shows us that when Abraham came to eulogize Sarah and cry for her, the word "to weep over her," *livkosah* (Genesis 23:2), is written with an unusually small *kaf*. This has been said to indicate that Abraham did not eulogize her publicly, as would be expected of a man of his stature to do for his wife, who was so loved and esteemed by the world.

Some sages say that Abraham did not eulogize Sarah publicly because she committed suicide. Was it suicide? Did Sarah actually take her own life? Would a woman like Sarah, a great prophetess who had bore such hardship with faith and strength in her life, commit suicide? Or did Abraham not eulogize his wife publicly for another reason? Might it be guilt?

Several rabbis of note actually have addressed Sarah's death and have explored whether it might even be considered as a suicide. Some say she died happy, fulfilled that her son was going to be sacrificed. It has even been said that she died of shock when she learned that he was not sacrificed. She received a vision that Isaac was not harmed and the shock and/or grief that he was saved and not worthy of being sacrificed killed her. Others say that on hearing the news that her son was alive she died of a joy so intense that her heart gave out.

The Baal Turim, the great biblical commentator, said that Sarah committed a kind of suicide when she said to Abraham, "Let God should judge between you and me." With these words, she invited judgment into her life and that is why she died before Abraham. The Zohar says that it was grief and anguish that killed Sarah and also that she gave up her soul so her son would live.

When Sarah died, the people wept deeply for they more fully realized what a source of blessing, materially and spiritually, she was to them. Rabbis say that Sarah obtained eternal life for herself and through her merit for all her descendants. Not only does the life of Sarah continue after she is no longer physically embodied, but righteous people like Sarah are said to be more alive when they are not confined to the limits of a physical body. She is to this day considered the mother of all people who choose to convert to Judaism.

Sarah is buried in the Cave of Machpelah, in Kiryat Arba in Hebron, where tens of thousands of women and men continue to visit her every year. This burial site was offered to Abraham as a gift by the owner; yet,

Abraham wanted to purchase it to ensure that there would be no doubt as to the ownership. He purchased it for a great deal of money. Sarah was the first of the matriarchs to be buried there in what would become the ancestral burial site for the patriarchs and matriarchs, with the exception of Rachel, who is buried on the main road leading eastward outside of Jerusalem, so that she could console her children centuries later as they were being led into exile. Legends speak of Adam and Eve also being buried at the Cave of Machpelah, a place of great holiness, a gateway between this world and the higher worlds.

Rebecca

According to hidden Kabbalistic teachings in the Zohar, Sarah bequeathed part of her soul to Isaac, her son, and the other part to Rebecca. Rebecca was said to be the image of Sarah and even considered a reincarnation of Sarah who herself was deemed a reincarnation of Eve. The same miraculous signs that were associated with Sarah were restored when Rebecca entered the tent of Sarah. When Isaac and Rebecca first saw each other, they immediately recognized each other as constituting one soul. Isaac was said to be thirty-seven years of age at the time of the death of his mother and forty years old at the time of his marriage to Rebecca.

Prior to his second marriage to Keturah, Abraham decided to look for a wife for his son and sent his most trusted and closest servant and disciple to look for her in the land of Aram, his birthplace. Abraham ordered him to not bring his son there but to request that the woman return with him. In the biblical account of the selection of Rebecca as the wife to Isaac, Eliezer, Abraham's servant, devised a scheme by which he would recognize the woman who would be worthy of being the wife of Isaac and the matriarch of the Jewish people that is recorded in detail in the Torah. "Let it be that the maiden to whom I shall say 'Please tip over your jug so that I may drink, and who replies, 'Drink, and I will even water your camels'" (Genesis 24: 14). The Bible very rarely includes an internal conversation such as the words of prayer or a dialogue between people and so to do so is to consider the act of finding a wife for Isaac very important. The Bible furthermore records not only Eliezer's prayer, but also his conversation with Rebecca, his lengthy conversation and retelling of the story with her brother and father, and his report to Abraham.

When Eliezer entered the town of Aram, he consciously left outside of the town the camels and entourage that would have identified him as a wealthy man. He wanted to make sure that he would not receive special treatment in the town because of his wealth. According to the oral tradition, Rebecca had gone to draw water from the well herself for the first time when Eliezer arrived there. Rebecca offered water to Eliezer and then to the camels and fulfilled the conditions as prescribed in Eliezer's intentional prayer. Carrying water required much effort but Rebecca offered to do this on her own initiative. By this conduct Rebecca demonstrated that she was surely an outstanding woman who had the capacity to truly give of herself. Eliezer then knew without doubt that she was indeed the girl worthy of wedding Isaac. He gave her jewelry that she accepted and she, in return, offered him hospitality.

Once in her home with her brother and father, Eliezer insisted that he explain the purpose of this visit prior to eating a meal with him. In his account of what had transpired, Eliezer sought to demonstrate the miraculous nature of these events that fulfilled his prayer to meet a suitable woman to marry his master's son. Acknowledging the hand of the Divine in this quest, Rebecca's brother and father agreed to allow Rebecca to marry Isaac. Rebecca was then asked directly if she would be willing to go with Eliezer. She consented with a simple statement, "I will go."

When Rebecca first saw Isaac, she fell off her camel. Isaac, returning from his afternoon prayers, was shining like an angel. Commentaries say that she fell off the camel because she foresaw through divine inspiration that she would birth the wicked Esau. Could it not have been simply possible that she was so taken and even shaken that she was to marry such a holy man and that caused her to lose her balance? She had never seen a holy person like Isaac before. It has been said in some *Midrashim* (legends) that Rebecca was three years old when she married and some people take it literally. Perhaps she was older but had the purity of an innocent child.

In another *Midrash,* Isaac waited for Rebecca to age to fourteen years old and then married her. The Bible so beautifully tells us "Isaac brought Rebecca into the tent of Sarah, his mother, he married her, she became his wife, he loved her, and thus Isaac was consoled after his mother" (Genesis 24:67). Love grew out of marriage and not before marriage.

Rebecca as the Shechinah

With the advent of famine, there was a necessity for Abraham and Sarah and then also Isaac and Rebecca to travel for food. Isaac and Rebecca were following the footsteps of Abraham and Sarah on route to Egypt when Isaac received a direct God revelation to not leave the Land of Israel. Instead, he and Rebecca traveled to Gerar, located within the boundaries of the land God had designated for the Jewish people.

Because both Abraham and Isaac feared the lack of morality in the land they were visiting, they introduced their wives as their sisters. "She is my sister," they both proclaimed. The Zohar informs us that the *Shechinah* is often called sister, so it is said that Isaac was not lying when he called Rebecca sister. The *Shechinah* (the Divine Feminine) existed within Rebecca to such an extent that Rebecca was more of a sister (the *Shechinah*) than a wife to Isaac. When Isaac recognized his wife as the *Shechinah,* he knew that he would be protected. According to the Zohar, Abraham and Isaac were considered as archetype chariots for *Zeir Anpin* (the Divine Masculine, "The Holy One Blessed be He") so it was fitting that their wives who embodied the *Shechinah* be called sisters.

What is most important to highlight is that like Sarah, also acknowledged as an embodiment of the *Shechinah*, Rebecca similarly had to enter a land of impurity and immorality, be at risk, and leave unharmed. This descent seems like a soul correction for Eve, for these women, both deemed incarnations of Eve, encounter expressions of the *nahash*, the serpent, embodiment of evil, and yet unlike Eve, they can leave unscathed. Both Sarah and Rebecca as embodiments of the *Shechinah* were reported to be so beautiful that even in their elderly years men greatly desired them. Because these women embodied the beauty and Godliness of women, their visit to these communities raised the respect that men had for women and the general level of morality there. They were both able to enter and depart from lands of impurity without any harm to themselves.

The Birth of Jacob and Esau

When Rebecca is pregnant, she is unclear about what is occurring within her. The Jewish oral tradition tells us that when she would walk near a house of idol worship or to a Jewish place of worship there would be intense movement in her womb. She is confused and overwhelmed by this occurrence. At this time, she did not know that she was birthing twins. She consults Shem and receives the prophecy that guides her actions later in her life.

The Bible describes Esau, the firstborn, as "a man who understood hunting, a man of the field," and Jacob as a simple-minded man "dwelling in tents." Even though these two brothers were so different in temperament and constitution, they were still twins. Yet the Bible tells that Isaac loved Esau for the venison he hunted for him and Rebecca simply loved Jacob. No reason is given for this love. When Isaac was old, he requests Esau to make a special dish for him to precede the monumental event of transmitting to him the blessing of the covenant. Rebecca overhears the plan of her husband and quickly schemes to deceive her husband and secure the blessing for her son Jacob.

Why would Isaac want to bestow the blessings to Esau in the first place? The Bible tells us "Isaac loved Esau for the game that was in his mouth" (Genesis 25:28). It could not be simply that he liked that Esau was a hunter who gave him venison. That seems rather shallow. What was really going on? Was Isaac's judgment impaired? Did he not see that Esau would not live in accordance with the principles of the faith he received from his father? Did the trauma of the *akeida*, the Hebrew word that refers to sacrifice by the hand of his father, affect his judgment? Does the Bible tell us that he was blind in his old age to indicate that he could not see who Esau really was? Why did Isaac favor Esau? Why did he want him to hunt for game prior to giving him the blessing? Why couldn't he just give the blessing directly to him?

The teachings of Kabbalah provide important insight into why Isaac wanted to bless Esau. It is said that Isaac clearly saw that Jacob's soul was rooted in the world of *tikkun*, the world of correction, and that he came into this world to heal and transform this world to be a place of blessing. He was so pure and really did not need a blessing for himself. The soul of Esau came from a more primal world, which is known as the world of *Tohu*, the world prior to creation. As such, Esau was capable of creating chaos, but he also could affect a higher level of redemption if he channeled his negative tendencies to good rather than evil. Had Esau been righteous, he would have surpassed Jacob.

According to the awesome Kabbalist Rabbi Isaac Luria, Esau and Jacob are reincarnations of Cain and Abel. In that lifetime, the brothers were given an opportunity to rectify the murder of Abel by Cain and restore the world to its intended perfected state that existed prior to the sin of Eating of the Tree of Good and Evil. Unfortunately, the rectification was not achieved. It then became necessary to take the blessings from Esau to safeguard the world.

There is a question in rabbinic commentaries whether Isaac knew that his son had been engaged in negativity and evil. Let's assume that Isaac knew that his son Esau was a thief, a murderer, and an idolater, and yet he still wanted to bless him. Why? Were Esau able to serve God fully with his soul, Isaac reasoned, he would be able to do more good than Jacob. Esau had certain talents that Jacob did not have that would be important to this mission. Isaac hoped that the blessings would magnetize the divine sparks buried within Esau to come to the forefront and motivate him toward holiness. Esau needed the blessing to be able to overcome his tendency toward evil and be part of the building of the Jewish nation. With the blessing, Esau would be able to transform the negativity within himself and that within the world as well. It is one thing to be pure and bring more light into the world, but to transform evil and negativity takes the capacity to know it and confront it directly. Esau was a hunter and fighter after all and would be better able to eradicate evil than Jacob who was so pure, always praying and meditating like his father.

Abraham, Isaac's father, was extroverted, traveling to many places to spread the teachings of God. Isaac stayed in Israel, internalizing what he received from his father and did not proselyte like his father. Isaac knew, however, that it was the mission of his sons to share the light of monotheism with the entire world. The plan most likely in Isaac's mind was for the two brothers to work together, in a partnership that he was not able to do with his half brother Ishmael. Esau, as a man of the field, would have prominence in the physical material world, and Jacob, as a man of the tent, would have prominence in the spiritual world. The work of the brothers need not be in conflict but would actually support and complement each other. Together they would be unstoppable. But Rebecca knew that her son Esau would not be willing to work alongside of Jacob as she revealed in the interview.

When Esau returns from his hunting and discovers that the blessing intended for him has been given to his brother Jacob, he is angry and pleads with his father for another blessing. "Do you not have a blessing for me?" Esau cries. Though Isaac gives him a blessing, Esau's blessing may hardly be seen as a blessing. Rather, it is more of a prophetic forecast of events to come in the future. Though Esau is blessed with material abundance, he is also blessed to live by the sword until he is humbled and surrenders his bounty to his brother Jacob. He may conquer the world, but in the end, he will indeed surrender to his brother, or rather to the spiritual principles and ideals embodied in Jacob. Perhaps it will be upon the realization of the futility of physical conquest and war that he will ultimately surrender.

The blessing that Isaac gives to Jacob when he was to depart from his home was what was originally intended for Jacob. "May *El Shaddai* bless you, make you fruitful and numerous.... May He grant you the blessing of Abraham to you and your offspring ... that you may possess the land of your sojourns which God gave to Abraham" (Genesis 28: 3–4). Jacob was indeed always the spiritual heir for the lineage of Abraham and Isaac. It is important to highlight that in Isaac's blessing to Jacob the gift of the Land of Israel was always intended solely for Jacob.

The final biblical comments about Rebecca include her instructions to Jacob to seek shelter with her brother Laban. She also then complains to Isaac about the wives of Esau and expresses her despair if Jacob were to marry similarly. While her concern for a wife for Jacob is indeed real, her main motivation at this time is to protect Jacob for she now fears that Esau will seek revenge against Jacob and kill him. She also wants Jacob to leave Isaac with a blessing, not have to run away in the middle of the night like a criminal. Again she so cleverly uses her feminine wiles to have Isaac do exactly what she wants, to bless Jacob and direct him to Rebecca's brother to find a wife among his daughters. It is all Rebecca's idea but Isaac pronounces it to Jacob. At the completion of this incident, Rebecca withdraws from the biblical narrative and we hear of her no more.

The Application of Rebecca's Prophecy to Our Lives and Our Times

Our study of this biblical chapter, as with all biblical study, cannot be confined to the events recorded in the Bible. The Bible according to Kabbalistic wisdom is less of an historical document, a record of actual events, but is more importantly, a coded prophetic forecast for the future. In this regard the story of Rebecca is most important. Within this chapter are the secrets of the shift of power between nations that will ultimately lead to the final redemption and perfection of the world in the End of Days. At this End of Days scenario, the harmony between the feminine and the masculine, between Israel and the nations of the world, will be realized. There will be peace, there will be well-being, and the *Shechinah* will be revealed throughout the world.

The prophecy of Rebecca reveals the ongoing battle between Esau and Jacob that takes place on micro and macro levels. According to Kabbalah, Esau represents Rome, Christianity, and the nations where Christianity is a state religion, as in Europe, Russia, and the United States. Jacob represents the Jewish people, Israel, which also refers to the quest for spirituality and holiness within a person.

Teachings for the Individual

On the micro level, within the individual, there is a battle between physicality (Esau) and spirituality (Jacob). This battle is resolved favorably when the body, the physical nature of the individual, serves the spirituality, the soul of a person. When this correct alignment occurs, the body is uplifted by the soul and there is well-being and happiness for the individual. The soul, that is a part of God, entered into the physical world to channel blessing to it. The body must be a vehicle for the soul and not the other way around to be able to receive her blessings. According to Kabbalah, it is not that the body is lower than the soul. When the body is in proper alignment with the soul, the body can contain more spirituality than the soul and is even higher than the soul itself. The physical is very important in Judaism. It does not contaminate the spiritual as in most religions, but the body becomes holy only when it embodies the spiritual. Holiness is the elevation of the physical to the Godly.

The Bible, along with the rabbis, prescribed a series of physical and spiritual activities that outlines a path of a life of holiness known as *mitzvot* to Jews. Many of the *mitzvot* address the sanctification of the body and its physical activities, such as eating, sleeping, sexual relations, and even going to the bathroom, etc. According to Judaism, when the body is refined and enters into harmony with the soul, the body enjoys the properties of the soul. As the soul is immortal, the body can also ultimately become immortal by its total attachment and alignment with the soul.

On the other hand, when a person is ruled primarily by his physical desires, he is vulnerable to addiction, he loses contact with the soul and God, and is therefore plagued with feelings of emptiness, futility, and unhappiness. He becomes impure (*tammeh*), which means he is closed and blocked to the flow of Godliness.

Teachings for the World

On the macro level, according to Kabbalistic commentaries, what is happening in Rebecca's womb may be understood as a prognostication of the outcome of the ongoing battle between the Christian nations and the Jewish people. As the Bible says, "Two nations are in your womb: Two regimes from your insides shall be separated. The might shall pass from one regime to the other. And the elder shall serve the younger" (Genesis 25:23–25) It is important that we understand this prophecy as well. It is taught in Kabbalah that when the Christian nations of the world, that are symbolic of Esau, the older son, are powerful, the Jewish nation derived from Jacob is weakened, and vice versa.

According to Rebecca's prophecy, in the "End of Days", Israel and the Jewish people will be seen as a blessing to the world. The Christian nations who represent Esau in the world will seek their fulfillment and protection through their alignment with Israel. There is already an expanding movement of Christians in the world who feel a debt of gratitude to the Jewish people for providing them with the essentials of their faith and are ardent Zionists. Until that movement becomes more prominent, the ongoing battle between Christian nations and Israel represented by Esau and Jacob continues under the banner of anti-Zionism. Rebecca's prophecy reminds us at times of despair that there will be a time when it will end and there will be peace.

In regard to the Jewish people, there have been two primary orientations within Christianity that are important to understand. The principal theology guiding the Christian world, particularly in Europe, where the Jews were exiled and persecuted, is known as "Replacement Theology." When the Roman Emperor Constantine and Augustine, the most influential Christian thinker of his day, converted to Christianity, Replacement Theology became the primary church doctrine of this new official religion in the Roman Empire. This guiding principle in Christianity asserts that the covenant marking the special relationship that the Jewish people had with God in the Old Testament has been replaced by Jesus, Christianity, and the New Testament. Accordingly, Jesus brought with him a new spiritual order that negated the previous contract that God had with the Jewish people. There remains no meaningful role for Judaism or Jews after JC.

The persecution and suffering of the Jewish people in Europe, according to Replacement Theology, was due to their rejection of Jesus Christ as the messiah and as an incarnation of God. If they had accepted Jesus, they would be "saved" and integrated into the new world order. If God had favored the Jews, according to Replacement Theology, they would have been protected. "Where is your God now?" were the words Christians used to taunt the Jews. Replacement Theology blames the "victim" rather than taking responsibility for the cruelty the Christians have showed to the Jews.

For thousands of years, European Jews were treated like second-class citizens in Christian countries. In addition to discrimination and persecution, there were expulsions as well. The Jews were expelled from England in 1290, expelled from France in 1306, from Spain in 1492, all said to take place on *Tisha B'Av*, the very same day that the Holy Temples were destroyed by Rome.

The most recent horror perpetrated by the Christian nations upon the Jews was the Holocaust in the 1940s. The Holocaust perpetuated by Nazi Germany was also an outgrowth of Replacement Theology. Even though Nazism was not a Christian ideology, most members of the Nazi Party identified as Christians. The Catholic Church did not even take a stand to confront Nazi ideology. Because Europe already had a long history of anti-Semitism and persecution of the Jews, it was easy for much of Europe to accept this obsession that the Germans had with annihilating the Jewish people or even anyone who had any Jewish blood within them. Under the banner of Nazism, it was no longer possible for a Jew to "convert" to Christianity to be saved.

In present times, anti-Semitism in Europe has morphed into anti-Zionism. This should be understood, quite simply, as an altered expression of Replacement Theology. After the Holocaust, Europe could not be outwardly anti-Semitic. It may even be illegal to be anti-Semitic in many countries, but there is no prohibition to not be anti-Israel. "Zionism is racism" is chanted about the only democratic country in the Middle East by non- Jews and Moslems who are increasing in numbers as immigrants in European countries.

Lies continually widespread to delegitimize the State of Israel, to misrepresent her, to not honor the historical or biblical ties of the Jewish people to the Land of Israel must also be seen as expression of Replacement Theology. Because anti-Israel propaganda is rampant, even Jews have difficulty discerning truth from falsehood. It is now "politically correct" to be anti-Israel. Businesses and churches in America even boycott food products from Israel. It does not seem to matter what kind of injustice is perpetrated in other nations, there is no or little outcry. All the good and generosity Israel displays to all its inhabitants, even its Arab citizens, is generally ignored, while it is accused of activities that it did not do. Many have noted that anti-Semitism in recent days is reaching levels that are comparable to that during the Holocaust.

If we understand Replacement Theology, we might appreciate how the existence of a Jewish state in the Land of Israel poses a spiritual threat to Christians who believe that Jesus abrogated the Old Testament. If Christianity truly replaced Judaism as the true religion, the Jews should be weak, poor, or cease to exist. If the Jewish people are strong and the Land of Israel is vibrant in Jewish hands, the promises contained in the Old Testament may still be operative making some Christians fear that their power and domination of the world as they have achieved is vulnerable.

The lesser known theology guiding the Christian world is known as "Dispensationalism," which found a spiritual home more in the United

States than in Europe, though there were always and continue to be pockets of it in Europe. After the Holocaust and the establishment of the State of Israel, much of the Christian world in America engaged in an introspective process that led to the rejection of Replacement Theology. The State of Israel as a refuge for the Jewish people was seen as the fulfillment of ancient biblical prophecies and a clear indication and testimony of the faithfulness of God. Christians who follow "Dispensationalism" affirm that God did not reject the Jewish people and Christianity does not replace Judaism. Furthermore, these Christians believe that they owe the Jewish people much for providing them with the essentials of their faith: Jesus was a Jew, as were the apostles, and Judaism gave them the Old Testament and inspiring prophets. These Christians recognize the holiness of the Jewish people, as well as the State of Israel, and they as Christians see their role and mission as one of service to the Jewish people and protection of the State of Israel. This trend within Christianity does seem to be a fulfillment of the prophecy of Rebecca.

Dispensationalism forms the foundation of Christian Zionism. Israel's best friends are found in the Christian evangelical community of America. Not only do Christians give millions of dollars each year to Israel, they visit Israel on spiritual pilgrimage in even greater numbers than Jews. These Christians believe that the blessings of America may be attributed to a pro-Israel policy as stated in Genesis 12:3. It is therefore important and in America's best interests that America support Israel. The idea of being a fair broker between the Arabs and the Jews in settling the Middle-East conflict is not, however, one that is embraced by evangelical Christians.

Rachel and Leah and Bilha and Zilpa

Rachel and Leah, the daughters of Laban, along with their less known handmaidens Bilha and Zilpa, were the wives of Jacob and the mothers of the Twelve Tribes of Israel. Rachel and Leah, along with Bilha and Zilpa, represent the principal archetypes for women, the *tikkun,* the fixing of Eve and Lilith, and the pathway for the revelation and healing of the feminine.

Rachel, known for her revealed beauty, is associated with the *Sephira* (divine emanation) of *Malkut*, and is a reincarnation of Eve. *Malkut* is the revelation of the *Shechinah* in this world. As we learned earlier, *Malkut* initiates the arousal from below. That is one of the reasons that Rachel is buried on the road and that crying at her grave is deemed to be so powerful. When the Jewish people are in distress, it is to Mother Rachel that they turn. Gatherings of thousands of women are held on the *yahrzeit* (death anniversary) of Rachel. No such gathering would take place for Leah. Mother Rachel as *Malkut,* as the *Shechinah,* is viewed as the intercessor for the Jewish people in times of trouble. As stated in the prophecy of Jeremiah, "A voice is heard in Ramah, lamentations and bitter crying. Rachel is weeping for her children; she refuses to be consoled for her children, for they are gone.... Hashem said, 'Restrain your voice from weeping and your eyes from tears, for there is a reward for your accomplishments.... They will return from the land of their enemy'" (Jeremiah 31:15).

The Rachel archetype is associated with *Mayim Nukvim*, the lower waters, also known as the *Shechinah.* Rachel and women embodying the Rachel archetype must not be seen as entirely passive recipients. Rachel's very beauty, her openness, and her vulnerability, is responsible for stimulating and arousing *Zeir Anpin* (The Holy One Blessed be He) or Jacob to bestow light and blessing upon her and the world. When Jacob first met Rachel, the Bible tells us that he "kissed" her and lifted up his voice and wept. According to the Tanya, Rachel represents "Knesset Israel," the Community of Israel, the fount of all souls. Jacob by lifting up his voice and weeping awakens and draws compassion to the Jewish people. By kissing Rachel he unites the Jewish people with *Yihud Elyon* (Higher Unity) of the Light of *Ain Sof.* It is Rachel who awakens this depth of love.

Because of the *Sephira* of *Malkut* that is associated with Rachel has no light of its own, it is the ultimate recipient and stimulator. Just like the moon that reflects the light of the sun, a woman who is primarily a Rachel archetype reflects the light of her husband. Not having light of her own must not be seen as indicative of low self-esteem, spiritual deficiency, or lack of intrinsic worthiness. It is actually the opposite, for it is necessary for a person on the path of holiness to be able to surrender one's sense of self so as to reflect the light of God. Of course, one first must have a sense of self to be able to surrender. Surrender is not about being a doormat at all, but to have the courage to nullify oneself before that which is greater than you. For example, if you were a good student, you would place yourself in a position of receptivity before your teacher and humbly be willing to absorb the teachings presented to you. By your questions and thirst for learning, you would bring forth greater teachings than would otherwise be given. This is the role of *Malkut*.

Leah was Rachel's twin sister, though slightly older than Rachel. It is said that she was intended to marry Esau, who was Jacob's older twin. Leah is associated kabbalistically with the *Sephira* of *Malkut* of Ema (*Binah*), the Divine Mother. Leah is a greater revelation of the Divine Feminine than Rachel, even higher and greater than Jacob. In this capacity, she exerts an influence upon Jacob and Rachel. According to the Arizel, Leah is also considered the reincarnation of a refined and purified Lilith. When Leah "purchased a night with Jacob and went out to greet him with the words, 'It is to me that you must come for I have clearly hired you with my son's *dudaim* (fertility herbs).' So he lay with her that night" (Genesis 30:16). Leah took the initiative in sexual relations in a manner that was reminiscent of Lilith, according to the Arizel. Her assertiveness may have made her less desirable to Jacob. Leah might have reminded Jacob of his mother Rebecca and that was why he was not able to love her in the way that Leah so much wanted. Both Leah and his mother Rebecca were assertive women who used trickery when they felt necessary. They each coerced Jacob to do what he would not have done on his own.

Because Jacob represents *Zeir Anpin,* or Adam, he is the connector between the higher and lower spiritual worlds. Just as Adam had two wives, Jacob had two wives. Much of the Zohar is concerned with the dance between *Malkut*, *Binah,* and *Zeir Anpin.*

Meditative Practices for Rachel and Leah: The Two Faces of the Shechinah

Rachel and Leah, according to Rabbi Isaac Luria, are not to be viewed simply as mortal human beings but primarily as representative of the two faces of the *Shechinah,* the Divine Feminine within the Godhead. Leah is the higher *Shechinah,* Rachel is the lower *Shechinah,* and Jacob is *Zeir Anpin,* the Divine Masculine, "The Holy One Blessed be He', who makes the connection between *Binah* (Leah) and *Malkut,* (Rachel). It is for that reason that Kabbalists recite daily prayers for their *tikkun* (fixing) of Rachel and Leah. Each day when Kabbalists wear *tefillin,* they meditate on making unification between the higher spiritual worlds with our physical world. The box of *tefillin* that is placed on the head represents Leah, and the box on the arm represents Rachel.

Kabbalistic Meditation for Tefillin

Through imagining themselves in the place of *Zeir Anpin,* Kabbalists with their *tefillin* envision Rachel, the lower *Shechinah,* standing next to Jacob (themselves) with her head only reaching to his chest. *Zeir Anpin,* the Divine Masculine (Jacob), receives sustenance from higher *Partzufim* (Faces of God), *Chokmah* and *Binah,* who are also called *Abba* (Father) and *Ima* (Mother). Through permutations of the Divine Name associated with these *Sephirot,* the light of *Binah* is then transferred through *Zeir Anpin* (Leah's union with Jacob) and then this higher light is transferred to Rachel (*Malkut*).

Because Rachel has no light of her own, like the new moon, Rachel is totally dependent on *Zeir Anpin* and receives her sustenance through the hole in the center of his chest, the heart of *Zeir Anpin.* Leah, on the other hand, is spiritually higher than Jacob, so we can envision her feet resting on Rachel's head. Not dependent on *Zeir Anpin* (Jacob) for sustenance, Leah receives directly from the Divine Mother, who she is identified with, and she gives in turn light to *Zeir Anpin* through their union. Since Leah is so much higher than Jacob or Rachel, she is also not as grounded, or connected to the practical things in life, in the way that Rachel is. Both Rachel and Leah are necessary. So in this meditation, the connection between Rachel and Leah, the *Shechinah* (*Malkut*) and the Divine Mother (*Binah*) is strengthened. (As an aside, I always encourage my male friends and clients to put on *tefillin* on a daily basis to strengthen their positive masculine loving energy.)

A Kabbalistic Meditative Practice with the Four Mothers

Kabbalistically, Zilpa and Bilha, the handmaidens of Rachel and Leah, embody the *Ohr Makif*, the surrounding light of God, whereas Rachel and Leah embodied the *Ohr Penima*, the more inner concentrated light. The light of *Ohr Makif* is transcendent, large, and expansive, without bounds, while the light of *Ohr Penima* is concentrated, smaller, hidden, and constricted. Taken together, these four women embody four aspects of the Divine Feminine that correspond to the four worlds in the Kabbalistic paradigm.

Meditation on the Four Mothers

Rachel corresponds to the world of *Assiyah*, this physical world, represented by the final letter *Heh* of the Divine Name YHVH; Bilha, the world of *Yetzirah*, the world of the heart and angels, represented by the letter *Vav*; Leah, the world of *Beriyah*, the world of the soul, and the archangels, represented by the first *Heh* of YHVH; and Zilpa to the world of *Atzilut,* the highest spiritual world with the greatest proximity to *Ain Sof,* the limitless light of the Divine, represented by the *Yud* of YHVH.

Sit or stand in meditation. Take a few moments to center yourself, letting go of extraneous thoughts, so the mind is quiet. With each breath, allow the body to relax, to open more and more. Imagine yourself as an empty vessel with a capacity to truly receive.

Meditate on the selflessness and devotion of beloved Rachel who willingly gave her secret signs to Leah so her sister would not be embarrassed. Meditate on Mother Rachel who sits outside the city limits of Jerusalem to pray for her beloved children. Meditate on Mother Rachel who so much wanted to have children that she was willing to risk her life to do so. Feel her and identify with her and her beautiful qualities. Focus on taking deep breaths and absorb the love and blessings of communing with our beloved Mother Rachel. Then visualize the final *Hay* of the Tetragrammaton, the four Hebrew letters usually transliterated as YHWH, used as a biblical proper name for God, that represent Rachel and this physical world. See this letter shining brightly on your inner screen with your eyes closed. This letter represents *Malkut* (*Shechinah*), and the arousal from below. Continue to breathe and meditate on your yearning to receive. Then place the letter *Hay* by your waist and legs.

Now meditate on the selflessness and devotion of beloved Mother Bilha who lovingly served Rachel without thinking of any personal reward. Meditate on Mother Bilha who was constantly loving, and seeking to make the connection between the higher worlds and this lower world. Then visualize the letter *Vav,* which represents Bilha, and connects the pelvis, the genitals, (*Yesod*) to the heart (*Tipheret*) to the crown (*Keter*).

Bring your awareness to the top of the head, the seat of the higher self, the soul, and *Binah* (Divine Mother), and meditate on the love and devotion of Mother Leah, who is so beyond this world yet yearns to descend and have a place in this physical world. Meditate on Mother Leah, identify with her, connect with her, feel her love and determination to do what is necessary to actualize her holy purpose. Then visualize the letter *Hay,* which represents Leah, resting on the top of the head.

Now meditate on Mother Zilpa, that joyous blissful feminine energy that is so pure and beyond this world. Zilpa is willing to descend into this physical world, not because of any need on her part, but only to radiate love and joy. Meditate on Mother Zilpa, identify with her, commune with her. Then place the letter *Yud*, which represents Zilpa, about six to twelve inches above the top of the head.

Repeat as long as you like the meditation on the mothers and the letters of the Divine Name as you travel through the spiritual worlds and make their connection with the physical world.

A Kabbalistic Meditative Practice
Crying for the Shechinah:
Tikkun Rachel and Tikkun Leah

Crying for the *Shechinah* opens the gates for grace that purify and heal not only ourselves but the whole world. After the destruction of the Holy Temple (*Beis Hamikdash*), several prayers called *Tikkun Hasot* (midnight supplication) to be said in the middle of the night, twelve hours after sunrise, was established for Jews to pray, plead, weep, and mourn for the Holy Temple. *Tikkun Hasot* has two parts: *Tikkun Rachel* and *Tikkun Leah*. *Tikkun Rachel* consists of Psalm 137, 79, Lamentations 5, Isaiah 63:15, Isaiah 62:6–9, Psalm 12:14–15, and Psalm 147:2. *Tikkun Leah* consists of Psalms 42, 43, 20–24, 67,111, 51, and 126. It is customary to sit on the floor, place ash on one's forehead, and wear a sackcloth garment. This is a most powerful spiritual practice. With the exception of several holidays, Sabbath, and other designated times, Kabbalists do these prayers nightly followed by hours of Kabbalistic learning, and concluded with morning *davening*.

The destruction of the Holy Temple diminished the revelation of the feminine and caused the *Shechinah,* the Divine Feminine, to once again be in exile with the Jewish people. Rachel (the lower world) and Leah (the higher world) together represent the Holy Temple, that precious and holy place in the world in which the Divine is fully embodied in this world, the place where Heaven and Earth meet. Through the particular service of the Jewish people conducted in the Holy Temple, all the nations of the world were blessed. Since its destruction two thousand years ago, Jews pray daily for its rebuilding. It is said that in the messianic times the nations of the world will ask the Jewish people to rebuild the Holy Temple because they will know what a source of blessing it is to them.

Dina
Dina Transforms Lilith

In the Bible, as we learned earlier, Dina is called "Leah's daughter." Dina likely identified primarily with her mother because her father lived in Rachel/Bilha's tent and he might not have spent as much time with her as she wanted. Like her brothers, but perhaps even more so, within her heart Dina may have carried her mother's anguish of not feeling so loved by her father. Additionally, Dina may have also been more estranged from her father than her brothers because it was probably easier for Jacob to father the sons he had with Leah, and less comfortable for him to father a daughter, Dina, who was herself a miniature Leah.

The pain of her mother's rejection by her father Jacob and her own possible rejection may actually have emboldened Dina to venture beyond the boundaries of what she knew would be acceptable. Dina would have been safe as long as she stayed in the parameters of the holiness of the family. Archetypical Leah women often value freedom and self-discovery more than security. Dina similarly needed to explore beyond the narrow confines of what was available to her.

Dina is, however, called Leah's daughter in the Bible because, according to the Arizel (Rabbi Yitzhak Luria) , Dina carried some of the dross from Lilith that remained in Leah that still needed purification. That may be why she was raped and harmed. Though the rape by Shechem was horrifying to her, it may actually have purified and cleansed her. A woman, according to the Arizel, is purified by rape while a man is made impure by raping a woman.

Interestingly enough, the Talmud actually blames Jacob for Dina's rape, rather than Dina. In preparing for an encounter with Esau, Jacob hid Dina in a chest, under lock and key, because he feared that his brother Esau might be attracted to his daughter and demand to marry her. Because Esau embodied some of the *nahash* (serpent) energy within him, and Dina contained some of the Lilith energy, there would have been attraction between the two of them. Jacob knew that so he hid his daughter to protect her. In its discussion of this episode, the Talmud suggests that Dina could actually have been the soul mate to Esau and that she would have been able to facilitate his *tikkun* because she contained within her both the holiness of Jacob and the residue of the *klippah* (shell) of Lilith from her mother. Because Dina did not marry Esau due to Jacob's intervention, she became vulnerable to Shechem, another embodiment of the *nashash*. Consequently and unfortunately, Dina was raped rather than married. And the *tikkun* of Esau did not take place.

Dina as the Shechinah

Dina's story is very important for understanding the secret legacy of biblical women. The Zohar views Dina as the *Shechinah,* the Divine Feminine, in her generation, just as the previous biblical women occupied this position before her. Like her foremothers, Dina wrestles with evil and makes a major contribution, at such a young age, toward the *"tikkun* of the feminine." In the end, Dina's story is redemptive and inspiring.

Both Sarah and Rebecca, like Dina, were also kidnapped when they also entered lands of immorality. Sarah and Rebecca at the time of their kidnapping were, however, older, married, and had the needed spiritual protection to escape unharmed. They entered and departed from contact with impurity without harm. Dina, on the other hand, was a very young girl, alone, vulnerable, innocent, and unprepared, and was indeed harmed.

Dina's kidnapping, as the previous kidnappings of Sarah and Rebecca, may be viewed as an reenactment of the seminal story of Eve (Chava) and the serpent (the *nahash*). The *nahash* refers to an entity that is ruled primarily by Samael, or Satan. Shechem is called the *nahash* in the Zohar. Lavan, the father of Rachel and Leah, is also viewed as an expression of the *nahash*. The Pharaohs who kidnapped Sarah and Rebecca were also considered embodiments of the *nahash*. The work of the holy mothers who embody the Divine Feminine, as begun by Eve and continued by Sarah and Rebecca, Rachel and Leah, and now Dina, has been to descend into the places of evil and impurity to uplift the fallen divine sparks there so as to transform, weaken, and destroy evil by their very presence.

The story of Dina must also be understood very much as a Jewish story, foreshadowing the perils to be confronted by the Jewish people, when they are exiled from their homeland and forced to reside in other countries that host the most impure and evil people and forces on the planet. Wherever the Jewish people go, they bring blessing. Unfortunately, after a certain amount of time, jealousy occurs and anti-Semitism rises, until it reaches a point that the factions within these countries rise up against the Jewish people to persecute and/or annihilate them. Eventually, through miracles and divine intervention, these countries are destroyed, weakened, or transformed, the Jewish people survive, yet often it is at the cost of much Jewish suffering and blood. Like Dina, Jews have suffered and died for the "sins" of the nations. That may be why the Bible calls her the daughter of Jacob only after the rape.

The Patriarch's Jacob's entire life was filled with trouble and challenge. Rabbi Samson Raphael Hirsch's commentary on Psalm 20 verse 2 " May Hashem answer you on the day of distress. May the God of Jacob fortify you" offers us the spiritual strength that Jacob accessed whenever we are similarly brought to grief and pain.

The Reincarnations of Dina and Shechem

According to Kabbalah of the Arizel, Dina and Shechem reincarnated later in the bodies of Zimri, the chief prince in the tribe of Shimon, and Cozbi, a Midianite princess. For this encounter, Dina was the non-Jewish princess and Shechem is the Jewish prince. This second and important meeting of these souls took place during the time when the Jewish people were wandering in the desert. Balak, king of Moab, had asked Balaam, an incarnation of Lavan, the father-in-law of Jacob, to curse the Jewish people.

Not being successful in cursing, Balaam devised a scheme to weaken the spiritual protection of the Jewish people by ordering the Midianite women to seduce the Jewish men into idolatry. Though it was said that Cozbi really wanted to seduce Moses, she settled for Zimri, the head of the tribe of Shimon, when Moses rejected her offers.

According to the Arizel, the Shimeon part of Zimri was drawn to Cozbi because she energetically carried the Lilith energy that was reminiscent of Dina and Leah. So captivated by Cozbi, Zimri urged the Jewish people to intermarry with the Midianite women to merge these two cultures and usher in a new dawn for both cultures. To initiate this new order, Zimri, an old man, and Cozbi, a beautiful young woman, stood at the tent of Moses to engage in public sexual relations that may have resembled the Goddess sex orgy worship of Midian. A plague ensued and Pinchas, a young zealot, then thrust a spear into the joined bodies of Zimri and Cozbi, killed them instantly, and the plague ended.

According to the Arizel, the souls of Shechem and Dina again reappear in the Talmud as Rabbi Akiva and his nameless second wife, the former wife of Turnus Rufus, the Wicked. In this story, she, however, converts willingly before marriage, but in the end, Rabbi Akiva dies a painful death by the hands of the Romans. Like Jacob, Rabbi Akiva also interestingly enough has two wives; the first one was Rachel, who was a total embodiment of the selfless beautiful Rachel archetype, and the second wife, an embodiment of Leah. With this marriage, the great Rabbi Akiva helps to complete the *tikkun* of Leah and through her Lilith.

Miriam, Batya and Chana
(Kabbalistic and midrashic material incorporated into interview)

Esther

According to the Chida, Rabbi Chaim Yosef David Azulai, and others, Esther was a reincarnation of Eve, and the serpent was embodied in Haman. The story of Adam and Eve is once again reenacted. The *Midrash* states Hadassah (Hebrew for "myrtle") is another name for Esther. "In the same way that myrtle has a sweet smell but a bitter taste, Esther was sweet for Mordecai yet bitter to Haman" (Esther Rabbah 6:5). Esther as a reincarnation (*gilgul*) of Eve was bitter to Haman, who was the serpent who had brought her to sin, and sweet to Mordecai, who was a reincarnation of Jacob, who was a reincarnation of Adam.

There are some *midrashic* teachings that address Esther's sexual relations with King Asherverous. How did she maintain her purity and worthiness to receive the "holy spirit" and embody the *Shechinah* when she was forced to have sexual relations with such an evil man? One popular teaching in the oral tradition is that Hashem put in her place a "double" with her identical image so it wasn't really she who was having relations with the king. Though that may be quite possible, anything is possible, what I understand this to mean is that the soul of Esther was so elevated that she was truly not affected by sexual relations with such a despicable man like the king. Because she was so identified with the higher realms of her soul, during sexual relations, it was like she was not really there, even though her body was present. Esther was said to be totally passive in sexual relations, except when she went to the king on Mordecai's command. By initiating sexual relations with the king at that time, she was said to have committed adultery and forfeited the possibility of returning to her marriage with Mordecai.

In the month of Adar, in the week before the holiday of Purim occurs, we are told to read the following: "Remember what Amalek did to you. You shall erase the memory of Amalek from beneath the heavens, you shall not forget" (Deuteromy.25:17–19). It is considered so important that the rabbis have asked that everyone be present to hear these words. Historically, Amalek was a descendent of Esau who had sworn to hate and kill the Jews. His tribe, the Amalekites, waged war on the Jewish people as they wandered in the desert. The Amalekites went out of their way to battle the Israelites because they could not bear that they had a special connection to God. The spiritual energy of Amalek is so bent on the destruction of what is positive and good, on destroying the spiritual entity and integrity of the Jewish people, even if its proponents receive no benefit from Israel's destruction and it costs them their lives. The hatred that Amalek feels toward the Jewish people is not logical and cannot be placated with bribes.

In every generation, throughout time, Amalek, as the sworn enemy of the Jewish people, tries to destroy the Jewish people, spiritually and even physically. The face of Amalek has changed throughout time, but is embodied in anti-Semitism. Amalek was Hitler of Germany, Amalek was Nebuchadnezzar of Babylonia, and it appears now that Amalek is now Ahmadinejad of Iran who is continually threatening to wipe Israel off the map.

Haman was considered a descendent energetically and even biologically from Amalek. Haman was identified as the son of Hammedatha, the Agagite (Esther 3:1–2). In Shmuel I (15: 1–9) "He took Agag, the King of Amalekites." Queen Esther rectified the previous shortcoming of her ancestor King Saul, who due to misplaced compassion, failed to kill Agag, the king of the Amalekites, as he was divinely ordered to do so. Because of this weakness, Haman was born.

According to my teacher Reb Shlomo Carlebach of blessed memory, Haman is connected to the verse in the biblical story of Adam and Eve when God asks Adam, "Did you eat from the Tree of Knowledge," "*Hameen ha etz*"? This is the hidden reference to Haman, who embodied energetically the power of Amalek, the same evil that the original serpent (the *nahash*) represented in the biblical story. This is the primordial evil that Esther subdued in her time. Though Eve may have fallen a victim to the seduction of the serpent, Sarah, Rebecca, and Dina encountered it, Esther as a reincarnation of Eve and Sarah returns to subdue this primordial evil. In this battle, she gave her very life as she remained married to the king. As the queen, she exerted much influence over the king and gave birth to a son, Darius, who later became king and went on to liberate Jerusalem and rebuild the Holy Temple as his mother had instructed

In the common usage, Amalek also refers to the negative force, the *yetzer hara*, the evil inclination, within people. Amalek has the same numerical value as *safek,* the Hebrew word for "doubt." The energy of Amalek causes us to doubt ourselves and our capacity to accomplish what we want to do, especially in regard to spiritual growth. It is the evil inclination within us that makes us self-critical, judgmental, fearful, and vulnerable to depression. The energy of Amalek says, "Things just happen," or "Everything is random." Amalek is also the negative inclination within people that is spiteful, jealous, and willing to be hard on oneself or others even though it serves no purpose and will bring no benefits. Addiction is an expression of this evil inclination. Generally speaking, people who have internalized the evil inclination and even identify themselves with their ego rather than their soul tend to be self-critical, judgmental, and filled with fear and doubt. Amalek is the force within a person who wants to receive only for himself. Amalek has won this inner war if these people cannot take the steps to move forward in their lives with faith and joy.

Within every person is an ongoing battle between the good inclination (the soul) and the evil inclination (ego). To become a true servant of God, we must wage an internal battle between the inner soul, who wants to nullify herself, and the ego, who wants to control, receive, be recognized and honored. This is a lifelong process requiring much work and divine assistance. Though we may not fight the battle with the external Amalek, we do fight this battle internally, within ourselves. The story of Purim reminds us that we can most effectively fight the evil inclination internalized and externalized when we are united with others. Evil feeds on fear and doubt of the ego mind and a sense of separation from others.

According to Chassidus, the teachings of Chassidic Rebbes, evil does not have any real existence because only God has real existence. In a section of the Tanya, *Shaar Hayichud* (Gate of Unity), the Alter Rebbe provided the following illustration to explain this idea: Compare the light of the sun to the sun itself. The light may spread a great distance, but what is it in relation to the sun? The light is a part of the sun and has no existence by itself. So similarly, this world and all its inhabitants is nothing in relation to God. If I feel that I am a ray of God's light, I experience oneness with God. We may like to think that we are independent but we are not. Our separation, our independence, is only an illusion. In the higher realms, there is only God.

The final destruction of Amalek is anticipated for the messianic time in a battle that asks us all to participate. Some battles are to be fought with guns and bombs, but the greater battles are ones of consciousness. They must be fought with spiritual weapons like joy, faith, and a little holy wine to "cut off evil " at its root, for evil feeds only on fear, doubt, illusion, and falsehood. This is what we learn in the celebration of Purim. Though we may not be called to the front lines, nevertheless, we must all utilize our spiritual weapons to engage in this battle that is also taking place within ourselves and in our small corner of the world. From our experience of September 11th, we also know firsthand that our enemies are quite willing to fight their war on civilian populations. There is ultimately no physical protection from evil.

Each year, during the month of Adar, and especially during the celebration of Purim, the full moon of that month, the energy of Amalek, is erased a little bit more by the joy and love that we open up to on this day. On Purim, we send gifts to our friends, we party, we eat, we drink, and all these actions that you think of as physical and mundane are actually the most holy. Joy and love are actually considered powerful spiritual weapons.

In the Purim story, God's deliverance comes in the midst of feasting, drinking, and sexual intrigue, revealing a most important teaching that God is everywhere and in everything. For many, there is a perceived split between the spiritual and material. Purim teaches us that God occupies all realms equally. Since the miracle of Purim took place through parties and alcohol, we reenact these scenes. Purim is party time. There are concerts, spoofs, and a tremendous spirit of joy and love, and the widespread use of alcohol.

On Purim, the rabbis encourage people to drink so they do not know the difference between "Blessed is Mordecai" and "Cursed is Haman." These phrases have the same gematria so as to indicate their equivalency. Why would the rabbis elevate alcoholic drinking so much? Whether we drink so much or not, the rabbis are reminding us of a very powerful spiritual practice to transform our lives and the world. To see God in everyone and everything that happens is to reveal the oneness of God. To know the oneness of God is to defeat the illusion of separation, falsehood and evil. Purim signals a return to the unity consciousness of the Garden of Eden, that existed prior to the Eating of the Tree.

The name Esther is derived from the root *hester*, meaning "hidden" or "concealed." Megillat Esther, the Scroll of Esther, is a revelation of what is hidden. God's name is not mentioned in the scroll at all, yet divine providence is obvious through the series of circumstances that take place. We only have to read between the lines to see God's hand at play. The word Purim means "lots" to make it appear that everything is happening by chance, but the whole story of Purim comes to teach us that nothing is by chance. Purim is the holiest day because it is clear that God is masquerading as people and circumstances in the whole story. The rabbis have taught that Purim is higher than *Yom Kippur*. *Yom Kippur* is a day like Purim. What we accomplish on *Yom Kippur* through fasting and intense prayer, we accomplish even more on Purim through drinking, partying, and giving gifts to friends and poor people.

According to the teachings of Rabbi Shlomo Elyahiv (1814–1926), one of the greatest teachers of Kabbalah, Avraham Sutton records in his book

Purim Light, that for six thousand years, the light of *Arich Anpin* (Infinity or Higher Faces of the Divine), *Abba,* and *Ima* have flowed down into *Zeir Anpin* and *Nukva* (the root of all creations) only in accord with their limited capacity. It is in this sense that *Zeir Anpin* and *Nukva* are said to dominate during the entire six thousand years of this world, which are associated with the six *Sephirot, Chesed, Gevurah, Tipheret, Netzach, Hod,* and *Yesod,* and the six initial days of creation. With the *Shefa* (divine illumination)that *Malkut* (kingdom or *Shechinah*) receives from these six sephirot, She governs and oversees all that transpires in the lower worlds. Everything that *Ain Sof* (the Infinite God) does in our world, it does through *Nukva,* known as *Shechinah. Nukva* also descends into the realm of evil to return sparks that she extracts from the realm of evil allowing them to be rectified. There are times when the higher modes of *Abba* and *Ima* are revealed directly to us in the form of a divine revelation or miracle. These times are exceptional because when the higher revelations of *Ain Sof* are revealed directly to us, there can be no free choice. Infinite mercy and love pours down gloriously upon us irregardless of our merit. In these kind of miraculous times, the face of God known as *Ha-Kodesh Boruch Hu* is diminished, even hidden. **We receive directly and lovingly from *Ima*, the Divine Mother.**

This revelation of *Abba* and *Ima* to *Malkut* is what happened in the story of Purim. This is a kabbalistic explanation of why *Ha-Kodesh Boruch Hu* (the Divine Name) was not mentioned in the *Megillas Esther* read on Purim.

The second *Hay* in the Divine Name that corresponds to *Malkut* will rise to the first *Hay* Bina and there will be a reunion between the two. This is the healing of Rachel and Leah.

Divine Light will flow to people irregardless of their merit. **The Shechinah is revealed.** This will be the return to the Garden of Eden.

Chapter Twelve

Meditations and Contemplations on the Shechinah:

Make Yourself a Dwelling Place for Her

1.

Before there was time, before there was space, there was only *Ain Sof.* Limitless Light. That was all there was, only Ain Sof. There was nothing to bestow goodness upon, no one to be known by. The light of *Ain Sof* contracted and withdrew to create a void that would allow worlds to emerge as receptacles for the light of *Ain Sof.* A line known as the *kav,* a rod of light, was extended into the void to sustain creation within *Ain Sof.* Not too much light to overwhelm creation, but enough to sustain it as the light became increasingly differentiated. The vessels that contained the light are also of the light. Everything is of the light, even the forces that oppose the light. Though divine light is most concealed in our physical world, it was our physical world where the divine intention is most realized. If the light would be too revealed, there would be no choice but to love God.

The goodness, the love, and the light of God are so overwhelming that we would be totally defenseless to choose otherwise. Only in this world of concealment is love possible. Love requires freedom, the free will to choose love. Because of God's concealment, we feel a separate existence. Otherwise, there would be no one to love God in return. God wants our love too. We are told to love God. Hear the words within you, "Love me with all your heart, soul, and might." Hear the divine call for love resounding within you and rebounding back to God. God lives in your open loving heart. There is only one call to love. God's call to love is at the root of all expressions of love.

2.

Imagine you can travel back in time before there was time and space. Visualize 100 years, 10,000 years, 100,000 years, travel back through time, until you realize that you can conceive no further. You touch a place that is called Infinity. Beyond Infinity is *Ain Sof.* With your imagination, travel forward in time, ten years from now, 100 years, 10,000 years, until you once again touch a place called Infinity. Beyond Infinity is Ain Sof, Limitless Light.

In your imagination, travel eastward, journey past China, leaving the orbit of our earth into the galaxy until you recognize that your imagination can take you no further and you again touch a place that we will call Infinity. Beyond Infinity is *Ain Sof.* Now travel westward, going past California, Hawaii, and out again into space, continuing as far as you can visualize, until you arrive once again at Infinity. Beyond Infinity, there is *Ain Sof.* Repeat this meditation in all directions. Travel north and south, up and down similarly in your consciousness. Arrive in consciousness at a place that you recognize as Infinity. Know that even beyond infinity is Ain Sof.

Ain Sof surrounds Infinity. Then, sit, stand, and live in the expanded perception of *Ain Sof* and yet be simultaneously fully aware of the individualized expression of life that you know as you. You are alive in the middle of what you have identified as Infinity of Time and Space. Every point, every person, is the center point, the mid-point in Infinity.

Repeat silently to yourself, "I am the center point in *Ain Sof.* I am in the center of God." Internalize this awareness. Breathe and expand or contract your consciousness as much as you like, to the highest heights, to the deepest depths, to the greatest joy, to the most painful despair, yet you still remain within *Ain Sof.* There is truly nowhere else to be. *Ain Sof* encompasses all that was, is, and will be, in all places simultaneously.

Just as you were born out of your mother's womb, imagine that you are in God's womb. This is the truth. You are in the womb of the Divine

Mother. This awareness is called the *Makom,* "the Place of the World." You feel yourself unconditionally loved and embraced when you live in the awareness of *Makom.*

"Bridle your mouth from speaking, and your heart from thinking, return to the Place," instructions from Sefer Yetzirah, the ancient manual for Kabbalistic meditation.

"Be Still and Know that I am God," Psalm 65.

3.

Your soul, created out of the light of *Ain Sof,* descended into this physical world to reveal a greater light for light shines brightest amidst the darkness. It was a dangerous mission because it required that you forget what was previously known and discover it once again anew.

For a limited time of years while you occupy a physical body, you have been charged to bring the light of the upper worlds to the lower worlds, to make unifications between the physical and spiritual. Godliness is revealed through these unifications. Your spiritual wings have been clipped while you occupy a physical body so you remain grounded enough to fulfill your mission. You can still however ascend to the upper worlds when you take time to quiet the mind, open the heart, and attune to your soul frequency.

Listen, deep inside, to Her voice, within your own heart and soul. She will speak of Her thirst for the light and even of her yearning to return home to the place of luminous light revealed. She will remind you of your mission, and guide you to fulfill your purpose. Reveal Godliness in your midst. Be God's candle and shine the light for all to see. What one can do in the physical world is very great. Do not delay. The world is depending on you.

4.

Because you now live in a physical body, you may lose perspective from time to time, and entertain illusions that you are separate, independent, and limited. You are not. You may feel separate, but as the divine soul, your true essence, you are not. You may feel yourself an independent entity, but you, as the divine soul, are a part of God. You are interconnected with all of Creation. Your reality is not confined to the physical world nor limited by the five senses you have been gifted. You may feel limited by time and space, but you are not.

Even though you live in a designated space known as a physical body, you need not be limited or defined by it. You may live in a material world, but you are not of it. You are so much more. You are an expression of *Ain Sof*. You have even been told that you are created in the likeness and image of the Divine.

Repeat, "I am created in the image and likeness of the Divine." Internalize this message by repeating many times and meditating upon it often. You are not separate from the Light that created you, permeates, sustains, and surrounds you. You are a ray of the light of *Ain Sof.*

Meditate to enter the doorway into the consciousness of *Malkut,* or *Shechinah,* who lives within you, at your core, in your heart of hearts, as you. See Her through the garments that She wears in the world. Everything that happens is a message from Her. She is homeless, so let Her enter your heart and take residence there. There is no Holy Temple for Her to dwell in yet, but She does live within an open heart.

When you truly welcome Her into your life and invite Her to reside within you, She is the most holy loving treasured guest who will never leave you. Because She is faithful, She is with you at all times, in the good and in the bad, even when you are unaware of Her. From time to time, know that it is She who orchestrates events in your life so you will call out to Her, and receive all the love and wisdom that She has hidden away for you. It was for this love and knowledge you were created. Words are inadequate to express our appreciation for all that is bestowed upon us each day.

5.

The *Shechinah* is not an entity separate from us. She is us. She is the sum total of all the souls who ever were and will be. She is hidden within us, yet She stirs our hearts to love. So full of love and compassion for us, She adapts herself to be available and present for each of us. She is the love we share with others. When our hearts are broken, She sheds tears though us and with us. And when we cry, we cry for Her too.

She was shattered in the primordial breaking of the vessels, and descended into the lowest places of darkness, where Her light was entrapped, imprisoned. Instead of donning beautiful garments befitting her, She is covered with *klippot,* shells that entrap and imprison Her light. She is with us and she is us. Our pain is Her pain. "I will go down to Egypt with you. When you are in a contracted place, I am also contracted and I am with you." She suffers when we suffer. How tragic it is to devote so much energy to destroy Her creation when She wants to give us so much love. In the End of Days, She will be redeemed and we will bask in Her love.

6.

The Holy Torah begins with *"Bereshit Bara Elohim,"* which means "with a beginning was *Elohim* created." *Bereshit* means *Bara* and *Sheet,* which means Elohim first created six, which refers to the creation of the six *Sephirot: Chesed, Gevurah, Tipheret, Netzach, Hod,* and *Yesod.* These six *Sephirot* constitute *Zeir Anpin,* known as *Ha-Kodesh Boruch Hu,* *"the Holy One Blessed be He."* The other higher *Sephirot were and are* still *concealed,* beyond *creation. Zeir Anpin* is called the Small Face in comparison to *Arich Anpin* (the Long Face) and *Atik Yomin* (the Ancient One of Days), also called "Great Grandfather and Grandmother," who remain beyond creation, both filled with even greater infinite love and mercy that extends to all regardless of merit.

The Zohar teaches us so beautifully that "The Hebrew letters *Aleph, Lamed,* and *Hei* (in the word *Elokim*) are drawn from above, from *Binah,* who is the Divine Mother, downward to *Malkut*, "it is as if a mother lends her clothes to her daughter who is *Malkut.*"

7.

Our God, known as Hashem, literally means "The Name", is *Yud , Hay, Vav,* and *Hay. Hashem* is both masculine and feminine. The Tetragrammaton is the code to convey this deepest wisdom. The apex of the *Yud* is *Arich Anpin.* The *Yud* refers to *Abba,* the Hay is *Ima,,* the *Vav* is *Zeir Anpin,* and the final *Hay* is *Malkut, Nukva*, or the *Shechinah.* Hashem is balanced, male and female, upper and lower. When we are aligned with Hashem, we are balanced too. Zeir Anpin is commonly known as the Holy One Blessed be He. Nukva is known as the Shechinah. HaShem is both masculine and feminine.

8.

Upon being inseminated by *'Abba'*, the Divine Father (*Chokmah*)," *Ima*" the Divine Mother (*Binah*) went through contractions to birth you and this entire magnificent, awesome, beyond beautiful and amazing physical reality as a garden of delight for all Her creation. She created you and everything for love and through love. Abba and Ima are our Divine parents. It was for the sake of love were you created. Out of an act of love, were you empowered to emulate Her; that is, to create and give birth like She did with so much joy, love, and ecstasy.

"I was created out of love and for love." Repeat this until you internalize it deeply. Only out of love. The Divine Mother never forsakes you, and never forgets you because you are a part of Her.

9.

"Let him kiss me with the kisses of his mouth." King Solomon was speaking of the love between the upper world, *Zeir Anpin,* and the lower world, *Malkut.* Just as kisses are the beginning of the arousal of every love, Song of Songs begins in this way. Sometimes according to the Zohar, *Malkut* is under *Zeir Anpin* and sometimes on top and sometimes in the center. Just as *Abba* and *Ima* are inseparable, *Zeir Anpin* and *Malkut* are always united. Their love is constant. When we pray to one, the other is revealed to us. God is transcendent and immanent. There is a love affair between them. We celebrate and share in the joy of their unification. On *Shabbat* we call the Bride (the *Shechinah*) to come to the Beloved One (*Ha-Kodesh Boruch Hu*); Shabbat is a wedding. "Honor the *Shabbat* and keep it holy." God remembered the *Shabbat,* and on *Shabbat,* we remember who we truly are.

10.

God is one, yet we say " On that day He and His Name will be one". Is God not one now? *Zeir Anpin* (*Ha-Kodesh Boruch Hu*) and *Nukva* (*Shechinah*) are the male and female aspects of the one God operative in our world. They may appear to us to be distinct, but they are not. When one is revealed, so is the other. Yet, we live in a world where the oneness of God is not fully revealed. There appears to be a separation between *Ha-Kodesh Boruch Hu* and the Shechinah, particularly when the Jewish people reside out of the land of Israel. For that reason, Jewish prayers often begin with a Kabbalistic intention. "I now prepare to thank, laud, and praise my Creator. For the sake of the unification of The Holy One Blessed be He and His Presence ..." or I pray to unify *Yud Hay* with *Vav Hay.* Everything is done to make unification and reveal the oneness of God. All that is false, all that seemingly causes division and masquerades as the light will disappear in the true revelation of Her. May She be revealed in our days.

11.

The mission given to Abraham, Isaac, and Jacob, their wives and their children, and later given to the Jewish people as a whole when they received the Torah at Mount Sinai, was to repair all of creation by restoring and revealing the divine light and the proper intrinsic connection of the physical with the godly. The purpose of all of the *mitzvot* is to strengthen the connection between the physical and the spiritual. This unification enables the revelation of the Divine in this physical world. This is the *Shechinah* who is at the heart and soul of all the spiritual work done by the Jewish people. When necessary, the *klippot*, the shells that block the flow of divine light to allow evil to exist and operate in this world, have to be destroyed. As a result, there are many wars throughout history between the forces of good and evil. Too often the Jewish people are at the center of these battles.

12.

The Divine Names are the keys for anything a person needs in the world. We respond to our name, so does God. We do not pronounce the Divine name YHVH, but we say 'Adonai" instead. YHVH is Zeir Anpin and Adonai is Malkut, Shechinah. We are constantly making unification each time we say God's name in prayer.

Place yourself in a meditative state. See the letters of the Divine Name in front of you. Carve out each letter individually. See the *Yud*, the *Hay*, the *Vav* and the finale *Hay*. Now breathe the *Yud* into you head, exhale the *Hay* into your shoulders and arms, breathe in the *Vav* into your torso and exhale the *Hay* into your waist and legs. Alternate between seeing the letters on you router screen and seeing them within your body. Then say the Divine Name Adonai silently to your self as you visualize the letters in your body and also on your inner screen. According to the Arizel, the name Adonai is a treasure chest of blessings. Keep repeating the Name as you visualize the letters.

Chapter Thirteen

Summary and Blessings

Summary and Blessings

When I dedicated this book to the memory of my beloved mother Corinne Ribner of blessed memory, I expressed my hope that you the reader open your heart to honor your personal mother and acknowledge your debt of gratitude to her. What an awesome responsibility it is to be a mother. Can we ever pay back our mothers for all the love and all that they have done for us? I do not think so. I hope that this book has made you aware of the debt of gratitude we owe to our Biblical mothers as well. How can they ever be sufficiently acknowledged for all the good they have done for humanity!

Mothers are so important. Who we are as men and women is in large part due to the love of our mothers. How they hold us, speak to us, respond to our cries, play with us when we are infants inform us whether the world is safe for us to be authentically true to who we are. When we venture out of the home environment where the mother was dominant to the expanded world more associated with the values of the fathers, we are challenged to grow, achieve, and adapt in ways that may be quite different than the unconditional love and acceptance that we ideally and hopefully were blessed to receive under our mother's tutelage.

Individually and collectively, we are confronted continually with dichotomies between the masculine and the feminine, between doing and being, achieving and allowing, between the ego and the soul, spirituality and physicality. There is an imbalance between the masculine and the feminine within our world and possibly within ourselves. As a result, our external world is

THE SECRET LEGACY OF BIBLICAL WOMEN

fragmented, beset with wars, crimes, natural disasters, failing economies, Our inner world may similarly be plagued with feelings of anxiety, depression, and insecurity. We all need healing particularly if we did not receive the unconditional love from our mothers needed to grow and thrive.

Sister Miriam, our beloved prophetess and advocate of the feminine, highlighted the costs we have each paid for the societal domination of the masculine over the feminine during her interview.

"The world suffers due to this imbalance. Masculine energy has made tremendous accomplishments in the external world, for that is the nature of masculine energy, it is always expanding. Unfortunately, these accomplishments have occurred at the cost of the feminine. For example, modern societies in your time have made great technological advances, but they lack intimate loving communities where people can be authentic, vulnerable, and caring with each other. It is the wisdom and the heart of the feminine that nurtures real intimacy between people. What good is technological advancement if more and more people are depressed, anxious, isolated, and unhappy because of the lack of meaningful relationships with other human beings. Societies pay dearly for the imbalance between the masculine and feminine. So if women become more like men, who will do the nurturing needed to make a person feel totally loved and validated?

An ancient story in the Talmud about the sun and the moon is offered as an explanation for the imbalance of power between the masculine and feminine. According to the Talmud, God created two great lights, the sun (masculine) and the moon (feminine), that were equal in stature initially, but the Bible states, "a great light to rule by day and the small light to rule by night." What happened? According to the Talmudic tale, the sun and the moon were initially two great and equal lights but then the moon complained to the Holy One, "Is it really possible for two kings to share one crown?" Even though it was true, the Holy One responded by saying "Go and diminish yourself." She answered him, "Sovereign of the Universe, because I spoke rightly must I diminish myself?" The Holy One made several gestures to appease her anger. For example, God told the moon that she would rule by day and night unlike the sun that shone only in the day. The moon objected "What is so great about that? Of what benefit is a lamp in broad daylight?" After a few more exchanges, the Holy One requested that he-goat offerings be made on the new moon to atone for His diminishment of the moon. Until the light of the moon is restored to be equal to the that of the sun, the Holy One asks us at the time when the Jewish people have the Holy Temple to make offerings to atone for the diminishment of the feminine. These " sin" offerings are recorded in the bible. Much of Jewish practice is devoted to restoring the proper balance between the masculine and feminine.

Every time we pray, every time we do a mitzvot (a prescribed commandment or good deed) Jews hold the intention that they are unifying the Holy One, (Divine Masculine) , with the Shechinah (the Divine Feminine). The " Shema" the fundamental prayer in Judaism affirming the oneness of God is recited and meditated upon two to three times each day. " *Shema Yisrael Adonai Eloheynu Adonai Echod*'. When we say God's name (Adonai) the first time in the recitation of the " Shema", we meditate on the transcendence of God, the Divine Masculine. When we say God's name the second time in the "Shema", we meditate on the immanence of God, the Divine Feminine. We close our eyes when we say the Shema. If something is far away from us, we need to open our eyes wide to see it. If something is close to us, we relax our gaze. If something is very close to us, we must close our eyes to more fully sense its presence. People close their eyes generally when they kiss. Similarly, to have a taste of God's unity, we close our eyes. Sometimes in prayer we have a taste of the higher unity of God, when we *know* that there is nothing by God. God is one and everything is a part of God. As physical human beings, it is not our fate to remain in the spiritual world of unity. God created this world of differentiation. We then say after the six words of the "Shema" , " Blessed be the name of your glorious kingdom forever and ever" so as to see God reflected in the multiplicity of forms here on earth.

In the deepest truth, in the highest worlds, from God's perspective, God is one, has always been one and will always be one. In the lower worlds, where we live in this physical world, in this world of separation and fragmentation, God's oneness is not totally revealed.The divine sparks of the Shechinah have been shattered throughout history, throughout nations, religions and all of creation. There is good and evil in our world. Our spiritual work in this world is to do a *tikkun,* a cosmic fixing, so as to reveal God's oneness by restoring the balance and unity between the masculine and the feminine.

It may be helpful to highlight the deeper implications of the Talmudic tale mentioned earlier. In the beginning, the moon shone with her own light, equal to the outward light of the sun. The masculine and feminine were equal. Adam and Eve were one being. Then due to her complaint, her own external light was stripped from her. Her light would now be hidden and concealed. She would possess no manifest light of her own so she must now reflect the light of the sun. Her own inner light would be felt rather than seen. The masculine light would be externally seen, but would lack the hidden depth of the feminine. The sun (masculine) and moon(feminine) are complementary, equivalent, necessary but not the same.

The light of the sun shines brightly during the day, yet it is not seen in the night. The moon may be seen slightly during the day, but it is in the night, in the darkest depths, that the light of the feminine illuminates. The moon also models fluidity, how to live gracefully and inwardly through life cycles, how to surrender to a greater light. Like the moon, there are times when our light is waxing. We are shining for the world to see. Other times, our light is waning and and we are called to return to the depths inside ourselves. There is much we learn from the moon in addition to grace and patience.

As we learn Kabbalah, we understand that the feminine principle represented by the moon is one of receptivity, but it need not be one of passivity. In each chapter of this book, we saw clearly that it was the love, courage and vision of biblical women that rose at critical and dangerous times to save humanity and alter the course of history. In the Kabbalah commentary of this book, we learned how the arousal from below of *Malkut,* the domain of the *Shechinah,* initiates a flow of blessing that creates miracles and transforms the world. Most everything begins with this arousal from below.

Let's conclude this book this book, remembering the words of encouragement by Mother Sarah.

"Now is the time to reclaim the path of the feminine that I began. You will be supported on high by many great ones. Doors to palaces of spiritual delight that have been closed for so long will now easily open for you to enter, but you must stay clear and focused. Know your worth. Keep yourself pure. Be strong. May you be privileged to lift the veil of the *Shechinah* so Her light may shine throughout the world. May the peace of Her revelation come soon and easily to the Land of Israel and the entire world."

Blessings to the Readers

Whether you are a Jew or not, a woman or a man, your personal efforts are needed to restore the balance and make this world a dwelling place for the Shechinah. In large and small ways, we each participate in Her redemption. The more that you do in this effort, the more you will be inspired to do, and the more joy and love you will experience in your life.

How do we do this? We follow the path that our holy mothers carved out before us. We simply stand on their shoulders and continue their holy work as outlined in each chapter. As Queen Esther told us, "Everything that you need is already given to you. You have all the resources you require."

Let's hold the intention to reveal and embody the intrinsic Godliness that is at the heart of who we really are. We do not have to wait to do this. God is present with you right now. Right now, let us consciously choose to simply open our hearts and create opportunities to deepen intimate authentic connections between others. When we do a simple kindness for another person, we reveal the *Shechinah.* The Lubavitcher Rebbe said once, " It is more important to be kind than right." If ever you find yourself in an argument, if you find yourself criticizing a person, blaming another person for the feelings that have been triggered within you, please remember those words. It is easy to win a battle. It is easy to be right, but to be kind, you need to quiet the judgement of the ego-mind and open your heart even more. If you are angry, you block the revelation of the Shechinah within you. According to kabbalistic teachings, illness is often rooted in these blockages.

Being compassionate and engaging in acts of love and kindness is healing to all. In all our acts of love, compassion and kindness, the *Shechinah* is revealed to us if we open our hearts to Her. When we heal ourselves, when we heal others, we redeem Her, for we each are a part of Her. We do not and cannot do this work alone. We must do it together.

*   *   *

Please take a few deep breaths, quiet your mind, and open your hearts to receive the blessings that are contained within this book that I extend to you now with my full heart.

May this book inspire, educate, and guide you to reclaim the path of feminine spirituality that our biblical women so courageously walked. May we each be blessed in our own unique ways to be strengthened by their examples.

May these biblical women become so alive to us that we routinely ask ourselves, "What would Sarah do, what would Miriam say, when we make the choices that impact on ourselves and others?" May our hearts open so wide that we are filled with love for all of creation as the hearts of biblical women were.

May we truly value the fullness and holiness of life itself over any abstract idealization or ideology as our biblical mothers did.

May we be blessed to create holy sanctuaries in our homes, relationships, places of worship, and even in our own bodies where the *Shechinah* can dwell, be known, revealed, and experienced.

So may it be that with our love, our tears of joy and sorrow, may we reclaim the path of the feminine and redeem the *Shechinah,* the Divine

Feminine, from Her hiding. May Her light shine in all Her splendor for the whole world to see. Amen selah.

* * *

P.S. I thank you from my heart for reading, studying, and sharing this book with others. More than anything else, this book is an outpouring of my heart. I pray that it has touched your heart as well. May it continue to inspire and comfort you throughout your life journey. To reap all the gifts of this book, share this book with others, practice the meditative and spiritual suggestions associated with each biblical woman so you can deepen your understanding of each woman through discussion. I am excited about sharing this book with you because I believe that it will also empower you to be your most beautiful authentic self. I received many gifts through its writing, so thank you. If you are interested in Jewish meditation, I encourage each of you to study and practice the meditations that are in my books *New Age Judaism, Everyday Kabbalah,* and *Kabbalah Month by Month.*

Always feel free to contact me at Miriam@Kabbalahoftheheart.com. Sign up for my weekly newsletter on the Kabbalistic energies of the months, holidays, meditation, healing, etc. If you are interested in further integrating and applying the wisdom of the heart of the feminine into your life or in the practice of kabbalistic meditation, please contact me directly at melindaribner@gmail.com. If you are part of a woman's group, and you would like to study this material in the book further so as to deepen the experience of feminine spirituality within the group, please also contact me at melindaribner@gmail.com. There is so much more that I have to teach and transmit about the feminine that could not be contained within the confines of the written word. I would love to hear from you. Please feel free to write me and post reviews on Amazon. I hope that you will share this book with the members of your community. If invited, I will come to you. Before your very eyes, I will become each biblical woman in a theatrical performance in person or online.

Melinda Ribner L.C.S.W. has taught Jewish meditation, ecstatic Kabbalistic meditation, Jewish spiritual healing, and "Kabbalah of the Feminine" for over twenty-five years at synagogues of all affiliations from Chabad to Jewish renewal, national conferences of Jewish learning, and through her own organization Beit Miriam. At Beit Miriam she offers ongoing classes and workshops on a variety of topics as well as alternative meditative gatherings for *Shabbat* and the Jewish holidays.

Melinda Ribner is the author of *New Age Judaism, Everyday Kabbalah,* and *Kabbalah Month by Month, The Gift of a New Beginning* and the producer of two CDs, *Holy,* meditative songs and chants, and *Arousal from Below,* guided Kabbalistic meditation. She is also a licensed psychotherapist (L.C.S.W.) who uses meditation and Kabbalistic teachings as part of treatment. Ms. Ribner is single and divides her time between NYC, Florida and Jerusalem.

For more information about her workshops and counseling services, please visit Kabbalahoftheheart.com. For a speaking engagement, workshops in meditation, feminine spirituality and performances of biblical women, please contact her directly at MelindaRibner@gmail.com.

Other Books by Melinda Ribner

New Age Judaism
(Simcha Press: Health Communications Inc.)

Many people will be surprised to find that Judaism is fundamentally aligned with what we think of as the New Age. Many of the things we associate with the New Age are not new but are part of kabbalah, the Jewish mystical tradition. For thousands of years, Judaism has been involved with meditation, angels, vegetarianism, holistic healing, personal transformation, unity consciousness and many other things which have concerned the New Age movement.

"Believe it or not, I have read *"New Age Judaism"* probably a hundred times & every time I read it, I get more out of it-it has become a daily part of my life, as well as many others it has touched! I try to share with everyone its words of encouragement and insight!" *Lori Hana, unsolicited review to author.*

"New Age Judaism is a tonic for the soul. Through her extensive knowledge and wisdom of such subjects as reincarnation, kabbalah, angels, you learn how vibrant and relevant Judaism is in the 21st century, "the New Age." Melinda Ribner is the rare author that combines scholarship with first hand experience. She not only knows what she writes, but will inspire you with all that a faith based life can be. She is truly a spiritual guide and as you travel with her in this wonderful book, you will most certainly feel God's presence leading the way." *A Customer review on Amazon.*

"The path that leads to Jewish spirituality can have many false steps. But if you begin your journey with *New Age Judaism*, your feet will be firmly planted in the rich soul of divine wisdom. From the first page to the last, *New Age Judaism* has something to teach. More importantly, it is an inspirational treatise that transports the reader beyond time and space with a gentle landing at the doorstep of enlightened awareness." *Larry Lieblin*

"*In New Age Judaism*, Melinda Ribner does a remarkable job interfacing ageless Jewish spirituality with new age life today. For this we owe her and her book a deep debt of gratitude." *Rabbi Simon Jacobson, Author of "Toward a Meaningful Life."*

Kabbalah Month by Month
(Jossey-Bass: A Wiley Imprint)

The ancient wisdom of kabbalah outlines a month-by-month guide for personal healing and transformation. It is the original twelve step program, as each month has its own unique energy and opportunities for healing and spiritual growth.

"A remarkable contribution for helping to make the month by month Jewish spiritual journey. It is inspiring and informing and transforming. This book is a treasure" *Rabbi Zalman Schachter- Shalomi , ALEPH.*

"*Kabbalah Month by Month* is one of the most amazing books that I have ever read. Melinda Ribner combines kabbalah, astrology, numerology, torah portions, and psychology. It is well-written and accessible. I turn to it again and again to connect with the energies of the month" *Ninah Kessler*

"I continue to read *Kabbalah Month by Month* each month from the time when I purchased it in 2006 until the present. There has been no other book that I have read so continually and consistently for so long except the Bible." *Sarah Blum*

Everyday Kabbalah
(Citadel Press/ Kensington)

Everyday Kabbalah is the first step-by-step manual integrating the spiritual teachings and meditation lessons of the Musar, Hasidic and kabbalistic schools... While all the meditations and teachings of this book are designed to promote personal healing, some are intended to give spiritual fortitude to individuals undergoing particular hardships such as the loss of a loved one, divorce, physical pain, unemployment, low self-esteem and loneliness.

"This is a great book to read if organized religion leaves you cold or if you would like to learn to do meditation with Jewish content. Mindy Ribner was my teacher so I was able to learn some of these meditations directly from her. I can tell you that the meditations in this book are really tremendous experiences." *Amazon reviewer*

"*Everyday Kabbalah* is extremely well written with great background, Biblical and Talmud excerpts, and extremely practical 'How to" approaches to beginning Jewish meditative practices. Her practical approachable writing style will encourage the reader to try the methods she writes about and the methods themselves are powerful. *"Amazon reviewer"*

"This splendid book provides an immersion in the wisdom of the Jewish and kabbalistic tradition. It will answer the hunger many people are experiencing for a return to Western spirituality... Highly recommended" *Larry Dossey, M.D. Executive Editor Alternative Therapies in Health and Medicine*

16207400R00180

Made in the USA
Charleston, SC
09 December 2012